# CAPTAIN ABBY AND CAPTAIN JOHN

*Books by*
# ROBERT P. TRISTRAM COFFIN

**POEMS**
- CHRISTCHURCH
- DEW AND BRONZE
- GOLDEN FALCON
- THE YOKE OF THUNDER
- BALLADS OF SQUARE-TOED AMERICANS
- STRANGE HOLINESS
- SALTWATER FARM
- MAINE BALLADS
- COLLECTED POEMS

**ESSAYS**
- BOOK OF CROWNS AND COTTAGES
- AN ATTIC ROOM

**BIOGRAPHIES**
- LAUD: STORM CENTER OF STUART ENGLAND
- THE DUKES OF BUCKINGHAM
- PORTRAIT OF AN AMERICAN
- CAPTAIN ABBY AND CAPTAIN JOHN

**AUTOBIOGRAPHY**
- LOST PARADISE

**LECTURES**
- NEW POETRY OF NEW ENGLAND
  (*Frost and Robinson*)

**NOVELS**
- RED SKY IN THE MORNING
- JOHN DAWN

**HISTORY**
- KENNEBEC: CRADLE OF AMERICANS
  (*Rivers of America Series*)

**TEXT**
- A BOOK OF SEVENTEENTH-CENTURY PROSE
  (*With A. M. Witherspoon*)

Mrs Abby J Pennell     Capt J D Pennell

# CAPTAIN ABBY AND CAPTAIN JOHN

*An Around-the-World Biography*

BY ROBERT P. TRISTRAM COFFIN

ISBN: 0-942396-86-3
© 2002, Estate of Robert P. Tristram Coffin

Originally Published by The Macmillan Company, 1939

All rights reserved

Front Cover Photo "Oxen at Bow of the *Benjamin Sewall*"
Courtesy of Bowdoin College Library Special Collections

Cover Design by Beth Leonard
Typesetting by Jen Feldman

Blackberry Books
617 East Neck Road
Nobleboro, Maine 04555
chimfarm@gwi.net

TO
BROOKS LEAVITT
A LATER SON OF MAINE
WHO HAS BUILT AS SHINING A LIFE
IN THE GREAT WORLD
AS CAPTAIN JOHN PENNELL BUILT
WHO IS
ONE OF THE BEST READERS OF MY BOOKS
AND
ONE OF MY BEST FRIENDS

# Preface

I HAVE MANY PEOPLE TO THANK for helping me make this book. Aunt Nell Pennell, while she lived; Mrs. Carroll Pennell; Andrew and Catherine Pennell, James's grandchildren; Mrs. Helen Baxter, Charles's daughter; Lucy Hinds, Lettice Hinds's daughter; Mary Gilman, of the Curtis Memorial Library in Brunswick; Miss Alta Reed, Elias's daughter; Emery Booker; Alice Furbish; Samuel Kamerling; my children, Margaret and Robert, who helped me with the diaries; and many others who assisted in one way or another. I thank them all now.

But it is to J. Fred Pennell, the son of Abby and John, that I owe the greatest gratitude. He trusted me with the best of family treasures, the log-books, diaries, account books, maps, and letters of his father, and the diaries and letters of his mother. He gave me the chance to erect this memorial to his mother and father. I shall always be grateful to him.

I am glad to publish this book, in addition to my poem, as my part in the celebration of the Bicentenary of Brunswick's incorporation as a town, in this year 1939, as well as a thank-offering for the two decades of lovely living I have enjoyed in Pennellville—anciently Middle Bays—thanks to the builders of my house and the planters of my elms. I hope this book will excite others in Brunswick to do something similar for other people, other houses, other events that make up the

## Preface

whole and true history of the town of Brunswick. No real town history will be available until each section and each house have been explored with an eye not merely for facts but for human nature and the small but everlastingly enduring details of everyday living. And each historian must work by another lamp as well as the lamp of truth; he must work by the lamp of love.

I have taken the liberty to re-spell some of the less essential spellings of Abby and John Pennell. But I have kept the essential idioms as they spelt them. I have repunctuated, too, a bit, in order to make their words clearer to the modern reader. Especially I have put in exclamation points now and again. For both Abby and John, like many Yankees, were quiet and unexclamatory people.

All incidents and characters in this book are real, and every reference is to some actual person, living or dead. Every word within quotation marks was written or spoken.

ROBERT P. TRISTRAM COFFIN

Pennells' Shipyard,
Pennellville, Brunswick, Maine,
July 19, 1939.

## Contents

| | |
|---|---|
| *Preface* | vii |
| *The Blue Chest* | 1 |
| 1. *The Birch Switch* | 4 |
| 2. *Oak Fever* | 8 |
| 3. *Houses by Euclid and Ships' Carpenters* | 17 |
| 4. *Begetter of a Chapter of American History* | 25 |
| 5. *Young Mizzenmast* | 66 |
| 6. *Abby Signs the Papers* | 77 |
| 7. *The Bark Is Made Ready* | 88 |
| 8. *A Housewife Looks at a House 25,000 Miles Wide* | 101 |
| 9. *The Carnival of Venice* | 130 |
| 10. *The Long Way Home* | 149 |
| 11. *Reunion at Middle Bays and Harpswell* | 173 |
| 12. *Farewell, Deborah! Hail, Elias!* | 185 |
| 13. *The Cradle at the Mainmast* | 201 |
| 14. *A New Ocean and a New Son* | 231 |
| 15. *Sunshine on Abby and John* | 265 |
| 16. *Last Page Out of Homer* | 279 |
| 17. *Happy Family at Sea* | 287 |
| 18. *Earthquake, Loup-Cervier, and Reunion* | 321 |
| 19. *Where Rio's Mountains Preach Eternity* | 334 |

## Contents

| | |
|---|---:|
| 20. *Captain Abby Ashore* | 344 |
| 21. *The Roll Call on the Headland* | 349 |
| *Appendix 1: The Roll of Pennell Vessels* | 355 |
| *Appendix 2: Brunswick Shipmasters* | 358 |
| *Index* | 361 |

## Illustrations

*Abby and John Pennell* — *Frontispiece*
*Oxen at Bow of the* Benjamin Sewall — *page* 64
*The Bark* William Woodside — " 90
*The Bark* Deborah Pennell — " 190
*The Ship* Benjamin Sewall *on the Ways* — " 284
*The Ship* Benjamin Sewall — " 318

CAPTAIN ABBY AND CAPTAIN JOHN

# The Blue Chest

MOST NEW ENGLAND FAMILIES have left a large house full of furniture and portraits and haircloth trunks behind them. They have even left wreaths of their hair —long curls such as used to cascade down the sailor collars of boys too big in their velveteen pants to spank, rankling with golden life, white locks of aged men, curls of fine-spun hair from brides' heads, stiff wires from spinster crowns. New England families have left albums of daguerreotypes and tintypes, showing uncles who sat for minutes with flies tickling their noses. They have left cupboards full of dishes, attics full of hoopskirts and bustles. You can walk into whole rooms full of history. You can climb upstairs and find out easily what kind of people they were. You can build them up again into the company of the living out of the solid substance of their beds and comforters, and armchairs and pots and pans.

But the man and woman I am going to bring to life in these pages are shut up in a very small room. It is five feet long and only a little over a foot wide. Smaller than a coffin even. It is shaped something like a coffin, though, and it is made of clear Maine pine. It is painted blue. It is that old-fashioned thin and greenish blue that runs in most Maine families as the color of their eyes. No one can look at that blue and not think of the sea. This narrow chest in which my two Maine captains

## Captain Abby and Captain John

lie buried and waiting the word to rise went to sea all its days. It went around the Horn many times. This small box is full of tremendous courage and great tenderness. It has sweat and the love of children in it. It has details of simple everyday living. Great storms and earthquakes are shut up in it. There are wide wings of albatrosses and half a thousand white-sailed ships. It has far-away shining cities and Maine farmers' gossip. It is filled with huge cargoes of sugar and white pine, and of life and death and love.

This box is the sea-chest of Captain John Pennell, of Middle Bays, Brunswick, in the County of Cumberland, State of Maine. It is stuffed with maps on which many voyages are penciled in. It is filled with tall log-books of more voyages than Captain John had fingers and toes. It contains cash-books and account books, bills of lading in the captain's bold hand. It also has several diaries and many letters written in an ink as bright as the day it flowed out into the delicate lacework of a New England housewife's hand. For the captain's wife wrote, too.

Here are the bare bones of fine and brave and godly living. Here are the complete anatomies of two who followed the sea all their life together. They had no other roof to their heads than the swaying one of a ship's planks or the one studded with nails of stars. They begat and bore their children and brought them up among winds and high waves. Here is all the furniture of a house built on water, all the household goods of a home that leaned and swayed as it moved around the world many years. This home held babies and pies made of Maine apples, socks to darn and shirts to starch and

## Captain Abby and Captain John

iron. It had schooldays and birthdays, and death days as well. It was a complete home. It held a small and warm Maine household in the coldest and windiest places of the world. Here it all lies in small words on old paper, in this chest that is smaller than a coffin and blue as the middle Atlantic at sunrise.

Here are the bones. They need only two hearts and the flesh. I must make the small words come to life. Like Elijah of old, I must put my mouth on the mouths that have grown cold. I must put my hands upon these marks made by dead hands. And I must make this woman and this man stand up again and breathe.

And if I can do this, I shall restore to history, without the risk of its being lost again, a small chapter in the vast history of Maine's seafaring people, so young in the world's measure of time, so ancient already beside the empty Atlantic which washes the coast of Maine today. It will be a family history, but it will, in the small, be America's amazing history as well. It will be a chronicle, I hope, full of that vital mixture which is so peculiarly American, plain living and grand living. It will be the history of a captain who is also a working man, of a seaman who is a father with his family around him always, the history of a ship's first lady who is also a busy housewife, knitting and mending and ironing. It will be that paradox that confounds Europeans when they study our ways of life—the lordly and the humble, the bold and adventurous and the tender and homely combined. It will be the story of a plain Yankee home that went to sea.

May I be the man to bring this house and home to life!

# 1

## The Birch Switch

IT WAS EARLY APRIL. The clear sun was rolling big as a cartwheel through the golden green new leaves on the birches. It was a day full of a thousand bright new frogs. They were so new and bold and full of Spring that they were going it full cry at nine o'clock in the morning down in Cap'n Ben's swamp. They were daring all the boys in Christendom to come and chase them. They were sassing every boy within a mile.

But Johnnie Pennell wasn't headed their way. He was headed south-by-west, and he was going fast away from the frogs. His feet were sending up quick puffs of dust on the road. He was headed bee-line for the yellow schoolhouse. He was going so fast his tight long trousers were threatening to slice him up from the bottom and make two Johnnie Pennells of him. His trousers were tight across his stern. And his stern had three horizontal lines where the dust of Middle Bays he had been sitting on as he contemplated frogs was neatly flicked off and three lines of clean blue cloth showed.

Two steps and a half behind the boy puffed Deborah Pennell. She had a long birch switch in her hand. She had hard work to keep within business distance of the

## Captain Abby and Captain John

boy ahead. Every so often she got up to what she thought was the proper distance. She lashed out with the switch. But Johnnie seemed to have eyes in his back. For he hitched his stern ahead with remarkable nimbleness in the middle of his stride. There was only the whistle of birch on empty air. The woman lost a step or two and most of her balance as her right arm swept its empty arc. But she recovered her balance, made up for lost time with three quick steps, and began to measure once more with an artist's practiced eye the distance to her plump double target again. Her eye lighted up like the eye of an eagle.

Mrs. Deborah Pennell was seeing her eighth and youngest son to school.

Deborah had seen seven sons to school, and they were all doing men's business now in the family's shipyard or on the family's ocean. The Pennells looked upon the Atlantic as theirs. They had begun to cover it with ships as fast as they could, under the encouragement of their mother Deborah. They didn't hear the whistle of birch now, the older Pennell brothers, but they heard their mother's tongue. Deborah never shirked her duty. She was not the mother to shirk on her latest baby. If oil of birch could do it, the baby would take his place and tend to business beside his brothers. John Pennell would be a sea captain yet, by the Great Horn Spoon, as long as the Middle Bays birchwoods held out! There would be no playing with frogs on an April schoolday morning. She had smarted up seven backsides in her time and sent the young men at the front of them on into life and glory. She wasn't going to stay her hand on

## Captain Abby and Captain John

the last witness of her husband's manhood presented to her before her husband died. She was the head and manager of the Pennells now. She was going to make the Pennell Brothers' new blue-and-white flag known from the Arctic to the Antarctic, from Batavia to Buenos Aires, or her nose didn't have a mole on it halfway down.

Deborah took an extra long step. She drew her arm back and took another fierce switch at her hurrying son. This time she got home. Johnnie yipped loud and left the ground with a smart leap. Another blue mark joined the three already stamped across the Capes of Good Hope before her. Her son's school trousers were made of Cap'n Jacob's own best blue Sunday ones. It had cost her a pang to cut them down for her youngest. But time moved on, and new men must come up to handle the times. Johnnie stood in his father's trousers. She'd dust the dust out of them!

The thirteen-year-old boy reached the wide stone doorstep and leaped into the open door like a frog into a deep pool and safety. Deborah halted at the stone and waited grimly. The sound of excited childish voices came out to her through the door. Then there was the deep bass of the teacher's stern voice. Deborah still waited. There was a dramatic silence. Then the sounds began, with perfect regularity. The sound of leather lighting on what schoolhouse leather loved best. Deborah counted the cracks. Ten of them. Then she tucked her birch sapling under her right arm, for the tomorrows. She put up the sunshade she had thought to bring along under her left arm, and she walked slowly back

## Captain Abby and Captain John

up the Pennells' Wharf Road towards the little cottage on the hill, second of the Pennell houses, where all the Pennells had begun in the wiry loins of her husband's sire, Thomas.

Benjamin, Jacob, Jr., James, Job, Charles, Joseph, and Robert—the three daughters did not count until they got sea captain husbands to make up for their mistake in sex. Deborah had seen the seven sons to school on bright April mornings when frogs were calling and robins were playing truant in the trees. She had seen them all to school. She had tingled them all into great ambition to do their sums and get ahead to adzes and hammers and tree-nails and wives and babies. And now John, the last. The last of her sons to see to school. She was kind of sad about his being the last. But boys grew up. Maybe she could begin on the grandchildren soon. She had an eye on three who were almost at school age. Maybe there would be no break in her April mornings. She put up her birch switch carefully over the door on the gun-rack. It might do for many years yet. It was well seasoned. Her sadness lifted from her.

The last pair of boy trousers were safely throbbing under a boy with his head full of fractions instead of frogs, full of Dakota Territory and Nebraska and Kansas Territories and Van Dieman's Land.

John Pennell would make the finest shipbuilder or sea captain of them all. He was built in his backsides the leanest and likest his father.

2

Oak Fever

To KNOW THE REASON why Deborah Pennell was driving her son John to school with a switch along the road on that bright morning of the Year of Our Lord 1840, it is necessary to make a study of a fever. It was a fever that swept the New England coast from one end to the other after the War of 1812 had made it possible for a Yankee who was built handsome and wanted to follow the sea to leave Harpswell and Yarmouth and come home without having served some years in His Majesty's British Navy. The war had made the sea safe for American merchantmen, and so the fever set in. It was a lovely fever, though, and the brightest chapters of the State of Maine's history rustled past during its rise and fall. For the years from 1820 to 1880 were the only years when the State of Maine was able to keep her smartest children home and give them all something to do, and not have to breed them for states farther west, Illinois and Michigan, Wisconsin and Minnesota, Oregon and Washington. Those states had to look elsewhere, during that spell, for good farmers and fishermen and boatbuilders and lumbermen, and not rob the

## Captain Abby and Captain John

Maine cradle of its best lumbering and fishing babies. And this was thanks to the fever.

The fever began in the oaks—white oaks which grew taller and straighter here than they grew anywhere else —that came right down to the shore and even waded out into the ocean on the many islands of Maine. These trees had been there before the coming of the white men. They had pushed up and up for years and years, seeking the sun in company. They had killed out all rivals for light and air, their heads were very high, as high as the bald eagles flew. For twenty, thirty, forty feet, they might be without a big bough, pure, white wood inside, without a knot. The fever started in that sheer whiteness. Men along the shore had been putting it into barns and houses. Now they discovered it turned into something tougher than iron itself when it dried out in the wind. Now, after 1820 especially, they began to put that white metal of a wood into houses that were piked at the front door. Those houses moved out from the shore, to southern ports first, then to the West Indies, then to England, and at last around the two capes which separate the Atlantic from the Indian and Pacific oceans. The winds moved them, and they went wherever the winds blew.

And so the years crowded on fast when every farm that had its feet in salt water had houses which went around the world annually. As almost any farm in Maine that wants to can have its feet in salt water, since the ocean obligingly keeps going up into the middle of the state and coming back every mile or so, that meant that many farms had these round-the-world houses. And

## Captain Abby and Captain John

the farmers went off in them, just as soon as the oats were cut, and did not come back till the leaves were red on the swamp maples again and peepers calling in the marshes, and it was time to think about sowing oats again. The men wanted to be husbands as well as sailors and traders, they wanted to have their socks darned at night, so they thought to take their wives right along with them, with the makings of Maine apple pies hung on strings and the cows and chickens of home. For even the hens and cows of Maine became nautical ones. And, of course, family events took place, as family events will take place when husbands are around, and many of Maine's babies were rocked to sleep in their earliest naps by the motion of oak cradles weighing 700, 800, 1200 tons at last. For the ships grew in size as did the families.

Maine boys began to have strange names in front of their plain Yankee family names, Blanchard and Merriman and Linscott: San Lorenzo, San Sebastian, San Fernandez. For they first saw the sunlight in lost and forsaken jumping-off places, far volcanic islands in all the lonely places of the sea. And their fathers named them for what little of land they could see with a spyglass the mornings or evenings when they were born. Maine birthplaces became world-wide ones, and fathers filled in proud little crosses where the blooms of their manhood flowered on the charts where they marked the paths their ships made from continent to continent.

These were the days when every front dooryard along the Maine coast did not stop at the sea's edge but went right along down the earth's curving sides and took in

## Captain Abby and Captain John

the great fireflies of a Javanese night and the windy escarpments of the end of the earth at Cape Horn. Every Maine man of the coast was a citizen of the big world, did business in Genoa and Leghorn and Calcutta, rowed ashore to Cadiz in a smart Yankee boatload of clean and shining men, and came home again with fine furniture and stuffs and china dishes bought at the four corners of the globe. A State of Maine farmer lived a life in the round, in long straightaway lines which turned to circles and brought him home clean as a die. He erased the seasons. He lived all in Summer, hanging head down from the sphere at Table Rock in Summer when the snow flew back home, standing head up under the Dipper in a Maine August night snowed over with stars and nebulae when the Winter blew bleak across the southern Pacific. These farmers erased the seasons and the geography of small inland minds. They were at home wherever their white-oak homes could sail.

The homes sailed everywhere. The lonesomest wastes of the Pacific saw Yankee captains' wives paying calls and drinking tea with one another as their ships stood hove to in spells of fair weather. Gossip of little Maine hamlets rippled out under coconut fronds in the velvety heat under the Line. Wives mended their husbands' trousers after an afternoon at the palace of the Doges of Venice. Children went to school for arithmetic to their own mothers alongside the fairyland mountains of Borneo, and their mothers became distant and severe blue-eyed taskmasters and allowed no boy at the beginning of his multiplication table to rest his cut-me-downs from his father's trousers on her prim lap. The boy had

## Captain Abby and Captain John

to sit up straight and toe the line and say his two-times-three like a Trojan. And the girls had to put their dolls one side and sit up sober at the dough-dish with their brothers. And their mothers collected a schoolteacher's pay for schooling their offspring, once they were home again where there were school committees to collect it from. There were American babies smiling up blue-eyed among naked brown strangers; many and many

> A woman knitting baby things
> Under the albatross' wide wings,

for babies arrived in port and for babies coming.

And these people kept the Yankee thrift and worship of homely solid things in expensive capitals of the older worlds and among the careless living by the day in places too sunny and lazy for hurry and hard labor. They kept their plain living among the palaces and glories of ancient lands. They came back from the Grand Canal and the Rialto and shops that looked like the insides of giant butterflies' wings and mended men's shirts and thought how the haying was coming on at the other side of the sea, how the old mare, Kit, was standing the gaff on the one-horse farm they had sprung from. They kept their decks and cabins as spick-and-span as the barn and parlor back home. Captains' wives scrubbed their floors on their marrow bones, darned and ironed and knit. Their husbands mingled with their crews and sweated with them at lines and winches. Their sailors were most of them cut from the same piece of Yankee cloth, all wool and a yard wide,

## Captain Abby and Captain John

as they were themselves. The seamen in the yards might well be the captains tomorrow. The ships' masters worked with their hands, harder than the men. For they were harder workers at home, and they had come up fast by such hard work. These were Yankee seafarers. They often startled the British captains they fell in with by their democratic ways and their love of doing things for themselves with their ten fingers and ten toes.

This fever of prosperity in shipbuilding and sailing hit Casco Bay, Maine, especially hard. The oaks were unusually tall along the hundred coves that ran deep into the land there. Fine harbors were as common as thrushes. Almost every farm had one, and the farmer-sailors could run their brigs right up to the kitchen windows and say good morning to their wives, being still on board. Every man around the bay began turning his trees into ships and turning his farm hands into carpenters and ironworkers. Every farmer built him his bark in his cove among the June daisies where they came down to the shore, and went sailing away to make his fortune in sugar and molasses or tea and pepper.

The fever spread inland. It spread up along the rivers that were navigable. But it did not stop at the head of the tide. It spread to the very heart of Brunswick town, which had once begun as a seaport but had thought better of it and moved inland five miles to the water power of the Androscoggin River falls. The fever swept right on over Brunswick, to Lisbon, eighteen miles from the Atlantic. A big ship was built there. They launched it when the Spring freshet came. It

## Captain Abby and Captain John

came a-fluking down the river to the high stairway of the falls at Brunswick. There it was drawn out on rollers, and a hundred yoke of oxen towed it over to McKeen Street, thence to Main, through the town's heart. And then it was launched anew into Merrymeeting Bay, at the town's end, and went on its way rejoicing. In 1815, a family built themselves a schooner right in the middle of Mill Street, Brunswick. It was hauled to the Landing, below the falls, and so to sea. And in 1822, farmers of Durham, high over Rocky Hill, built a ship and dragged it on rollers to the ocean road to fortune. Nothing could stop such men. Not hills, not mountains. They cut swaths through the woods to get their family ships to the water. No farm was too far back or hilly to be out of reach of the fever. Any small stream might come out of its quiet meadows on the sound of hammers at the next bend, and the trout in the brook flashed away frightened by the immense thing that was rising from the shallow pools. The climax was capped when a man built a schooner, in 1823, in tiny Mair Brook, Brunswick, and hauled it overland to Maquoit Bay. There was not enough water in Mair Brook to do more than float the peapod schooners of boys in their first breeches with buttons, but this man could not resist the trickle of running water, and so he laid down his keel there and hid the brook from sight. It was like a goose trying to bathe in a saucer! But Mair Brook's banks served for braces as the schooner grew. People along Brunswick's streets might expect to look out any morning and see a ship going by higher than their housetops, bound for Sumatra and the spice isles. Deer

## Captain Abby and Captain John

of McKeen Woods might stop and stare at oxen with sunflower eyes, two hundred of them, leaning to their yokes and drawing a ship through the forest.

Brunswick was loud with hammers night and day. Maquoit pushed off its schooners, pushing the azure mud and quahaugs each way as they slid at high-run tides. Flying Point sent off its ships with the white furrows curling at their bows. Bunganuc's deep canyon of a harbor sent them out. The sawmill there showed its silver teeth night and day, turning out pine planking. Mair Point shoved ships off, both sides of its spine, white and new as its birches. Simpson's Point sent them off. New Meadows River was crowded with last year's ships coming home and this year's going to the Gulf for cotton. Boys with their first jack-knives stood waist high in curls of shavings under the high sides of sea-going houses, and picked up new and exciting words from the mouths of men who banged their thumbs with a hammer. Girls set up housekeeping in the half-finished hulls. Wives cooked their clams with chips from boards that would sail the seven seas soon.

And Middle Bays, the part of the township of Brunswick where the sea came nearest to the village itself, had been one of the first places to feel the stir of shipbuilding and trade. The Pennell family, who had settled by beautiful Middle Bay where meadows full of violets came down to the tide's way and who had built their mansions there, named the place for themselves, and taken over its fine stands of oak and pine, had been building ships from the eighteenth century on. They had moved their shipyard from time to time down Mid-

## Captain Abby and Captain John

dle Bay and nearer the deeper water as their ships grew in tonnage. They had turned the quiet place, where Indians had once drowsed beside their smoking shell heaps, into a hive. Men swarmed over the ways there, hot as hornets. The world's goods were coming in at the Pennells' doorsteps. By 1823, a steamboat was landing regularly at Pennells' Wharf. By 1825, a steamboat was connecting New Wharf, a stone's throw to the south of Pennells' Wharf, with Boston, carrying boxes and staves destined for the West Indies and sugar.

By the time Deborah Pennell came into the family, Pennell shipbuilding was almost at high tide.

It was no wonder Johnnie Pennell got his back struts tingled that April morning. There was no time for any boy to loaf or hunt frogs at Middle Bays. A boy there had to be up and coming. Especially if his last name was Pennell. Johnnie was a Pennell. There were ships—many ships—waiting for him to help build them in his front dooryard, and sail them around the world, afterwards. The birch switch was hurrying him on to glory.

3

## Houses by Euclid and Ships' Carpenters

VISITORS REMEMBER the Maine coast as edgings of fine point-lace, going back, row on row, towards New Hampshire hills or the local mountains which come down to take a look out over the sea. They recall it as wild evergreens, fir and spruce and cedar and hemlock, with feathery white pines behind. The houses are surrounded by wilderness, the forest comes up to the back doorsteps. They recall the whippoorwills singing in the apple orchard at night. It is a fact that Maine is mostly forest still.

But there is a place at the head of Middle Bay, where Brunswick township touches the sea, which has the tamed and trimmed look of old England. The wild is near enough to see. The laces of firs and pines hem the horizon on the west and north and east. But the wild is kept at a distance. The place is wide rolling meadows starred with millions of daisies in June and galaxied with Queen Anne lace in September. The air runs honey with hay making in windrows and haystacks. The land looks and smells like Hampshire or Surrey in England. Every so often there is a lovely

## Captain Abby and Captain John

island of tame trees, and fountain elms interlace their boughs over a house.

The house is more than a house. It is a whole hamlet. It is a mansion, with a housekeeping house, an ell, applied to it behind, carriage houses and woodshed hitched to that, and, last, a barn as big as a cathedral, white, with green blinds, and a cupola to finish off the whole white company of buildings. Everything about these places is exact and exquisitely planned. Each individual structure is so placed as to get the maximum of light and warmth from the sun. Many of the houses are oriented, as churches are. I have measured my own house among these mansions of Middle Bay. The rising sun on May first is centered exactly, huge and golden, in my open front door. These establishments are in L-form, in order to make a corner to hold what little of the South comes this far north. The flower gardens and roses of these houses are always within that L, where the sunshine is captured and hoarded. The side veranda is here, so that old bones may sit in warmth that lingers even into November. The grindstone is always at the bend in the L, under the grape arbor, for coolness' sake. This brings the wide barn door towards the east, too, so the fine horses that used to stamp here could come out of a cathedral gloom into the full day and begin their progress properly oriented, with carriage wheels radiating the light as they came past the house and went off into the world. It is a geometry which tells you at a glance that people who had fitted their lives beautifully into the laws of weather and wind have lived a long time here. It tells you they were artists in living.

## Captain Abby and Captain John

A lot of living creatures had their abode here. There are rooms large enough for, say, twelve children, two hired girls, three hired men, six cows, seven horses, a brace of pigs, and enough hens to keep all the two-legged in eggs. And all these creatures had elbow and wing and flank room. Which is another way of saying that these hamlets mean civilization. They were self-supporting, too. From beef and pork by the barrel, to caraway seeds for the hamlet's cookies. These hamlets had strawberry beds, they had looms for making clothes, they had vegetable gardens and orchards, asparagus beds, cucumber frames, a Dutch oven, big enough to bake up a whole family for a week, a cistern to hold all the drops that fell on the house roof, a well that went down deep to coolness in middle July, long shelves for butter crocks and preserves in the cellar, a woodhouse, and a dark pantry for milk and cream. Mine has even a hop vine. But then, my Middle Bay house began in the eighteenth century as an inn for thirsty workmen, hot from the shipyard up the cove. These houses were weaving, baking, poultry-raising, meat-curing, fruit-raising, horse-driving, farming, fishing, as well as ship-building centers. They were all-round places. And they raised good round families—families of six, ten, twelve good citizens in short clothes, and a lot of marginal boys and girls, children of the family retainers by furrow and wave. Not to mention colts and chicks, piglets and calves with morning stars on their foreheads!

These hamlets were high green islands in rich clay farmland, each decently distant from its neighbors; they raised the kidney beans for Saturdays and Sun-

## Captain Abby and Captain John

days, and the pork to go in them, the currants and apples for jellies, and the flour for the edgings around tarts filled with home-grown strawberries; they made their own butter and smoked their own herring; produced their own milk and cheese; and grew their own clothes. But they were not farms. They were greater than that.

If you walk up their long lawns and go in under their porticoed doors, you will see at once that they are also town houses, furnished from the whole circumference of the globe. For the residents here were Yankee farmers who went to sea and traded with the world. The carpet in the front room was brought from Brussels, the matting in the bedrooms was woven by the Malays, the colored prints are from Genoa and Pisa, the dishes in the pantry are from Birmingham and Limoges, the tables in the parlor are Sheraton and Hepplewhite, the convex mirrors are from Paris, the porcelain doorguards are from Holland, the vases are from Canton, the pampas grass in them from the Argentine, the marble figures of lovely ladies and human hands on the mantel are Carrara marble, and the seashells are from the far islands of the Pacific Ocean. The rooms are full of loveliness and usefulness wide as the world.

The rooms themselves are as nice a balance between usefulness and beauty as men have ever hit upon. For they were planned and built by ships' carpenters, and those men knew how to handle form and light well and fit them serviceably into the weather and the years. They were not architects. But they had learned the principles of architecture by making wooden shapes

## Captain Abby and Captain John

that could cleave storms apart and ride tall and graceful on the high old seas. So the porticoes and balustrades are pleasing to both eye and mind. Their mantels are exquisite central points in the rooms they made. They are fluted like a Parthenon pressed flat, they are scalloped into right lines of waves and winds. They are proper temples built around the central fact of life, fire, warmth. The windows and doors and panels and wainscots grow out of the rooms they are in. They carry on the white symmetry of the fireplace around the walls. There are nine houses in this Middle Bays settlement. Each house has at least ten rooms. Most of these have fireplaces, with mantels. And none of these are alike. But all the rooms are a delight to look at for their honest loveliness. The light comes in the right way and shows right designs. These designs were made by hand, out of good square Yankee heads. They were made by Yankees who had a Euclidian passion for usable, good-looking shapes. My own house happens to have in its closets—and every bedroom has its clothespress—mahogany pegs, whittled out by hand, curved over like a Greek vase or Middle Bay wave as it breaks, to hang the clothes on. Even the sheds and barns are full of a loving sense of right patterns. There are forked fir boughs, stripped of bark, to hold up the collar-and-hames and the dung-fork. And on top of the barn, on the cupola that was inspired by a Chinese pagoda some sea captain saw, is the crowning point of these hamlets whose life depended upon the winds and the weather, the long white arrows, barbed with carved wooden feathers which let the blue sky through and are

## Captain Abby and Captain John

lighter for that, the weather vanes which pointed at the wind through the days and nights of a year, of a lifetime, of years after the builder's lifetime was done.

I like to think that houses have a lot to do with people's lives going on in them. I like to think that a lot of the good sense, plain piety, tenderness and trust of wives in their husbands, and silent devotion of men to their wives and children and their hard work, came into these Yankee people of Maine from the mantels, the panelled doors, and the sunny goodness of their wide, square rooms. Their rooms are beautiful by elm-leaf light, beautiful by the bare sunlight of Winter, by the soft light of the moon of April. Make no mistake. Such geometry means civilization.

It gives a man strength to live in rooms so large and well-made, in these days of crowding and hurry and bad manners. I thank the Pennell family for a lot of the good feeling, these past twenty years, which has led me an easy way to poems and peace. For every last one of the houses I have been describing, as well as the one I occupy at present, was built by the Pennell family.

The Pennells were sufficient unto themselves. They built their own schoolhouse in the middle of this shire of theirs. They chipped in and owned a share in the schoolteacher who came here to instruct sea captains and shipbuilders when they were still damp behind their ears. They had their own graveyard, even, in a corner of their shire, flowered around with cinnamon roses and flowering almond, for the shipbuilders and captains who had finished with hammers and the sea.

But the real monuments of these Pennell people are

## Captain Abby and Captain John

these houses on this tamed land of Middle Bays. Every house you see here is theirs, save one. That is the square, plain house I have my sunsets behind, the one on the hill, color of the weather, with no elms around it, an eighteenth-century hostelry for the sun as it goes home for the night. But that house was built by a family that had good sense enough to marry in at once and often with the Pennells, the Giveens. The Giveens didn't go in for fancy things, like elms around a house. They were closer to the plain earth and the plain sea. Every so often a volatile Pennell went over to the sunset, went over courting at the bare house on the hill, to give his children a dash of the thick blood the Pennells sometimes lacked. The Pennells renewed their strength like the giant Anteus by touching the earth there. So the Giveens are really in the family. And I count their house as a Pennell one.

I do not know of another place in America where the unity and goodness of a family are so plainly seen.

All the Pennells who built these places a century or more ago are gone from all but one of the hamlets. The older ones sleep in the graveyard here. The younger ones lie under the songs of the Bowdoin pines in the town cemetery. Their children are scattered to the four winds. Some of them followed wooden ships as they ebbed away to other places, even to San Francisco. Their other children, the ships of many tons, are gone under the sea. Their wharf and ways are a ruin of stones and rotted wood. But their houses remain to show they were here once and built a good chapter in the history of our country.

## Captain Abby and Captain John

I am going to turn back through the pages of that chapter now, to the time when the Pennells' Wharf Road, so quiet and empty now, was smoky with oxen and men in full beards, when the quiet cove right under one of the loveliest of the Pennell houses resounded with the sound of hammers and axes, when the annual family ship was on the ways and the hum of work drowned out the bees and the thunder of a Maine Summer. The hamlets under the elms swarmed with children then, and this part of Brunswick was very much alive with a life all its own.

## 4

## Begetter of a Chapter of American History

YOUNG JOHNNIE PENNELL had a lot to grow into besides the frog ponds of Middle Bays. He had a town, and he had a family that expected a lot of him.

Brunswick was a peculiar town a hundred years ago. It was on the river, and it did not have many miles of coast on the Atlantic. But it made the most of those few miles. The population of the place did not much exceed 1500, on the average, in the years between 1830 and 1880. But during that time this little place was well represented on the sea. During those years Brunswick had two hundred sea captains. Two hundred that I know about. There were probably a lot more. I don't know for sure, but it seems to me this is some sort of a record, even for Maine coast towns. I have the list that Charles Pennell, one of the Pennell Brothers' firm, wrote out, in 1899, of his fellow citizens who commanded ships in the last century. Two hundred captains! And of course there were other hundreds of Brunswick seafarers who never got that far, because death or lack of ambition, matrimony or other hazards, kept them from going the whole way aft. Allowing for the wind and for the fact that some of the captains

Captain Abby and Captain John
were repeaters in the same family, let's say that for every ten inhabitants of Brunswick, there was one sea captain in full cry on some ocean somewhere. Some of the hundred were tacking around the Horn, some were in the China Sea, some on the Atlantic. But they were all busy.

It is interesting to see how the same names recur: Skolfield, Giveen, Woodside, Merryman, Woodward, Pennell, Melcher, Dunning, McManus, Otis, Boutelle, Minot. There are thirteen Skolfields: John, Joseph, Charles, Thomas, James, Thomas again, Alfred, Samuel, Lincoln, Robert, William, Samuel again, George; nine Giveens: Daniel, Robert, Robert 2nd, William, Lewis, John—who commanded the Pennell topsail schooner *Exchange*, Robert once more, Robert still again, Thomas; seven Pennells: William, John, James Henry, Isaac, Benjamin, Lewis, Samuel; seven Merrymans: Thomas, Richard, Alfred, Curtis, Jacob, William, Jeremiah—(Lord only knows how many dozens of Merryman captains there were two or three miles away on Harpswell Neck, but I am sticking to Brunswick); seven Otises: James, Albert, Henry, James 2nd, William, Edward, Albert 2nd; six Dunnings: Jacob, Minot, Benjamin, Joseph, Sylvester, Charles—two of these, Jacob and Minot, were over half Pennells, having a Pennell mother; five McManuses: Richard, Asa, Robert, George, and Robert again; five Melchers: Joseph, Benjamin, Abner, George, Josiah; five Snows: Jesse, Thomas, Jesse again, Charles, Harrison; four Woodsides: William—veteran master of Pennell ships and maker of more sea captains than he had fingers and

## Captain Abby and Captain John

toes, Benjamin, Arthur, Adam; four Boutelles: Charles, Joshua, William; Charles A.; four Jordans: Peter, Cowan, Frank, Francis; four Martins: Clement, Matthew, Thomas, Clement Jr.; four Minots: Harry, Thomas, Albert, Bradbury. And there are three Woodwards, several Chases, three Simpsons, three Badgers, two Thomases, two Stovers, two Stanwoods, and two Orrs. Practically all these names are found on captains in neighboring Harpswell, and are multiplied down two or three or four generations. One can see that the sea ran in certain families in place of blood! Calling the roll of sea captains in Brunswick and Harpswell is like calling the roll of whole families: grandfathers, fathers, sons. And when you recall that most of these families were related by marriage, you can see how small a chance any boy born then had of not commanding a ship!

John Pennell, youngest of the eight Pennell brothers, had no chance at all. The whole town was against him. He was never to have any home except one that had sails on its roof and rolled about round the world. Whatever children he would have would have to be cradled and brought up there.

When you remember that every captain must have a vessel, you can see that a fleet could have been assembled off Brunswick that would have taken Homer two books more to catalogue. And practically all these ships, remember, were built in Brunswick, of the white oaks the Brunswick Plains grew, and built by the same families that built the captains. This was a town that left its mark on the sea and no mistake! If there is any town

## Captain Abby and Captain John

that can stand up to Brunswick, I should like to know it and take my hat off to it.

It wasn't John Pennell's town only that forced him out to sea. It was his family, too. Ships had been in the family blood stream goodness only knows how long. For the Pinel family—as it was spelled sometimes in old records—came from the Isle of Jersey, in the Channel, across the sea. There the ocean was a natural road, and they must have travelled it long. The family, spelling its name in the ancient English and modern American way, had gone down there to the Channel Islands during the Wars of the Roses and had become big toads in that small puddle.

No family is worth much that doesn't have a cruel step-mother on its coat of arms or in the family tree. The Pennells have one, though it happens to be a wicked uncle and he happens to be a myth. The story runs that this uncle sent three Pennell brothers to America for their education, cheated them out of their patrimony, and left them in the New World to snuff ashes on the shores of Massachusetts Bay. Being penniless, they went to work. So runs the tale. And as in most families, there was the usual American dream of recovering vast estates overseas. As a matter of fact, there were only two brothers who came over, Thomas and Clement. I know why they came, too. It wasn't for an education. It was for the trees. They had used up all the available trees on Jersey, and they wanted more to build ships out of. So they came. And they happened to have shillings enough in their breeches to buy property when they got to Massachusetts early in the eighteenth century, and

## Captain Abby and Captain John

trees. Thomas, born in the year of the Glorious Revolution, 1688, was a mariner and shipwright, as most of his descendants were going to be. He naturally kept to the coast so his sons after him might follow in his trade. He settled in Gloucester and went on building ships as usual. He died in 1723. Thomas the Second, his son, born in Gloucester in 1720, moved up to the District of Maine, as the trees in Massachusetts grew thin, settled first in Falmouth, then bought the land around the head of Middle Bay, Brunswick, in 1760. He built himself a house and a shipyard, and set up housekeeping in the old family trade of shipwright. He brought his son, Thomas the Third, born at Gloucester in 1739 and second of the Pennells born in America, along with him, gave him a hammer, and put him to work, too. Thomas the Second became a leading citizen. He saw the Maine Pennells started right on their shipbuilding, and died around 1780. That was the beginning of the Pennells of Middle Bays. Like Moses, this man had led his children into the Promised Land.

When John Dunning Pennell was going to school that morning in 1842, with his mother escorting him, the house that Thomas the Second had built was only a green hollow in the ground where lilacs still grew and a clump of lonesome apple trees with lonely whippoorwills calling through the stillness. For the family had been by that time nearly a century on the bay, the old homestead had become a ruin, the shipbuilding had moved down towards deeper water. This was America, and civilization moved fast.

Thomas the Third flourished like a quahaug at high

## Captain Abby and Captain John

water by Middle Bay. He got him a wife, Alice Anderson, out of Freeport, a fine place to get a wife from. He had got to be Tax Collector of Brunswick around 1778 or '79. By 1791 he owned two horses, four oxen, eight cows, and twenty acreas of arable land. He also had added ten children to the land by then, five of them sons. He was also able to board the Congregational minister, as well as his numerous offspring, for in July, 1803, the First Parish paid him for Minister Brown's keep. He had his hands in the ocean and ships, too, as well as in soil and ministers. He had taught all five sons to build ships. By 1800 he and his sons, William, Jacob, Thomas, and others in the family had evidently spread out on a larger scale in shipbuilding and were trading on the high seas. Son William, around 1780, had built himself a fine story-and-a-half house—for which I thank him since it is now my own—and a shipyard lower down the bay than his father's, had sold it to his brother Jacob, and had become a sea captain. And now, in 1800, he had a fine new son, Thomas, growing up to follow him on the decks of Pennell ships. There was at least one schooner in the family by 1807, I am sure. For in the attic of the house Capt. William built for himself and me, I have brought to light a receipt by John Powell, dated February 13, 1807, for money Jacob and Thomas Pennell had paid him. It seems John had repaired the schooner *Farmer's* sails for $2.00, had supplied three yards of Russia duck, two pounds of twine, and three pounds of bolt rope. His bill totalled $10.21. That schooner *Farmer* appears again

## Captain Abby and Captain John

in a letter from my attic dated at Boston, July 17, 1807, and addressed to Thomas Pennell the Third and his son John, a partner with him, at Brunswick, Massachusetts, District of Maine. Maine, as you see, was not yet free of Massachusetts. This letter came by ship, was folded and sealed, without envelope, and it cost the Pennells fourteen cents to have it delivered into their hands. In it, the mate, Thomas Cloutman, writes the Pennell owners of his taking their schooner *Farmer* over, after the death of Capt. Hills, on the way from Havana. So the Pennells this early had their hands in Cuba and sugar. "The Schooner Behaves Very well, All But One Small Steady Leak, which I Suppose is a Nail hole. I shall Black the Spars & sundry Other Small Jobs With what we have to do with. Gentlemen, if you wish me to Do Any thing with the Schooner, you will Be so Kind as to Drop Me a Line ... Thos. Cloutman." The Pennells would keep their hands in sugar of Havana for three-quarters of a century more.

Somewhere around this time, too, there was another schooner, the *Independent,* in the family also. It is mentioned on another scrap of paper from my attic. This time it is a bill for labor on the schooner by George Minot, in shillings and pence. The items are on the back of a MS of a patriotic song of our very young nation, a eulogy of Washington, which some patriotic Pennell had copied off in a fine, cobwebby hand. Washington and the Muse have been sacrificed on the altar of shillings and pence! Only the eighth stanza remains on the scrap. Here it is:

## Captain Abby and Captain John

Should the tempest of war overshadow our land,
Its bolts could ne'er rend freedom's temple asunder,
Crowned at its portal would Washington stand
And repulse with his breast the assaults of the thunder,
    His sword from the sleep
    Of its scabbard would leap
And conduct with its point every flash to the deep.
For ne'er shall the Sons of Columbia be slaves
While the earth bears a plant or the sea rolls its waves!

The Father of his country, one can see, has profited by the experiments of the great Dr. Franklin!

The beginnings of every nation are found on little scraps of paper or stone someone forgot and left in an attic or grave. So it is with the nation of the Pennells. The beginnings of their glory as shipbuilders and masters are well-nigh lost. Only little sparks shine out here and there in the dark that has closed over the light that burned a century and a half ago along Middle Bay. How many craft the Pennells had built and sailed before the beginnings of fair records, around the year 1834, will never be known. But by that time the Pennells had made a bright name for themselves among Maine builders and sailors.

Besides the schooners *Independent* and *Farmer* I have already referred to, I have found mention, in scraps in the Curtis Memorial Library at Brunswick, of a sloop *Eliza*, a brig *Favorite*, and a schooner *Harmony*. The years around the War of 1812 are especially hard to find accurate information on. It was a time of confusion, and legends that spring from confusion, in

## Captain Abby and Captain John

our nation; and it was for the shipyard on Middle Bay, too. Thomas the Third, founder of the clan, died that year 1812. Of course, in the years just preceding, President Jefferson's Embargo Act had crippled the Pennells along with other Yankee shipbuilders and traders with foreign ports. But evidently there had been some shipbuilding in spite of the presidential prohibition of foreign trade. And Thomas the Third's last act in life, if we can trust a very old and strong tradition, had been a typical one. A privateer had been ordered for prosecuting the war against the British. Thomas, in his last Summer, turned out a fine one complete in ninety days from the time her keel was laid. She was christened the *Dash*. She sailed out of Middle Bay—so the tradition swears—with a crew of Brunswick men, and she was never heard from afterwards. But Thomas never knew that. He was safe in the grave at last, having died in November, 1812, on his own sweet soil, in a place he had chosen for all the Pennells to lie in, a corner of a field above a brook called Spinney's now, with white birches and pines leaning over. And his wife planted cinnamon roses over his place. The conventional memento was put over his head:

> My loving friends, as you pass by
> On my cold grave please cast your eye;
> Remember as I am so you must be,
> Prepare to die and follow me.

Time has obliterated the grave now, and the stone has disappeared. But Middle Bays swarmed for three-

## Captain Abby and Captain John

quarters of a century with the life he passed on to the nation and the future.

Another craft was surely built during the War of 1812. The memory of it was always a mournful one and bound to be in such a family as the Pennells, who had a Yankee passion for making good use of good things. Jacob Pennell, Thomas's oldest son, and father of young Johnnie Pennell of the smarting trousers, had built the full-rigged ship *Charles*. But the owners never dared to have their ship risk running afoul of the British men-of-war swarming off Maine at the time. The *Charles* lay for years beside Pennell's Wharf. The *Charles* lay there till her timbers were wormed and unseaworthy. And they left her there till she rotted away. Her keel, they say, was seen for many a year at low tide. It was like a scar on the Pennells' minds.

After the war was over, and American sailors could go to sea without ending up in the Royal Navy, the Pennells blossomed out again. They launched the ship *Fair American* in 1815, begun during the war. They built many others the names of which have not survived. Capt. William's son, from my house, another Thomas, took his first voyage on a Pennell ship in 1821 and died at sea. A whole batch of future sea captains probably perished in that young man. But there were many other Pennells now to carry on. Middle Bays was alive with them, good men with timber and rope, men who had cut their teeth on a hand spike. The topsail schooner *Exchange* was certainly built somewhere around this time, and in the Pennells' upper yard. She was as smart a little schooner as you will see in a month of Sundays.

## Captain Abby and Captain John

There is a painting of her in the Curtis Library in Brunswick, shining like a piece of the morning, with two square sails atop her schooner sail on her foremast, running along the wind into the port of Trieste on July 26, 1824. A topsail schooner was a rare bird of the sea. There were not many of them made. They were as jaunty a vessel as ever danced along the waves. John Giveen was this schooner's master. She was a thing to be proud of, and her smart, spruce Yankees must have cut a fine figure on the streets of a town like Trieste, a town that was to become almost as familiar as Brunswick to two generations of Pennells. There is a family tradition that Tadesco Beach, near Lynn, Massachusetts, got its name from the name of a bark of the Pennells which went ashore from her anchorage there with all on board and broke her ribs open and drowned every soul. That was in the great gale of 1851 when Minot's light was swept away. The bark's name, *Tadesco*, the Pennells say, was the name of an opera singer of the time.

There must have been a steady procession of schooners, barks, brigs, and ships going off the stocks at the Pennell yards after the commencement of the last century and so on up to the Golden Age of the Forties and Fifties. For by this time Jacob Pennell had started on the begetting of his long line of children, that ended in Johnnie Pennell. This was the Age of Jacob. And Jacob was a man who felt, like Abraham of the sons like the stars in the sky of night, that it was given to him to people a nation. And being a builder, Jacob felt that every son and daughter ought to have a vessel of his

## Captain Abby and Captain John

own. So ships must have gone into the Atlantic in the rhythm of his sons and daughters. Every year or so a son, every year or so a vessel. Whatever Pennells there were of the older days, they were soon crowded out by this growing young republic from Jacob's loins. They were crowded out to Portland and Brunswick town and Harpswell, to earn their bread elsewhere. They left Middle Bays to Jacob's sons and their wives and children and cattle and ships. It is the old story of the one best ear in the wheat, of the one chosen to found the chosen nation. All the other Pennells' lands fell into Jacob's strong hands. He sat at the center of the land, in the house he had built near the close of the eighteenth century. He sat on the Middle Bays hill, with a shipyard at his feet to keep his children busy, and he watched his children grow great around him. He was a man out of the Book of Genesis, and God's word to Adam and Noah and to Abraham was in his ears: increase and multiply as the stars in the sky. So the vessels came out fast as his offspring from his house and went away to the four corners of the sky. He was the first great builder and the father of the greatest. His ships went out white on the world.

There is a persistent legend in the family of the Pennells, which all Pennells swear by, that the young Longfellow, while a student and professor at Bowdoin, often came down to witness launchings at Middle Bays. They say he saw a Pennell ship named the *Union* take the waves, and it was around the sight of this ship being built and launched that the poet afterwards built his poem, *The Building of the Ship:*

## Captain Abby and Captain John

Thou, too, sail on, O Ship of State!
Sail on, O Union, strong and great!
Humanity with all its fears,
With all the hopes of future years,
Is hanging breathless on thy fate!

It is arguable that Longfellow was thinking more of our nation than of the Pennell ship *Union*. But the Pennells won't hear to it! It was their ship all right, they vow. Anyway, Longfellow probably got his local color at Middle Bays.

The poet Longfellow touches again on Pennell lives, for the Pennells swear that after his student and professor days at Bowdoin, in the interim between Mrs. Longfellow the First and Mrs. Longfellow the Second, Henry Wadsworth was practically on courting terms with Susan Chase, sister of the wives of two of the Pennell Brothers' firm, Jacob, Jr. and James, sons of patriarch Jacob. Susan lived in the vast Chase mansion, above the craggy glen where Bunganuc Creek empties into Maquoit Bay. The Chase place stood on a hill looking out on Mair Point and Harpswell Neck. It still stands there, though the big central chimney is gone, and the woods have grown up so that you cannot see much of Maquoit Bay.

This house did a good deal for the Pennell family, and shipbuilding in general. It raised six daughters for the cause. If the Pennell houses are hamlets, the Chase mansion is a whole town. It has a staircase for an army of children to go up in column of fours and rooms for them all when they got upstairs. The Chase house once

## Captain Abby and Captain John

had an oven large enough to bake for all Cumberland County. The house has a graveyard to it, too, out in front, for the children to lie in after they had finished with their long lives. The slate stones in it were brought from England. They are beautifully carved. One has a death's-head cherub grinning with perfect teeth, and one has the loveliest weeping willow that ever wept green tears over a grave. Nothing was too fine or too far for a family who boasted that the royal blood of the Stuarts ran in their veins.

The Chase house was full of fine china and fine furniture. The Pennells seem to have stocked many of their houses out of its pantries and parlors. May the Pennells who are now within my own family forgive me for saying so! Historians can have no family but the truth, and I may lose a good part of mine in writing as I write. But it does strike me that the Chase girls were fond of stripping the old nest for the new. It had always been so with the daughters of this house, it appears. For this great mansion had had an almost titled mistress once, an Elizabeth Stuart, who eloped, according to tradition, with a Maine sea captain, Dan'l Campbell, from her eyrie in Scotland. She was the daughter of a great laird and head of a clan, and they say she had the purple blood of the Stuart kings in her. Her mother was Lady Eleanor Stuart. So little Bunganuc probably had a swarm of small Pretenders in it around the end of the eighteenth century! Anyway, though Elizabeth left home in a hurry and on horseback, with the laird somewhere in hot pursuit, she apparently had time to gather up a few things. Her horse must have been a tremen-

## Captain Abby and Captain John

dous creature. For here's what the almost-Lady Elizabeth Stuart Campbell brought with her, by my own count: a four-poster bed, three complete dinner sets of dishes, a dozen wine glasses, a warming pan, a pair of andirons, six Hepplewhite chairs, a dresser, a grandfather clock, and a rosebush! I have the descendant of the rosebush in my side yard under the window as I write this. I thank Elizabeth for that. The rose is white with gold in the center. Everybody in Pennellville has a piece of the royal bush now. Oh yes, and Elizabeth loaded in the side saddle on which she escaped that day, too. The wilderness of North America should not find her unprepared for the nicer occasions of life such as riding to hounds!

This fetching of an heiress from overseas by the high-toned Campbells set the style for the high-toned Chases. They kept up the tradition by bringing over lead coffins and a wrought iron fence to go around the family lot and to shut in that weeping willow which is lovely as the tracery in a dream.

It was lucky Elizabeth stocked the Chase house so well. There were six Chase girls. And as the Chase daughters began to marry the Pennells one by one, early in the nineteenth century, each bride brought enough furniture and dishes to set up housekeeping in her new nest. I am rather surprised that Miss Susan, who remained at home, had anything to eat off or any bed to sleep in at all. Anyway, she still had the grandfather clock, though the Pennells would get that when she died. The Pennells all swear to a man and a woman and a child that this clock was the one Henry Longfellow

## Captain Abby and Captain John

had in mind when he wrote his *Old Clock on the Stairs.* The Cambridge clock that is pointed out as the one is a wretched imposter, they say. They had a letter to prove theirs was the clock when the timepiece came, as most Chase things did, to the Pennells at last. Longfellow wrote the letter, and it was pasted right inside the clock. But Susan's Pennell niece, Aunt Nell, must have removed it, when she removed other clues that connected Susan and the poet. At all events, the aspens which Longfellow mentions in his poem—they call them honest popples up here in Maine—are still right out there in front of the house, catching the wind from Maquoit Bay, a whole row of them, and their leaves still tremble in the breeze. This makes, the Pennells say, two poems Longfellow got out of the family, the ship *Union* and the old stairway clock.

I am treading on ground the angels would tremble to tread—and I shouldn't dare even to imitate an angel if Aunt Nell were still alive—when I resurrect this episode laid safely away in lavender. But the Pennell tradition declares that Susan and Henry Longfellow were closer than mere acquaintances, after his Bowdoin years, in the late Thirties and early Forties of the last century. The tradition is that he had gone often to Bunganuc in his days as professor at the college, and had got to know the Chases very well and their young daughter Susan. Tradition also says he had often tasted the cider made in the mill built right under the lovely Cape Cod cottage, where my apples are ground to this day. (I can think of no lovelier place to live than over a cider mill, with the soul of Summer seeping up through

## Captain Abby and Captain John

the floor. I've tried to buy the house. But the people won't sell.) The poet had admired Susan as a child, the story is, and now as a professor at Harvard renewing his lost youth at Bunganuc and bereft of his wife, his attention was centered on this lovely young lady at the Chase house. Tradition declares that Longfellow wrote many letters to Susan and that whenever he came back to visit in Brunswick the two of them were seen riding along the Bunganuc road. Whether on Lady Eleanor's saddle or in a chaise, I cannot determine. And I don't dare to ask. The two were as thick as thieves.

Whatever blight fell, I do not know. The Pennells don't, either. But nothing came of this promising beginning, and the belle of Bunganuc was never translated to Cambridge. So the family lost the chance to add a poet to its sea captains. Longfellow eventually married again. But Susan stayed single all her life. She had her art to comfort her. She painted wild roses and pansies on velvet for all the Pennell houses. She even dabbled in portraiture and essayed the Pennell faces. But faces are harder to do than pansies. The softness went out of Aunt Susan's touch there. The Pennells looked like a lot of granite headlands. Still, a lot of them did in real life. Susan returned to her studies of the wild rose.

Susan and the poet Longfellow corresponded all their lives. Susan collected a whole trunkful of letters, it was said. And when the poet came back in 1875 as a whiteheaded and bearded old centurion and cried *Morituri Salutamus* into the face of death in his fiftieth-anniversary poem, they say he sent a note down to Susan ask-

## Captain Abby and Captain John

ing her to come up to Brunswick and hear him. Susan, of course, did no such thing. She had her pride. She stayed at Bunganuc, with her letters. She gave those letters, on her death-bed, to Aunt Mary Ellen Pennell, and she made her niece swear that, before she lay on hers, she would consign them to the flames. I guess I may have blown up the flames when, in 1925, on the hundredth anniversary of Bowdoin's Longfellow-and-Hawthorne class, bull in the china closet that I am, I pleaded with Aunt Nell to let me see the Longfellow letters to Susan. At any rate, the letters—which her sister-in-law had seen—vanished, and not one has ever been found. Who knows what facts of history and sentiment went up in smoke at Pennellville in 1925!

Whether or not Henry Wadsworth Longfellow ever bombarded Susan Chase (or Chace, as she spelled her name and her sisters usually did not) with passionate letters, other lovers did. There were many moths around that candle in Bunganuc. I have found two memorials to passion that burned hotly before the belle of Bunganuc's shrine. At least two lovers sought her hand. And probably a third, as one of the two hints. One writes from Brunswick, December 11, 1838: "Madam," his letter reads—Susan was twenty at the time—"I can no longer do so grate violence to my inclinations and injustice to your charms and merits as to retain within my one breast those sentiments of esteem and affection with which you have inspired me. I should have hazarded this discovery much sooner but was restrained by a dread of meeting censure for my presumption in aspiring to the possession of a lady whom beauty have

## Captain Abby and Captain John

conspired"—the lover's heat involves his grammar here—"to raise so high above my reasonable expectations. Were our circumstances reversed, I should hardly take to myself the"—a gap where some wretched seal-collector has destroyed a phrase of love—"of doing a generous action in overlooking the considerations of wealth and making you an unreserved tender of my hand. I shall await your answer in a state of unpleasant impatience, and therefore rely on your humanity not to keep me long in suspense. I am, Madam, Your most humble servant, Elisha Snow."

The heiress's answer—and I hope it was mercifully speedy—must have been No. For we find her being besieged by another even warmer and more rhetorical tender of marriage on January 6, 1843. This one came from Portland, it came in care of Capt. Daniel Chase, and it cost the writer six cents to send. The suitor this time was a sea captain, he was just about to sail, and he embarked on three sentences at the beginning much too elaborate for any plain sea captain in his soberer moments ever to embark upon: "Madam, Those only who have suffered them can tell the unhappy moments of hesitating uncertainty which attend the formation of a resolution to declare the sentiments of affection; with which you have inspired me. Every one of those qualities in you which claim my admiration increased my Diffidence, by showing the great risk I run in venturing, perhaps before my affectionate assiduities have made the Desired impression on your mind, to make a Declaration of the ardent passion I have long since felt for you. If I am Disappointed of the place I hope to hold

## Captain Abby and Captain John

in your affections, I trust this step will not draw on me the risk of losing the friendship of yourself and family which I value so highly that an object less ardently Desired or really estimable could not induce me to take a step by which it should be in any manner hazarded." The captain threw rhetoric to the winds and came out with sea-captainly frankness, he exposed his naked heart, probably without any letter-writing guide before him: "I am ready for sea the first opportunity to sail, and expect to be back in April, if it is God's will, and shall call and see you and talk this over if you are not otherwise engaged, if you keep your promise good. And excuse me for sending this scribblin. I don't expect you can find this out, but you can gess at part of it, I suppose. Plees excuse me giving you the trouble of this, and you will do me a favour in letting no one see the insides of this. I am, Madam, your affectionate admirer and sincere friend, E. D. Griffin." And the captain adds a rather sour postscript that he supposes that Susan will be seeing a good deal of a Mr. Kelsey this Winter at her residence.

Yes, Susan knew passion.

The Pennell tradition, you see, makes out that the poet Longfellow practically jilted their relation. As a matter of fact, whatever Aunt Nell burned that day, it was probably a funeral pyre of something like a jar of old rose leaves cherished for half a century, a slender fragrance, maybe merely of friendship, that had meant life itself to a thrifty and beautiful woman, growing old alone after having had her chances at marriage and bearing young sea captains and having refused them

## Captain Abby and Captain John

all. It is like Yankee women, unmarried ones especially, to treasure a rose in a *Bible*.

Captain John Pennell's log-book of the bark *William Woodside* is full of pressed roses and pansies, smilax, pinks, forget-me-nots, and lilies of the valley. It is like going through a hothouse in Elysium to turn through the pages. After the tall captain was under earth and his ships under the sea, feminine treasuring turned hard, plain latitudes and longitudes and details of bending fore topsails and making sail into a garden of tenderness. Of such shy and fragile stuff is Yankee sentiment!

If Susan Chase was folding her life away like a rose in the *Bible* over in Bunganuc, the family her sisters had married into were not. They were bursting out rampant as a lot of sunflowers. Jacob, as we have seen, had taken over his father's mantle. That garment could have fallen on no more robust a pair of shoulders. He had become lord of all he could see. He was building more ships than any of the other citizens of Brunswick who had caught the oak fever. The old first Pennell house had been too small for him. He had built himself the house on the hill, a story-and-a-half but wide enough to hold the children he was adding to the roll of shipwrights. Jacob had overflowed in all directions. When he had married, he had taken Deborah. Deborah was a Dunning.

Now the Dunnings of Brunswick and Harpswell were as the sands of the sea or the silver-blue alewives that crowd all the Maine creeks in May of the year. They were also as the salt of the earth. They were myriads.

## Captain Abby and Captain John

They were Tartars. They were full of the Old Hairy, and also of a special Grace. They knew winds and sails as they knew their own right and left hands. Ships crowded their blood stream. Tradition said that they were descended from James Dunning, Lord Ashburton. Somewhere in the family there was a picture of him in full regalia. He had had a vast estate in England, but it had reverted to the Crown. So the Dunnings of the New World had to make sail for themselves. The Pennells had already mixed with the Dunnings. Thomas the Third's first-born, Agnes, who had been born on Christmas Day and who died on Christmas Day 91 years after, in 1856, had married one, Joseph, and given him a sea captain son; and when he died, she up and married his brother, Benjamin, a sea captain, and started bearing him prospective sea captains, too.

Now Deborah Dunning, cousin of Agnes's two husbands, came into the Pennell family like a northwest wind on a ship working south. She bellied things out in great style. She probably brought the starch that the Pennells needed in their spines in order to become the leading Brunswick shipbuilders for half a hundred years, 1834 to 1874, when Middle Bays prosperity stood at tip-top highwater mark. Deborah started bearing children in 1802, the year she was married, and she kept right on with her profession till 1828, when she had Johnnie, her eleventh child, broke off and called it a day. Calling the roll in her house on the hill was like calling the roll of a platoon in the army: Eliza, Benjamin, Jacob, James, Job, Charles, Paulina, Joseph, Harriet, Robert, John. She must have baked johnnycake

## Captain Abby and Captain John

by the square yard and prepared hulled corn by the hogshead. A good mother to fill up a nation—eight boys and three girls all brought up well and amounting to something. Life must have been a three-ring circus in her house. I know, for I grew up in a family of ten myself three miles to the eastward as the seagull flies. Luckily Deborah's husband Jacob was a fairly large man, so pants he put by could do for three or four boys at once. How the moderate-sized house she lived in held so many children is a Middle Bays miracle. But it did. And they began early to bend sail for themselves, so by the time she was seeing Johnnie to school with her birch switch, that April morning in 1842, she already had four grandchildren. Deborah taught them all to read and cipher, sent them to toe the line in the schoolhouse. Then she turned the boys over to their father. He gave them all a mallet or an adz and let them rip. They ripped right into the tall oaks still left around the shipyard, and built ships bigger than their father had ever dreamed of building.

Long before Jacob died, in the Fall of 1841, he realized he had accomplished·something. He had begotten a chapter of American history. He had begotten the best firm of shipbuilders this part of Maine ever saw. He had begotten the Pennell Brothers.

Jacob divided up his estate, for he saw his years were heavy upon him in.the land he had peopled with good seed. He was ready to call it a day and go off to his rest in his corner, under the cinnamon roses. He cut his land up into strips, the way it was cut up*in old townships. He gave each of his sons a whole strip of Middle Bays

## Captain Abby and Captain John

from woods to the bay, so each should have all kinds of soil, from sand to blue clay, and all kinds of chances to spread out handsome. Only John Dunning Pennell, his youngest, got left out. But then, Johnnie was still a boy, and he had the whole Atlantic for his estate. Let him live there. And so, as we shall see, John did.

The older children had spread out handsome, for certain. In the year 1840, Jacob's old eyes saw four big mansions already around his modest house on the hill. And more were a-planning. Eliza had married a Reed and was living over on Orr's Island. Benjamin had married a sea captain's daughter, Mary Giveen, and had built himself a fine house at the bay's edge. Jacob, Jr. had come into the old house Capt. William Pennell had made, and was keeping it shipshape for my use a hundred years later. He had married one of the girls from the Chase mansion in Bunganuc, Hannah, and had sired a son already, Samuel, who would be a captain one day and command one of the largest Pennell ships, the *John O. Baker,* until she was lost in the North Sea in 1878—the model she was built from is beside me in the cabin as I write—and then the mighty Bath ship *Oregon,* would round the Horn seventeen times, as mate and master of Maine ships, and come home to my house, which his father had finished remodelling, August 31, 1859—as I can read on the inscription on my shed plaster—and he would sit in the side chamber that looks out on the empty bay, dreaming of old days when that water was crowded with ships and he a citizen of the vast world, until they found him dead, last of all the

## Captain Abby and Captain John

Pennell sea captains in a world where sailing ships were forgotten.

James, his brother, had married a Chase girl, too, Susan's sister Julia, and had brought her home to the loveliest of all the Pennell houses, loveliest because he built most of it with his own hands, and his hands were the best that ever planed a board at Middle Bays, in a ship or out. His house has a cupola that is the envy of my life. James, the handsomest of all the good-looking Pennell brothers, with a twinkle at the corners of his eyes that would have made him a success anywhere in the world, had blossomed out into the greatest Pennell artist in ships of them all. No vessel went down the ways that had not felt the fine touch of this master builder. He had a son creeping around in his house already, James Henry, a sea captain-to-be, and one that would break his father's heart. Master James's house up the avenue of elms was already the heart of the shipbuilding world of Middle Bays.

Job, James's brother, was soon to be married, and to the handsomest wife of all the Pennell ones, in spite of his hare lip and halting speech. He, the marked for life, stood somewhat apart from the others. He did not go down to the yard with them. He was not one of the firm. He kept to himself. When he drove his mother Deborah, in all her jetty Sunday-go-to-meeting best, to the First Parish Church, he did not go inside. He stole away and hid himself in the livery stable, or in one of the ribbon roads that wound into Brunswick, and sat among the hot pines and cool ferns there.

And superstition and malice touched Job and turned

## Captain Abby and Captain John

people from him. Folks said he had marked more than one unborn baby with his deformity. Even no less a one than that of Brunswick's first citizen and Bowdoin's greatest professor, Alpheus Spring Packard. Wives about to become mothers shied away from the sight of him. Human cruelty did not burn out with the witchcraft days. It had not ended in Brunswick with that woman whose body was staked down through the ribs at the Harpswell highroads' meeting place because she committed suicide. Human hatefulness came right down to our own times.

Job avoided working with other men. He worked his father's acres. He became the only complete farmer among the Pennells. He lived quiet and silent and peaceful, and apart. But he had his triumph. The lovely woman who came to his side bore the handsomest child of all who wore the Pennell name. Providence also comes down into our times.

And Brother Charles had, in 1840, just finished his grand house on the hill at the shipyard for his new wife, another daughter of Capt. John Giveen, like Ben's wife across the way, and she would occupy it only the year remaining to her life, and then resign it and its twenty-odd rooms to Margaret Patten, Charles's second wife, and resign her infant son Benjamin to his Uncle Benjamin across the road. Charles was on his way to become, in the family phrase, "Charles the Great." And the second Mrs. Charles Pennell would see her husband become the business manager of the Pennell Brothers and the "ship's doctor"—the man who met the family's incoming vessels in Boston, New York, or Philadelphia,

## Captain Abby and Captain John

and took charge till they were ready to sail again. The second Mrs. Pennell would become the social light of the whole very sociable Pennell clan and would entertain under her roof all the big-wigs from far and near. She would fill the immense house with five beautiful daughters and two sons. And the Pennells would get a poet at last. For her talented daughter, Harriet Given Pennell, would, in addition to being vice mother to all her brothers and sisters when her mother was trailing clouds of glory and silk in the drawing rooms of Boston and Philadelphia, and an accomplished pianist and singer and church worker, become a poet and would contribute to the book of Maine poets, the *Boston Budget*, and the *Christian Register*. If her verses seem soft and sentimental today, we need to recollect that a lot of the stern work of the world was done successfully by a thousand such heroines of Louisa Alcott—baking and sewing and scrubbing younger children's faces, and making the men feel like the lords of creation they believed they were, before women lost the fine art of sentiment—as well as poems about the flowers of life.

The poetess's father, Charles the Great, would gain control of the Pennell shipping industry, with 51 shares to his name. He would pluck at his hair in fine nervousness over the firm's affairs until all his fine hairs were gone, and he would have to wear a wig. And a young nephew, son of John, would one day burst in upon Charles the Great in his office looking on the shipyard, and see him without his wig, and never think of him again as the demigod he had always supposed him to be! It would be like seeing Zeus himself with his am-

## Captain Abby and Captain John

brosial locks hung on a chair. And no matter for all his Uncle Charles's carrying a gold-headed cane, the boy would never think of him as a being in the clouds again. Charles the Great would make a name for himself outside of business, too. He would cultivate music and sing a golden tenor in the Congregational Church in town. He would require a town house for his expansion and would acquire one for the Winter social season. One in Boston also, for the season there. He would give his daughters the "advantages," not without some envious whispers among other Pennell daughters that maybe some of these "advantages" were coming from the community chest of the firm. And Charles would crown his days by jumping in, wig and all, when the belated saint out of Bede's collection of saints, that plowman-preacher of Harpswell Neck, Elijah Kellogg, fell through the ice at the Pennell shipyard, and by saving him from a watery grave in Middle Bay. That act alone would have made any man famous. So when Charles the Great laid hold on the author of *Spartacus to the Gladiators* and a legion of books that have made boys better boys, that chilly day, the Pennell family touched on literature once more.

It was altogether fitting that the fine house Charles built, when it went out of the family at last, should go into the hands, for some time, of Helen Keller, the woman who made a dark world a world of light. This great woman of our times was able one day to sense that something wrong was going on around her barn. Some men were digging out a woodchuck. Helen Keller sent out word forbidding them to do any violence on her place.

## Captain Abby and Captain John

The little deed shines like a spark out of the dark and the past. And I wager the little woodchuck was grateful!

I owned Charles's house, too, for a little while and gave it to my wife as an anniversary present. But our friends got the better of us and would not let us occupy two Pennellville houses at once. One lovely fact about that mansion is that nobody connected with the Pennells has ever died there. I will make a bee-line for the place if I ever get to feeling really ill!

Paulina, the seventh child of Jacob and Deborah, in this year 1840, was married to another one of the Dunning clan, Thomas, and she was nursing her first sea captain now, Jacob, who would be lost at sea in 1869. And there would be a second sea captain, Minot, to nurse next year, and he would also die at sea. Another son would die in childhood. It is not to be wondered at that Paulina, after her heap of troubles, should become a little "queer." She was the only member of the family to become so. And she had her reasons, Lord knows.

Joseph was not married yet. And Harriet had not as yet married and lost her Dunning husband, an artist and carpenter in the Pennell yards, nor had the little white cottage gone up just north of my house, where she was to live so many years. Robert was still a boy of fourteen. And John was two years away from the birch switch of the April morning with the frogs calling him away from school. But small John had more voyages in him, for all the brief length of his trousers, than the whole lot of the Pennells.

## Captain Abby and Captain John

It was a fine, upstanding family for a father's old eyes to gaze on the last year of his life. If Jacob Pennell could have looked around the corner of time and seen into the thirty years ahead, his old eyes would have glowed still more.

He would have seen enough ships go out of the Pennell yards in Middle Bays to fill Portland harbor. And Portland has a pretty big one. Ships growing larger and larger, heavier and heavier, and more and more beautiful. He would have seen the Pennell Brothers' flag spread over the whole world and Pennell ships in every port under the sun.

He had seen the beginnings of the blossoming, in any case. Enough to make him very proud. He had seen his old shipyard given up, and a larger one in deeper water built between the houses of his sons Ben and Charles. He had seen the brig *Charles*, 160 tons burden, slide into the sea in 1834; he had seen the schooner *Harriet*, 128 tons, named for his fourteen-year-old daughter go down the ways in the same year. He had probably seen the brig *Cyrus* go off, for I think that smart vessel which hangs painted over my mantelpiece was built in the Pennell yards, though I cannot prove it for certain. Andy Pennell gave me the painting, and it had always been in Master James's family. Anyway, the veteran captain of the earlier Pennell ships, William Woodside, was her master in 1839, as my picture declares. I like this Pennell painting especially because William is going *uphill*. The artist drew his legend out of line with the ocean, so everything is uphill. William was an uphill kind of man. Old Jacob Pennell saw the ship *Eliza*

## Captain Abby and Captain John

—he was getting all of his daughters into his vessels' names—launched in 1838. He saw the brig *Mary Pennell*, 233 tons, and the bark *Tennessee*, launched before he died, in 1840. And in 1836 he had reached the peak of his pride and had received the master of arts degree in shipbuilding and in life, when a ship of 233 tons rode into the Atlantic bearing his own name. It was written in the stars that his ship would go ashore on the coast of Ireland and go down with all the crew and 400 passengers, Irish emigrants, men, women, and children. But that would be after Jacob was finished with the stars and lay under the soil he had made richer by his life in his family graveyard. Untroubled with the future, Jacob could die in peace, seeing his family blossoming so and his life so crowned with success. The patriarch had founded his nation and seen his children enter the Promised Land.

And Jacob Pennell had left a good manager of his children behind him. Deborah took her place in her husband's shoes and drove her fine sons on, with words and birch switches, to greater and greater glory. For Deborah Pennell did not stop with boys young enough to switch on their back trousers. She kept a weather eye on all her children, even the married ones. And she added their wives to her children as they came along. She gave them all orders. She made them all toe the mark. She knew what was going on everywhere. Her house commanded the road and most of the children's houses. She knew all that was afoot. She knew when her sons went to work and came home. She knew what wives went to town, and what for.

## Captain Abby and Captain John

"Cat's hind foot!" she would say. "There's Hannah traipsing off up to the village again, and she was there just last week."

Deborah had a vinegary tongue to go with her gimlet eyes.

"Ben's wife better stop gallivanting in her fine feathers, or she'll have Ben on the town one of these days, I declare.

"There's that young sannup of a Sam going home crying again like a bullefant. I guess he got his going-home-a-crying at school today. His bladder must lie near that boy's eyes."

Deb would look out of her window and sniff. "What's she got on her head now?—A new bonnet! Glory to Gideon! Jacob can't afford it. A bonnet?—Sho! sho!"

Or Deborah would have her hands deep in her dough-dish and not be able to go to the window. She would ask somebody to go for her. "Run see who that is going by. Julia?—and on a wash day? She best stay home and get her sheets whiter, say I."

Two small granddaughters of Deborah, Nell and Harriet, six years apiece, were sent up once by Master Builder James to his mother's with a ten-quart pail full of russets he had bought from a hand in the yards. Deborah loved russets. But she wouldn't be beholden to anybody, not even a favorite son. She filled the pail right up out of her new hogshead of molasses. The little girls started home. Ten quarts of molasses is heavier than ten quarts of apples. It was a heavy load for little girls. Their arms ached at their sockets. They meditated emptying some of the stuff out on the road. But they

## Captain Abby and Captain John

were afraid of those eyes that could see to all the corners of Middle Bays. They staggered on home with the pail between them.

It wasn't that Deborah was a hard woman. She had to be severe, for love and money's sake. She was watchful of the interest of her children and their families because she wanted them all to amount to something. She was bound the young-ones should get their money's worth out of the school. She and Jacob had built that school, out of their own pockets. The Pennells paid for the teacher and boarded him around. Deborah worked hard, the way Jacob had worked in his shipyard. Only her work was not merely from sun to sun. It was all but the sleeping hours of her life.

So, under Deborah's stern eye, down the ways went, in 1844, the brig *Guadalupe*, of 188 tons. The vessel sailed from Portland, December 14, 1844, and the great gale came up, and she was lost on her very first voyage, with all hands. That did not stop Deborah and the PB firm, though. They set their jaws and went on building. In 1845, off went the bark *Oregon*, 347 tons. Before 1849, they had the brig *Robert Pennell* on the sea, as John Pennell's pocket diary proves. In 1848, the Pennell Brothers launched their masterpiece so far. She was named for their master builder, the *James Pennell*, and she weighed 570 tons. She was a landmark in the history of Brunswick shipbuilding. They were prouder of her than of anything that had happened. But the stars were against this vessel, too. She sailed once too often with wheat around the Horn. The wheat shifted in her in a terrible gale, she was "knocked down on her beam ends,"

## Captain Abby and Captain John

her crew took to the boats, as she stood on her nose, and pulled away. But two other ships saw her later. She had righted herself somehow, she was going along by herself, with her hurricane sails set, her wheel lashed. They boarded her and found all apparently in order, except for no crew. They were loaded themselves with wheat, or they would have tried to save her. They watched her sail away, with her flag flying, headed due south. It was a sight to abash any sailor. Maybe in some frozen bay of Antarctica she still flies her PB ensign and the Stars and Stripes. It was a sad day for the Pennells when word of her loss came. She haunted them for years, their lovely flagship, going mysteriously on some unknown errand off into the silence of the South Pole.

By the time of the *James Pennell*, Johnnie Pennell was no longer Johnnie, but John Pennell, a young carpenter in the yards, doing a man's work and drawing a man's pay. His careful workmanship was built into the *James* and the six vessels that followed her. For vessels followed fast now. It was at the high tide of American shipbuilding, and the Pennells were bound they should keep on the crest. So the roll goes on, with ships growing ever longer and heavier. In the middle Forties, the Pennell ship *Majestic*, 714 tons; in 1848, the ship *Cornelia*; November 1, the ship *Tempest*, 861 tons; October 5, 1850, the ship *Governor Dunlap*—which a single notation in John Pennell's notebook has rescued from the darkness of oblivion; in 1851, the ship *Calcutta*; 1853, the ship *Redwood*, with the unheard of tonnage of 1165 —they had to dredge Middle Bay to get her off. The bark *William Woodside*, 462 tons, named for the tough

## Captain Abby and Captain John

old teacher of sea captains, slid down the ways in 1854. And then came 1855, the year that was an epic in the Pennell family. I have not heard of any family shipyard that can rival this one. In that year of grace, the ship *Charles S. Pennell*, 986 tons, went off, and Charles came into his glory now; the ship *Ellen Hood*, 1046 tons, went off; and the ship *United States*, 1082 tons! The Pennell ships in that one year could have taken the whole Greek army to Troy, and could have taken most of the Trojans out for a ride with them! The year 1855 was a record any shipyard in Christendom could well be proud of. Three ships in one year! And this was a onefamily yard, remember. And remember, too, that a year in Maine means at the most five months of outdoors working. Three vessels in five months! 3114 tons of Maine goodness, beauty and usefulness! After the panic of 1857, the record runs on—without John Pennell now, for he is out sailing the Pennell ships and not building them. In 1859, the ship *John O. Baker*, 797 tons, rushed down into Middle Bay.

On November 20, 1860, in her last year of living, the eighty-year old steel-blue eyes of Deborah Dunning Pennell dimmed with the proudest tears an American mother probably ever wept. Deborah had wondered why her sons and daughters had manoeuvred her and kept her away from the shipyard in the Fall of that year. Then the day came when they were launching. She went down, in her best bib and tucker, in her carriage. And there on the high ship, in letters of real gold leaf, was her own name. The bark *Deborah Pennell*, 599 tons, went into Middle Bay like a flying seraph, with her

## Captain Abby and Captain John

namesake on her. And Deborah, blinded with tears she had held back for so long and had used sparingly, Yankee-like, went into Beulah Land with all sail set. All the tenderness she had repressed all these years came welling out. She wept among the children who had made her so proud. All of them were grown now, and most of them successful and famous. And they were all hers. To crown it all, her son John, her youngest son, already the head master of the Pennell Brothers' ships, was to go as her captain. Deborah had earned her rest by her husband. She died just six weeks later, in great pride and great peace.

Whether or not Longfellow took fire from a Pennell launching, another famous American writer did. She must have seen several, for she lived in Brunswick right at the highwater of shipbuilding. This author helped to start the bloodiest war in history, a war that would be a handwriting on a wall for the Pennell prosperity. She had had a vision in the gothic First Parish Church at a communion service. She had written the vision down, partly in one of the college dormitories, for she had a husband who was Professor of Religion at Bowdoin College. She went to the dormitory when her brood of children became too loud for the Muse or anybody else. The book she wrote was *Uncle Tom's Cabin*. But she had her lighter moments, as when she was describing a launching. She described one of them in the Pennell shipyard at Middle Bays, in a book in which Moses Pennel is a hero, called *The Pearl of Orr's Island*. Harriet Beecher Stowe let herself go when she described Middle Bay:

"On these romantic shores of Maine, where all is so

## Captain Abby and Captain John

wild and still, and the blue sea lies embraced in the arms of dark, solitary forests, the sudden incoming of a ship from a distant voyage is a sort of romance. Who," asks Harriet, "that has stood by the blue waters of Middle Bay, engirdled here and there with heavy billows of forest-trees, or rocky, pine-crowned promontories, has not felt that sense of seclusion and solitude which is so delightful. And then what a wonder! There comes a ship from China, drifting like a white cloud,—the gallant creature! how the waters hiss and foam before her! with what a great free, generous plash she throws out her anchors, as if she said a cheerful, 'Well done!' to some glorious work accomplished! The very life and spirit of strange romantic lands come with her; suggestions of sandal-wood and spice breathe through the pine-woods; she is an oriental queen, with hands full of mystical gifts; 'all her garments smell of myrrh and cassia, out of the ivory palaces, whereby they have made her glad.' No wonder men have loved ships like brides, and that there have been found brave, rough hearts that in fatal wrecks chose rather to go down with their ocean love than to leave her in the last throes of her death-agony.

"A ship-building, a ship-sailing community has an unconscious poetry ever underlying its existence."

Harriet Beecher Stowe knew her ships and Middle Bays, even if her personifications do seem to get the upper hold on her.

The roll of Pennell ships went on, without Deborah. The bark *Anglo Saxon*, 543 tons, in 1862. This proud vessel Master James could do only one thing with. He

## Captain Abby and Captain John

gave it outright to his oldest son, the apple of his eye, James Henry. And this vessel, white and shining as an archangel that she looks like in the portrait she sat for off Holyhead, North Wales, James the Second, son of the master builder, took out on the seas, like the young blood he was, and with a lot of other young bloods with him, and indulged himself in a lark by running the cotton blockade of the South. The episode took place off Hatteras, and James Henry got his wings singed. He had not meant harm, it was all in jest. But Charles the Great, his uncle, the ship's doctor, had to hurry down and doctor James Henry out of prison, and he, it was said afterwards, got small thanks for it. A shadow seemed to come over Middle Bays with this blow. The twinkles left the corners of Master James's eyes. The family paid dearly for the escapade. The white ship was lost. Master James may have thought of another king like himself who lost a white ship long before. He had loved James Henry, and he still loved him, above all else on earth. And the most promising of the young sea captains among the Pennells was lost to Middle Bays. It well-nigh broke his father's heart. James Henry had to live forever in exile in far-away Cardiff over the sea. He would watch Yankee ships coming in there, even if he could never sail them again. Some of the Pennell ships were sunk by the Confederate ram *Alabama*, as that dark cloud of the Civil War hung over the oceans. These were hungry years for the Pennells. The family tried later on to recover something from the *Alabama* award of Geneva, but were never able to. The shadow of James Henry stood over them.

## Captain Abby and Captain John

But still the Pennells went on bravely. Still the roll going on: 1864, the brig *George W. Chase;* 1864, the ship *Mary Emma,* 1067 tons. But the shadow lengthened and deepened, for it was nigh the sunset time. The bark *Istria,* 811 tons, was on the ways in 1865. But she was the "hard luck" ship of the Pennells. An evil star shone on her before her keel touched water. The ranks of the Pennell Brothers were broken at last. Master James, brains of the business, the tallest and kindest of them all, standing on the top of the first section of the mainmast, stepped on a loose plank a careless workman had left there, and plunged down to the bottom of the ship. His back was broken. And though they did not know it at the time, the back of Pennell shipbuilding. James never spoke or moved again, though he lingered on for some weeks. Then the shadows drew in, and maybe a son's face he had loved and looked for. When kindly and kingly James went to the Pennell graveyard among the cinnamon roses, all the carriages in town followed. They reached the whole length of the Pennells' Wharf Road. And most of the people in them were James's friends. James had put his hand into his pocket to help every soul that had known need, workman or ship owner. Things were nigh the sunset. Bad luck went with the *Istria* on all the seas. It was hard to get men to sail in her. She finally sailed away to the Pacific and was swallowed up as if she had never been in the great silence of that vast grave. No word came of her. But somebody fell in with a Pennell captain in San Francisco, and showed him a bit of wreckage picked up in the southern Pacific, and the Pennell captain declared

## Captain Abby and Captain John

it was a piece of the *Istria*. She had gone to pieces somewhere out in that silence.

The sunset was upon the Pennell yard. The ship *Oakland*, 1237 tons, designed and begun by James, the master builder, was finished in 1866, the Summer after his death. It was the largest ship so far. But no ship went off the ways next year. None for eight years. The death knell of wooden ships had sounded over all the oceans of the world. The knell was heard on Middle Bay. It was the twilight. But one last blaze of glory there was. In 1874, the ship *Benjamin Sewall*, 1433 tons, slid into Middle Bay with Captain John Pennell on her deck and all Brunswick looking on, in the most memorable launching that the town ever saw. But in 1878 the bell of the First Parish Congregational Church tolled the return of the greatest of Pennell sea captains, from Rio to the graveyard that lies in the shadow of the pines of Bowdoin. Captain John was home forever. The Pennell sailing was done.

That is how the chronicle reads, if you follow it through to the end.

The hundred years of the Pennells had been a glorious hundred years, though  Seventy-odd vessels—so the count stands, though the names of them are not all known—built in a bay that is really a large cove, by one family. The Skolfields, across Harpswell Neck, in the bay named for them, had nothing to show as fine. Twenty-four vessels to the Pennells' seventy-odd. The Simpsons of New Wharf could show only thirty-seven. The Pennells had led them all. Their ships had become famous all the world over. Their sea captains were

OXEN AT BOW OF THE *BENJAMIN SEWALL*

## Captain Abby and Captain John

among the best on all the seas. It is a proud record for any family on earth.

And the slim boy with the scorched backsides had helped, he more than any other, to make this family shine.

## Young Mizzenmast

JOHN DUNNING PENNELL never had to have his mother escort him to school again. He went there under his own sail and learned all that the Pennell school could teach. He learned to cipher, and he learned to write a fine scrolled hand in which every capital is carefully shaded in. That was a good thing. For John was going to deal in capitals all his life. Most of his words began with them. He tried them out in that small notebook of his. His own name and his friends'. He tried out some ships' prows, too, and scroll designs to go on them. All his life he did so, in his log-books among latitudes and longitudes. His mind was full of fine patterns.

Of course, John took time out between capitals and sums. He dug for old homemade bullets of the Indian wars on the hill back of the Simpsons' New Wharf, where a stockade had stood. He skated on Middle Bay when a January snap had made a floor solid enough for oxen to go right down the bay to Birch Island. My father drove his down that way thirty years later. He shot his partridges in the ancient apple trees his Great-Grandfather Thomas had planted when he took possession of this peninsula. He went to molasses candy pulls

## Captain Abby and Captain John

at his uncles' houses. He went to spelling schools and singing schools at the schoolhouse. He had a good voice. John went in swimming when the tide suited. He may have set a powder train or two under some boy's tail at the schoolhouse in business hours, and laughed to see the boy galvanized into swift action. But usually he tended to business.

John never had much to say. He didn't after he grew up. He was one of the quietest and soberest of the Pennells. But he did a lot of straight thinking. It made him shoot up very straight in his mind as in his body.

When he had finished all the spellers and readers in the Pennell school, John went on to the town school and exhausted theirs. Then he boarded himself out in Portland and went to a business school there. Nobody had ever told him. Nobody had to tell him. But he knew he was going to be a sea captain. He took it for granted, as so many Brunswick boys took it for granted a hundred years ago. He was sure of it as he was sure his eyes were frostflower blue, like the hillside by old Deborah's house in Septembers. He was sure of it as he was sure his brown hair was curly and his hands long business-like hands. So John learned methodically and thoroughly all that there was to learn in the schoolbooks. He had been learning the wind and the weather and tides the same way, from babyhood on. He knew when the tide was flooding even in the dusty Portland schoolroom. He got as much schooling handling things on the ships at the Portland wharves, and talking to mates and captains. His last name opened any ship's cabin door to him. He did not hurry to become a sea

## Captain Abby and Captain John

captain, as many other boys did. Lots of the hasty ones came to a quick end. John did not want to be one at seventeen. He wanted to know about things before that. For instance, the way the oak planking is fastened together under a captain's feet. He wanted to be a first-class captain. There were plenty of the other kind. So John studied, shot up, and got his growth on him.

At nineteen John Pennell came home and entered his brothers' shipyard. There was no formal announcement or celebration. It was tacitly understood that he was to be one of the Pennell Brothers. He put on his work clothes and went at it with adze and plane. He worked hard and took a common man's wages. Building came first, sailing afterwards. John wanted to know all about the house in which he was going to set up housekeeping for life. His children would be born in just such a thing as he was making. It was a large cradle. It would be good to make it a strong one. John Pennell came to know how important the least tree-nail was to a ship. A score of lives depended upon that thing no bigger than his thumb. Upon this very one. So he shaped it and drove it in right. And so it went on, honesty and good workmanship out to the tip of the jib-boom. He learned to handle chisels and to know the right curve in a white oak plank by the feel of his hands. He didn't talk much with the other carpenters. But they soon knew he was one of them. He became the best one in the whole yard. He was constantly drawing the fine scrolled designs for ships' sterns and prows, and he was putting them into wood now. At the front of his log of the *Deborah Pen-*

## Captain Abby and Captain John

*nell,* there is the design he made later for a two-masted sloop and the prow-piece of a ship. The fine work in modelling and finishing was given over to John now. The brig *Robert Pennell*—named for his nearest brother and the one John loved the best—the ship *James Pennell,* the ship *Tempest,* the ship *Governor Dunlap*—John's clear and clean mind was built into these four vessels. His life was a part of the life they would have out on the sea, under the wind, when every fibre and nail in them would come alive and work every minute of the time, as dead steel never comes alive. Four ships to John's name now.

Young Mizzenmast, the men in the yards nicknamed John Pennell. He was tall, and he was solid. The mizzen is the mast next to the captain's cabin. John was proud of his name.

It wasn't all work and no play for the young man John. It could not have been in such a family as his, for all John's natural soberness. The young Pennells themselves made up a good-sized society. Many of them were full of the proverbial Pennell liveliness. There were high old times along Middle Bay on Sundays and when the snow flew and stopped work in the yards. There were baked bean and Indian pudding suppers Saturday nights in the Pennell houses, in rotation. This saved firewood. And every Pennell house had an oven large enough to bake beans and brown-bread for all Middle Bays. This Saturday assembly of the clan was an institution that lasted all through the shipbuilding years. At the gatherings, Mother Deborah laid down

## Captain Abby and Captain John

the law, and also played the melodeon for the singing. The Pennells were renowned for their good voices. They made the starry Winter skies ring like a crystal vase over whatever house it was, Jacob's or James's, Charles's or Ben's, or the old homestead. The chosen house rang with the assembled voices of the clan.

The Pennells went to church *en masse* also. They were one of the sights of Brunswick when they came along the upper Mall, by chaise and horseback, towards the First Parish Church. The men wore tall hats and shawls, and the women sat in acres of taffeta and silk, with bonnet and shawl over all. They were a handsome cavalcade. People turned out to see them come on a fine Summer morning. Young John was one of the tallest and one of the best riders of all. The Pennells were famous for good horses. Their horses were high steppers, like their owners. Middle Bays had the best horseflesh in Cumberland County. They ran especially to finely matched spans. The Pennells' horses could take them to Portland and back in one day, a good sixty miles. The lowlier townspeople described the Pennells themselves as "heads up and tail over the dashboard." The Pennells sat together in a block in Harriet Beecher Stowe's church, and the center of the music was always there. But though they made a fine show at church, they did not go there for show. They went for worship. For they were a very devout and godly family. Young John was religious and pious even from his youngest years. In his pocket diary, under March 1, 1848, he writes this pious stanza in a young man's hand:

## Captain Abby and Captain John

> Remember all Thy grace
> And lead me in Thy truth,
> Forgive my sins of sober years
> And follies of my youth.
>                              John.

This stands right next to measurements and notations of wages paid men in the yards. John combined religion and business all his life.

Some Brunswick citizens regarded the Pennells as stuck-up people, and they often shouted at them in town meetings a word not unheard today—and usually used against the finer-grained persons—"Bourbons!" For the Pennells naturally gravitated to the side of property in their voting and speaking there, having a good deal of property themselves. But they were at heart plain and democratic Yankees, no Bourbons. If they wore good clothes, they earned them. And with their hands and by their own sweat. The women by sewing and ironing for a host of children, the men by driving nails and planing planks. They worked with their workmen on their ships. If they had fine ways and manners, it was because they thought fine manners and a sense of decorum were a part of right living and thrifty living. If they had a sense of family, it was for the reason that they knew that wise breeding was essential, that it took silk to make a silk purse, and not a sow's ear. They were farmers and working people, as well as ladies and gentlemen. It never occurred to them that people might not be both at once. It had never occurred to most Americans in that day. It was the unthrifty and the small-

## Captain Abby and Captain John

minded Americans, then, who thought that way. Maybe times have changed now. If they have, the people deserve hanging who have changed them. For they have gone a good ways to destroying America.

There were the Pennell sleighrides, between Sundays, in a dozen two-horse sleighs in procession, for the Pennells always went together, over to Harpswell Neck, to Freeport, to Maquoit, to Topsham, to New Meadows, to Gurnet. Sunlit December days and moonlit January nights were full of sleigh bells and Pennells. They were great visiting folks. They called on friends and relations in company. They carried charcoal stoves and soapstones for their feet, and they often sang as they slid along, a sight and a sound to remember for years, under the moon.

And there was another church, nearer home, the "Forest Church," on the Mair Point road. John and the younger Pennells especially frequented this place. The services were in the evening. Bowdoin students often walked down from the college, and the Pennell girls often walked up. So they met on neutral ground. It was a traditional place for the beginnings of courtships. Many life lines first wove themselves together there. There were printed cards which helped matters along. They read: MAY I C U HOME? These were passed around surreptitiously during the sermon. John Pennell handed out several such cards, with blushes on his face. He saw his share of girls home. But he never saw any girl there home for good. There are several girls' names in his diary, written in when the young man was thinking of something else and so was most

## Captain Abby and Captain John

himself. Only two, though, occur twice. One was Martha Randell. The other—and it was scrolled in most carefully—was Abby Reed. Abby Reed did not go to the Forest Church. She lived over on Orr's Island. John did not let love interfere with shipbuilding.

There were meetings even at the Pennell schoolhouse. John notes in his diary that they had a meeting there on February 22, 1852, with Elder Cushing holding forth.

There was good gunning along Middle Bay. John records that he shot a wild goose in April, 1851. He shot hundreds of the wild pigeons that used to come over the Brunswick Plains in such myriads that they made a twilight at noonday.

A lull came in the Pennell building. It was the time. John was twenty-four years old and knew what was inside ships. Capt. Thomas Skolfield, over on Harpswell Neck, needed a man to make up a crew. John Pennell went over and saw him. Then he came back and packed up his things. Big Tom Skolfield was known among his friends as the Rock of Gibraltar. It took a lot to move him. None of the oceans had moved him any. He was a good man to learn sail under.

Where John sailed to, and how long, nobody alive knows. The log of the ship is lost. The ship was the *Screamer*, I have been able to ferret out that much, though. A good spread-eagle name for a Yankee vessel! And she was built by a Dunning. That made it perfect. Built by a Dunning and manned by a Skolfield. I don't know where John sailed. But I know he sailed. And learned. He learned to balance his feet on an icy moon-

## Captain Abby and Captain John

beam at midnight a hundred feet over a sea that ran blackness and sudden death. He learned to man a pump. He learned all the forty-eight sizes of rope. He learned what each strand meant in the gigantic cobweb spread above a square-rigger, and how his life might depend on a single knot there. He learned to eat the forecastle beef and to drink ropy water that stank to heaven. He mastered the exquisite science, one of the most intricate and exacting professions human civilization has ever worked out, with Phoenician and Grecian angles to it, of making a world of wood and canvas move around a world full of winds and currents usually against a man, and smashing waves always against men, over a network which isn't there but which the mind of man has traced over the globe so that he may know exactly where he is at any hour of the darkest night. It took a lot of learning. John learned to live detached from all but those two webworks, the ropes over his head and the gridwork of latitudes and longitudes running imaginarily over the ocean around him. He learned how to erase time and the history of friends and home always going on around one on land. He learned to live by the day, by the watch, by the single lonely minute. How to live by the wind and the weather, too. He learned to eat his heart and say nothing, to let his freezing tears roll down his unbrushed cheeks as he silently made a line fast high in a gale of Winter wind. John learned a lot.

Enough to last a lifetime.

John began his sea life the right end to, as a common sailor. There was no short cut by a mate's berth to a captaincy. This was a science that began at the bottom. And this was democratic Yankee land. A man began at

## Captain Abby and Captain John

the foot of the ladder. This is a Maine history of a Maine man.

Then John came home to Middle Bays and went to work in his brothers' shipyard again. And he probably had the name of Thomas Skolfield, who had shaped his body and his mind to the sailors' life, written across the curve of his heart.

John Pennell was busy as a hot hornet in the yards those peak years of Pennell building. He had had his hand in most of the vitals of the vessels turned out in the past five years. And he had his hand and his heart very much in the ship *United States*, 1046 tons, the prize ship of all so far, in 1855. It was the last ship he would have a hand in making in his life. He put all he had into her. She moved like a whole universe down the ways at last, in the Spring of the year. She took her place on the sea. And John Pennell left the land with her. He went as her first mate. His blue chest was in the cabin, his *Sailing Directory*, and his *Bible*.

There are only one or two such moments in a man's lifetime.

Now there was only the ocean for him for the rest of his time.

John sailed to Mobile on the *United States*, J. D. Blanchard master. It was John who made the entries in the log. From Mobile they carried 3166 bales of cotton to Le Havre. Then back to New Orleans they came with a cargo of immigrants. They are a crankier cargo than cotton. Five of the immigrants died on the way, two on a single day, an infant child and an old man. They were all buried at sea. And fast. It was the fever. It worked fast, immigrant fever. One immigrant used unseemly language on Capt. Blanchard and was put in irons. Irons were a leading article of dress on ships in the Fifties. They landed at New Orleans on November 16. They had a sumptuous Christmas dinner there: turkey, oysters, "pyes," and cakes. January 11, 1856, cotton again, 2163 bales of it, for Liverpool, a much less perishable cargo! They arrived February 12, a quick crossing, for Winter. They loaded in freight. March 10, they put out for Boston. On March 15, during a gale, they were run into by a bark, "name unknown," their main fore braces were carried away, and they were damaged at the hull "considerable." John did not note what happened to the bark! Plenty must have. They had lots of weather going home, five gales of it. They made the ship fast at Long Wharf, April 23.

John sailed as Blanchard's mate still, through 1857. He was with him when he sailed, February 6, from New Orleans, with cotton, for Havre. They fell in with the Russian bark *Odessa* on that trip; she was headed for Haiti and entirely out of grub. They gave her what she needed. Havre, March 16. And John parted hawsers with Capt. Blanchard. He joined the ship *Wellfleet Harbour* on April 6, as chief officer under Capt. Westcott. They sailed May 4 for New York, with immigrants. All Europe seemed headed for America. It was the revolutions and hot water there. John had to put one man, "soused in liquor," in irons on the way over, met an iceberg face to face and had to crawl in jibs past it, and reached New York on June 3. John went home to Middle Bays in the middle of the Summer to tend to various jobs.

# 6

## Abby Signs the Papers

ONE OF THE VARIOUS LITTLE JOBS John Pennell had to do that year 1857, at home, was a ticklish one. Before he quitted the land for good he had one very special job to do. It was an intricate and sobering business, almost as hard as bending a heavy sail in a gale of wind or rigging out a jib-boom. It was on Great Island John had to do it.

It was signing up a mate for a permanent berth with him, once he should become a captain.

John had driven to the islands of neighboring Harpswell, by buggy or sleigh, ever since he was knee-high to a grasshopper. That shows his father's good sense and John's good sense. For the islands of Harpswell are a very special set of islands. Harpswell Neck is all right, but being mainland it is a bit too close to civilization and full of usual and expected people. Personally I wouldn't be found dead in it. There are some good houses there, though. But the Harpswell islands are a boy with different colored pants on. They have people and bays and hills and woods like none other on earth. I know what I am talking about because I was raised on one of those islands. Great Island, or Sebascodegan, as

## Captain Abby and Captain John

the old lobster-loving Abenakis used to call it. That one island has fifty bays, maybe, and more loveliness and cussedness and excitement on it than five hundred boys could soak up working in unison all their boyhood.

There were a lot of good friends of the Pennells on Great Island. The place bristled with sea captains. It was crammed with Dunnings. Wherever you locate Dunnings, you locate a place with lots of living in it. It was at Gil Dunning's that I won my first bird in a shooting match when I was wearing the sawed-off pants of my father, and went home feeling like Robin Hood and Dan'l Boone rolled together.

The creator of Little Eva and Uncle Tom had noticed Great Island. She had ridden along the blueberry-starred Brunswick Plains along the ribbon roads, down over Gurnet Bridge, and had looked west at Lost Paradise Farm, where I was to be a boy in clover fifty years later. Harriet Beecher Stowe put on her best bib and bonnet in describing it:

"The traveler who wants a ride through scenery of more varied and singular beauty than can ordinarily be found on the shores of any land whatever," writes Harriet, getting crouched for a magnificent start, "should start some fine day along the clean sandy road, ribboned with strips of green grass, that leads through the flat pitch-pine forests of Brunswick towards the sea. As he approaches the salt water, a succession of the most beautiful and picturesque lakes seems to be lying softly cradled in the arms of wild, rocky forest shores, whose outlines are ever changing with the windings of the road.

## Captain Abby and Captain John

"At a distance of about six or eight miles from Brunswick"—it is five, but miles in buggies were longer—"he crosses an arm of the sea,"—Gurnet, and look to your starboard and you will see Lost Paradise Point!—"and comes upon the first of the interlacing group of islands which beautifies the shore. A ride across this island is a constant succession of pictures, whose wild and solitary beauty entirely distances all power of description. The magnificence of evergreen forests,—their peculiar air of sombre stillness,—the rich intermingling ever and anon of groves of birch, beech, and oak, in picturesque knots and tufts, as if set for effect by some skillful landscape-gardener,—produce a sort of strange dreamy wonder; while the sea, breaking forth on the right hand and the left of the road into the most romantic glimpses, seems to flash and glitter like some strange gem which every moment shows itself through the framework of a new setting. Here and there little secluded coves push in from the sea, around which lie soft tracts of green meadowland, hemmed in and guarded by rocky pine-crowned ridges. In such sheltered spots may be seen neat white houses, nestling like sheltered doves in the beautiful solitude."

That's the kind of place I grew up in!

John Pennell was wise in looking for a mate on such an island. There was one there waiting for him, "with the apple pie and the tea all turned out," as Great Island folks say when they describe something very lovely. It was Abby Reed, the girl whose name was written twice in John's pocket diary years before. She had curls down to her shoulders, the color of new ginger-

## Captain Abby and Captain John

bread, Great Island style, when you first cut into it with a knife. I think she had dimples, though her son isn't sure. Sons take things too much for granted. It looks like dimples in the photograph. Anyway, she was a young woman any sea captain would stop and look at. A lot of the young ones had stopped and looked. But John Pennell was the only one Abby had looked at back. Yes, John knew which side his bread was buttered on when he went courting on Great Island.

Abby had not always lived on Great Island. In fact, only two years. But, before that, she had lived on an island next to it and almost as good. Fairyland and no mistake! Since we have taken Uncle Tom's maker along with us on this tour, let's allow her to describe Orr's Island, too:

"The sense of wild seclusion reaches here the highest degree; and one crosses the bridge with a feeling as if genii might have built it,"—I took a header on it on my first bicycle and skinned my chin—"and one might be going over it to fairy-land. From the bridge the path rises on to a granite ridge,"—I did alpine climbing there—"which runs from one end of the island to the other, and has been called the Devil's Back,"—I can point you out hoofprints in a ledge to prove the Old Boy walked along here on Orr's, mistaking it for the annex to Eden—which was Lost Paradise Farm on Great Island—"with that superstitious generosity which seems to have abandoned all romantic places"—influence of Lord Byron, whom, by the way, Harriet did a bad turn to—"to so undeserving an owner.

"By the side of this ridge of granite is a deep, narrow chasm, running a mile and a half or two miles parallel with the road, and veiled by the darkest and most solemn shadows of the primeval forest. Here scream the jays and the eagles, and fish-hawks make their nests undisturbed;"—I disturbed two there with a .22!—"and the tide rises and falls under the black branches of evergreen from which depend long, light festoons of delicate gray moss."—I used it for whiskers in our dramatics on Lost Paradise.

And a stone's throw from the head of this reach, over on the next cove, Abigail Jacobs Reed had been born and had grown up like an Orr's Island birch tree. She was never called Abigail again after her christening. She was too much a human being for that. She had been born in the oldest house still standing in the town of Harpswell, or Brunswick, for that matter, the Joseph Orr place, built in 1756. Joseph had come from the North of Ireland. The Orrs, of course, named the island for themselves. Abby's grandmother was an Orr, an old sea lion of a grandmother, if ever there was one, and Abby had known her, a blind but fiery old lady, before she went off to the everlasting sea, and had heard her tell wild tales of the Indians and wildcats and first settlers who were tougher than both of them tied together. Her name was Lettice. It seems an anticlimax. The Orr house of Abby's birth is still there, by the way. High on its hill, it looks north over Merryconeag Sound, probably the second most beautiful bay in the world, wide and trimmed with lacework of firs, with daisy fields here and there coming down to the tide's way. Arthur Reed's people had acquired the house. It was a "fitten" place

## Captain Abby and Captain John

for Arthur to bring his children into the world, first Abby, candidate for a sea captain's wife, then Caroline, then Elias, Arthur's strong candidate for a sea captain, and then "Sis," the youngest. There had been only one shadow to fall across that neck of land. Caroline had left them for an even brighter place than Orr's Island.

Arthur Reed had brought his bride home in the old saga manner. Elizabeth Jacobs was a schoolteacher in Portland, probably twenty-five miles away as the shad swims. Arthur rowed her on her wedding morning, history tells, the whole way from Portland to Orr's in his dory, with his two blistered hands. Then they had the wedding. It was the only day Arthur could spare from his lobster pots. So he combined the rowing and the bedding. Tradition declares that Elizabeth wore her wedding dress on the ride, though she had to bail once or twice. Elizabeth was willing to come to Orr's, for she had been a schoolteacher there and had got a look at the kind of children Orr's grew, and a look or two at Arthur Reed. He was a good oarsman.

There had been at least one other saga episode in the Reed family. That was the day Arthur caught the whales. A whole school of whales. And he caught them right in that cove which Harriet Beecher Stowe has just described so well. Piddling sticklers for fact have asserted that the whales were only small whales, called black-fish by the ichthyologists. But a black-fish can give any fisherman who hooks on to him a good day's sport, I will wager. I saw some last Summer at the Saguenay's mouth. They were about the size of a twenty-five-foot launch, and ten times as fast. They came out of the

## Captain Abby and Captain John

water and went back in like projectiles. When they sneezed, it shook the chimneys of Tadousac, and drowned out the little French-Canadian loreleis who were springing up along the mile-long quay and singing *Alouette*. I shouldn't care to hook a black-fish in a canoe. The way Arthur Reed caught his school of them was this: he and his henchmen herded them into Harriet Stowe's cove, splashing back and forth in their dories, at high tide. This human seine swept the fish up the cove. The men threw a cordon across and kept them there, though a dory or two got smashed, as the tide ebbed. Then when the whales were beginning to strand, the men sailed in with flounder darts, cant-dogs, and old scythes, and the sport began. It was like something seen under the walls of Troy. When the foam and the blood settled, there were thirty-eight heroes of the sea put to sleep by the sword. Orr's Island and all Harpswell ran with fatness and oil and fresh black-fish steaks for months after. It was a day that went down into history.

John Pennell had first met the daughter of the whale killer at her Orr's Island eyrie, beside Harriet Stowe's eagles. She gave him a bunch of mayflowers the first time he ever really noticed her. He was only just in his first man-shaped trousers. It was during a call his father was making on Arthur Reed. John had probably seen the girl before often but he was too busy being a boy to notice her then. It took a man's trousers and mayflowers. Now Maine mayflowers are all good ones, like all Maine lobsters. But those on the Harpswell islands have more sparkle and spice to them than mayflowers anywhere else. I wouldn't give the others house

## Captain Abby and Captain John

room. It is the same way with lobsters. The same difference is found between lobsters in Casco Bay and Penobscot. I know Lincoln Colcord will want to kill me, but honesty makes me say that the Penobscot lobsters are as so much tasteless cornmeal beside my native kind.

Somehow or other, John Pennell could never think of his wife, even after twenty years of being husband to her, without thinking of Orr's Island and mayflowers.

After the mayflowers, Abby Reed had been on John's mind. You can tell that from the little red notebook, which he carried in his trousers, carpentering on his family's ships. He wrote her name in fine scrolls and noted she had left Middle Bays, October 13, 1849. Probably after a trip to Topsham Fair with him, and a ride on the merry-go-round, a place where many a sea captain of Brunswick first rode with his future wife alone. And Abby was over where John could drink her in again on April 5, 1851, the same day John shot the wild goose. Maybe the goose was for Abby.

In 1855, because of the sorrows in the old place, Caroline's death and his mother's, Arthur Reed had got up his anchor and moved his family up to Great Island. He chose a bay almost as beautiful as Merryconeag Sound to live by, Quahaug. Quahaug Bay is capes and islands, like the fingers on your two hands, cedars and fir trees like something an artist would dream, shining out bright above fringes of white granite against a wall made up of rolling sapphires where the ocean goes uphill.—Let Harriet Beecher Stowe match that!—I swam and fished that bay as a boy. I

## Captain Abby and Captain John

won a spelling match once with its name, though, honesty compels me to add, my wife was giving out the words and it was up in Carl Carmer's state, where they call quahaugs clams.

Arthur Reed picked out a house right under Misery Hill. Misery is the Olympus of my childhood. I was sure Zeus had his home up there, at an elevation of maybe two hundred feet. Anyway, our Lost Paradise horses, Dick and Kit, had to dig their toenails in to get our hayracks up its fifty-two-degree slope. Misery Hill was also the hideout of Isaiah Jordan's Lion. Isaiah Jordan's Lion was an institution of Gurnet. He was a loup-cervier, about the size of a tool-house, the way my father described him. He had got his first name by attacking and half killing old Isaiah, patriarch of Gurnet and parts adjacent thereunto. My father had saved venerable Abram Linscott from being eaten by him. But Abram never gave him credit. He thought of my father as a desperate man running at him, in an abstracted moment, with two big stones, the loup-cervier having dusted over a wall when the old man turned and saw my father coming. Some of the folks at the new Reed home saw the big cat going home to Misery. For a time they meditated moving away. It is something to be asked to live on an island that has a mountain lion on it. But they thought better of it and stayed.

It was at this Great Island house that First Mate John D. Pennell spent most of his hours on land between 1855 and 1857. Abby was the reason. She was a handsome woman now, yet she still had something like mayflowers about her. John wore man-sized clothes all

## Captain Abby and Captain John

the time now, of course. They both had long ago taken it for granted that they would sail all the seven oceans in company. It was hard to put a finger on the day and say just when that idea began. They were both serious-minded, rather soberish, and very sure all things were right in the sky, and would turn out for the best, on every part of the sea. John had made up his mind that taking care of Abby was what his business in life was in all the thousands of times he would set his sails or reef them. Abby was sure that sticking to John and bearing him children were what she had been created for. It was all as simple and direct as that. They knew it at once and for good. Abby's family was not quite up to the brilliant Pennells over west on Middle Bay. Her people did not speak so well. They had not done so much in the world for all they had caught whales, hadn't risen so high. But they were sober, industrious people and good people. Abby knew she could improve her speech and writing in John's company. Neither John nor Abby ever gave family differences much thought. They knew they wanted each other.

People in Brunswick and Harpswell, late in 1857, received this card:

To Receive Friends
7½ O'clock
Mr. and Mrs. A. J. Reed
Dec. 3, 1857

The Reeds knew how such things should be done, as well as any of the Pennells. Mrs. Reed had been a schoolteacher.

## Captain Abby and Captain John

It was a lovely, quiet wedding, by candle light. A hundred or so people there, and all attended to first-rate. Over seventy of them Pennells or Dunnings or Skolfields, or other high-toned folks, from the big houses over on Harpswell Neck or from Middle Bays. There had been boned turkey and, after that, raspberry tarts. There had even been music. Arthur Reed had played his accordion, and old Deborah Pennell had played the melodeon. It was quite remarkable, at her age. She didn't have any music, she played by ear. Her son had looked very handsome in his blue, tailed coat and white trousers. Abby certainly had a lovely complexion, and her hair was beautiful in its long ringlets. The two of them would look well on the deck of a ship. It was understood by everyone that this was an ocean wedlock. John would follow the sea, and Abby would bring up her brood there.

Abby's dress was white silk brocaded all over with white roses. It had been bought in Calcutta. I have just been holding a piece of it in my hands. Abby saved it in her *Bible*, next to her children's birth dates. That piece of silk went across the seas, though it was never worn again until it was worn by her son's bride at her wedding, through blows and calms, many times.

## 7

## The Bark Is Made Ready

THE DAY John Pennell married Abby on Great Island, the vessel he was to take Abby to sea in was lying in the port of Barcelona, Spain, ready to discharge her cargo of flour. It was the bark *William Woodside*, built by the Pennells at Middle Bays, 1854. Her master was James W. Causland, of Freeport, the man who, according to Aunt Nell Pennell, corrupted the young Pennells' morals and taught them to swear. He was the master who would, in a few more years, teach young James Henry, Master James's son, how to become a scapegrace and blockade runner. This, according to that same authority.

Whatever the morals of Master Causland, he had his hands full now, and a good excuse for profanity. He had a crew on his hands that he blushed for. They were Tartars, as you can see from the *William Woodside's* log. Alec Reynolds was a problem. He was on shore "without liberty." But the second mate, given December 6 on shore with liberty, stayed right there till December 9. And when he came aboard, he demanded his discharge, "which was refused. He then commenced to insult the captain, also threatened to take his life.

## Captain Abby and Captain John

He was put in chains." He was locked in the forecastle, and he didn't get out to duty till December 14. Then Causland began unloading his flour, 563 barrels that day. But another man, Thomas Sherine, went ashore. Next day he missed duty "on account of liquor." Thomas got sick and stayed sick for a month, until the flour was safely off. And on Christmas Day, Master Causland put Charles—whoever he was—in irons and on allowance—which means hard-bread and water— and Alec Reynolds, too, for "disbehaviour on going on shore."

Causland finished discharging the flour on January 2, 1858. But the next day two "sailor men," Frank Somebody-or-Other and Santa Argo, sneaked ashore without leave. Barcelona was too much for Causland. While he was loading and trimming ballast and getting ready for sea, two more men, a Dutchman and Antonio, deserted. Santa Argo went ashore without liberty again. And just as Causland hired two men in place of the deserters, on January 7, the second mate came down with a venereal disease, souvenir of white Barcelona and her charms. But the master got the bark away from the city of sirens, January 8.

Skirting Minorca, they brought up at Gibraltar Bay on January 13. But the next four days they were "wind bound" there by heavy squalls. "All ship's company employed trying to get the ship out of the harbor, but impossible." They lost the starboard anchor. They got under way, January 18, all sails set, towards New Orleans. They overhauled a vessel of 300 tons bottom up, Latitude 32-33 N, Longitude 24-14 W. And on Febru-

## Captain Abby and Captain John

ary 4, Thomas Somebody struck Capt. Causland on the head with a big piece of wood. Next came a gale, a beauty: "February 18, at 8 PM, weather looking bad, took in all light sail. 9:30 blowing a perfect gale. Clewed down the topsails. 10 PM reefed them." Just after they made San Domingo, they were "hove to by the English sloop of war *Forward* and inspected." The whipper-snapper British second officer, I. H. W. Routh, forgetting evidently there had been such a thing as the War of 1812, calmly wrote into Causland's log: "No complaints to make and everything correct." He couldn't have seen the second mate or Alec Reynolds! One more gale, and the steamer *Anglo Norman* had them in tow taking them over the Bar of the Mississippi. They rigged in the jib-boom and, along with the ship *Cloud*, were towed up to New Orleans by the steamer *Conqueror*, March 7.

At New Orleans, Causland saw the last of the homicidal second mate. He "settled off" with the scabby crew. But the steward left. The new one he got lasted only one day. He got another. Meantime they were taking on cargo. A new second mate, Mr. Abbe, joined ship. Two steamers took them over the Bar, the ship's doctor took his departure, and they were under way towards Boston, April 1. They sighted Cuba, April 6, and Cape Florida, April 10, joining the Gulf Stream, that aided them at the rate of 2½ miles per hour. They made Nantucket Shoals and saw "several fishermen at anchor fishing," April 16, made Nantucket, April 17, sighted Cape "Cord"—as every Yankee sailing master spelled it and pronounced it—and on April 20, worked

THE BARK *WILLIAM WOODSIDE*

## Captain Abby and Captain John

the ship up Boston Bay, "several sail in company." It had taken twelve days from Cuba to Boston. Capt. Causland left the bark for good. He probably thanked God fervently.

And who should come on board to command the *William Woodside* next but grizzled old Master William Woodside himself, for whom the bark had been named, teacher of Pennell sea captains! He wasn't his natural old self. He was far from well. He had been broken up by a recent shipwreck. That was why he was without a ship now. His vessel had been stove to pieces, and for two days William had walked along the wild shore dragging his passengers, dead and alive, up out of the waves' way. He got them all, every body and every living soul. The survivors had given him a gold watch for his heroism. It had taken a lot out of him. He wasn't so young as he used to be. He was only half the old William. But a half was worth two James Causlands.

There were different works now. There weren't many more voyages in the old man, but what there were left were going to be shipshape. William got under way May 10, broached a barrel of beef on May 11—which he made last till they raised Cuba—made the Hole in the Wall, May 24, with several sail in company, anchored at Orange Keys becalmed for a day, made the Dog Keys and the Double-Headed Shot Keys, May 31, the Marrow Bone, came to anchor, furled sails, and cleaned up decks in Havana harbor, June 1. Twenty-one days, with no wind worth noticing and against the Gulf Stream. Not bad.

It is a different log, with William Woodside handling

## Captain Abby and Captain John

the sail and pen. Everything for the better. Except the spelling. Old William's hand is much like an aged hen scratching in the dark—he was nigh the dark himself —and he spells by the moon. "Pumps regley tended," spells he, and "threw out the 24 hores," and again, "Capt som beter." The captain is himself. It is "breses" instead of breezes. And of course William puts in an *r* and puts an *r* on the tails of words wherever he can. But that was the Yankee cropping out. And William got things done. He discharged 274 barrels of potatoes, June 4. Then one man got sick, then two men got sick, then three. Barrel fever, probably. It comes on after you have taken about twenty barrels ashore. But Capt. Woodside got men from the shore, and he got his potatoes off, and then his blocks of paving stone, 3080 of them. June 27, he got under way, passed the Morro— he spells it "Morrer"—made Matanzas in one day— you should see how he spells that!—discharged four lighters of ballast, took on 648 hogsheads of sugar and 500 boxes, wood and water, and sailed for Cork, July 17.

William took just 43 days from Matanzas to Cork. And he was a sick man. On July 27 he records his own illness, in his own spelling; "At 4 AM the Capt was taken voilent sick rasing grate quant of Blude from the stomack. At 8 Am giting now beter thot it advisable to git to the nerist port for medical aide." But William did no such thing. He kept right on for Cork. He got better, according to the log. He ran through some bad going August 6, then thick weather, and took on a Cork pilot on August 29. But he was taken ill again in Cork.

## Captain Abby and Captain John

And when the *William Woodside* "hove short and commenced making sail" on September 4, the moonlit handwriting is replaced by one better in spelling. It is Mr. Card's, the mate's. They went round the north of Ireland, struck a gale and ran into Belfast Loch, hove anchor and set anchor watch, got under way again at midnight, September 7, were picked up and towed by the steamboat *Nimrod* into Greenock, September 8. And next day William Woodside's hand, very shaky, resumed: "Gails from SW, haled ship to her berth and commenced discharging cargow." The crew took a vacation, without liberty, but William got the cargo off with help from the shore, took on 7 tons of "cole," got the tug *Defiance* to tow him to Troon. A new mate, Mr. Thorne came aboard, September 18. The crew began to dribble in. Then on September 21, Master Woodside's shaky hand finished writing in this bark's log. It is a hand like a dying man's: "Two men came on board on duty." It is the last entry William Woodside ever made in any log-book. He, the maker of sea captains and father of one, had finished the long day's work. The old centurion was through making sail forever. He left the ship that wore his name. He went to take a ship that would get him home quickly. There were only a few weeks this side of the grave.

Mr. John Card, fellow townsman of Brunswick, stepped into the captain's shoes, though he did not sign himself as master for 13 days. He got his cargo of coal and sailed for Havana, September 24. Without her namesake, the bark seemed marked for trouble. She passed Black Head, Kish lightship, spoke an English

## Captain Abby and Captain John

brig Liverpool-bound from Bermuda, went in light sails, the wind "hauling to the southard," sighted "an English fleet of ships of war in company, 8 line of battle ships, one steam frigate," struck a gale, "took a lee lurch and shifted cargo, 3 streaks list." All hands fell to and trimmed the coal in the lower hold. The next bit of hard luck was October 3, when the main topgallant sheet parted and two hours later the fore topsail split. Next day they sent a new fore topsail up and bent it, repaired sails. October 6, a sea carried away the stern dead light and damaged the hull. The carpenter stopped the leak. October 9, a jib split. Next day, the flying jib parted the clew rope. October 16, the main royal split. They were having a spell of weather. And on October 17, a good sailor went home. "At 12 AM, during the time of reefing the spanker, Fred Oman, a native of Gothenburg, fell from the boom end and was lost, having sunk before assistance could reach him. All efforts to save him being useless. Put the helm hard down, hove a tub and a hen coop overboard. Launched the boat with 5 men, but could see nothing of him. Veered to the southard and stood till 4 PM, sea day. Gave up all hopes of him. Blowing strong at the time. Heavy sea."

And the next day, another seaman, Davey Lewis by name, took sick. Lightning and tremendous squalls, next day. The laboring bark lee-lurched again and shifted the coal. They reefed and stowed most of the sails. Davey still sick. The crew trimmed the coal at midnight. Davey sick. It was no ordinary sickness. For on October 21, he went out of his head completely:

## Captain Abby and Captain John

"Davey, the sick man, turned crazy, had to lash him to his bunk to keep him from destroying and injuring himself."

There are no logs that tell the history of the secret life and agonies of common sailors. Why did a Yankee seaman begin to sink into insanity the day after a Swedish sailor was lost and hunted for over a wild sea? Were the men friends? Or did something in the fall of the man take the starch out of another one? Or was it the look of the wicked dark waves rolling high over a tossing ship's boat and making a shadow on a mind that would not lift again?—No one will ever know. The sea and insanity keep their secrets.

The barometer fell and fell. "High old sea to the southard." The gale beat at the *William Woodside* six days. "Secured everything on deck. Preventer gaskets on sails. Decks full of water. Squared the yards and run to the southard." Screaming wind and pounding waves outside. And inside the seaman shouting louder and louder. Hell inside answering the hell without. "Fits on him. Real crazy." They put him in a strait jacket. He broke loose and got his hands on a jack-knife, "swearing he would kill all hands." Irons for Davey.

The storm petered out at last, with Davey still in irons. He scandalized Capt. Card by his language. This was not Master Causland, who taught young Pennells to swear! "Davey still in irons, using the coarsest language, swearing he will kill all hands if let loose." Davey would not take his medicine. They took one of his arms out of irons to wash and shift him. They cleaned his place out. On November 3, he asked for more to eat,

## Captain Abby and Captain John

being "still on his allowance." Irons still for Davey. The Gulf Stream at last. "Comes in with calms," November 17, and they made the Bahama Keys. But no calms for Davey, "more noisy than usual." November 20, Benini Keys, Davey tried to break his irons, and they put him below hatches "for safety." Next day they added coffee to Davey's bread and water, "Riding Rocks bearing NE, dist. 5 miles." Calms again, though still none for Davey. They painted the bark. A wind again. More. The jib split. Double-Headed Shot Key. November 25, "comes in with strong gales and high old sea." Matanzas, and up came another saucy Britisher, a steam frigate, just when Card had succeeded in getting all his sails set. All the work for nothing. The Britisher made Card show his papers. Master Card hopping, hopping mad! One more split sail. November 26 brought the pilot at last. The anchor: "Let go the best bower in 12 fathoms of water." Havana. Rest. Two doctors came on board to have a look at Davey. Next day: "Took David Lewis on shore with his clothes." And Davey passes out of history forever. Did he get home? Did his brain ever clear again? Captains do not annotate their logs with footnotes. They live by the day. For the day. And the Daveys go into oblivion.

The coal was discharged. A bag of beans came aboard, a bag of flour, a barrel of potatoes, and two new shovels, the 200-gallon cask was filled with water, the 160-gallon one. A Dunning came aboard for duty, Minot, a future sea captain—it would be a small port of the world that did not have a Dunning in it around 1858! —and the boy John got sick and went ashore. The bark

## Captain Abby and Captain John

got foul of a steamboat and lost her spanker gaff. The crew cleaned up ship for Christmas. They got a day's liberty to see the sights of Havana, as a Christmas present, 1858. They loaded in 141 tons of stone ballast—the bark weighed 462 tons—eight more casks of water, and 49 fathoms of 2½-inch rope. They "blacked" the ship, December 29 and got in a barrel of molasses. They sailed for New Orleans, December 30.

Up in Maine, John Pennell, husband of a year, home for some months from the *United States* and loneliness for Abby, had kissed her goodbye again, at Brother Robert's house, and was being driven to the steam cars in Brunswick. The blue chest was packed for sea. And on it was written in bold letters CAPTAIN JOHN D. PENNELL. John had reached the top at last. He was going down to meet the first ship of his very own. And down on the Gulf, on the vessel that was sailing to meet him, Master Card was writing in at the top of the log's page, "Cap. J. Pennell, Master."

On January 6, 1859, the *William Woodside* was in tow, along with the ship *George West* of Newburyport, of the steamer *Mary Kingsland*, going up the Mississippi. The boy John was sick again. They brought to off Slaughter House Point, at post 22, January 8, and the crew went ashore to glory. The ballast was discharged, the decks caulked. A new second mate, Mr. Sprague, came aboard. They started loading.

And on January 21, 1859, John Pennell came on ship, captain for the first day of his life. On January 24, a new hand writes the *Woodside's* log. It is a bold and clean scrollwork, and every capital is beautifully

## Captain Abby and Captain John

shaded in. The birch rod of Deborah had blossomed like Aaron's rod! From now on, the log of the *William Woodside* is a different book. There is no careless scrawl. No disorderly entries. You will look fairly long for misspellings, save the natural Yankee ones. Capt. John spelled it Cape "Cord," as a Yankee should, to his dying day. Everything is neat and shipshape as the vital statistics in a family *Bible*. Log-books were John's bibles, along with his family one, for the rest of his time.

John finished taking cargo. A new crew came on, eight of them "blacks." They started down river. Fog and thick weather held them up eight days, at the S. W. Pass. John kept the crew busy in the rigging and getting wood from the shore. On February 9, the steamer *Anglo Saxon* towed them down to the Bar and put them aground on it. They cleared it all right next day, and got to sea. John headed for Boston. There was one more member of the crew to come aboard. A member with a berth for life. It was Abby. She had never been to sea before, but from now on her life with her husband was to be all sea.

It was rather rough going across the Gulf and around Florida. February 15, "made Tortugas light, bearing NE by N, dist. 18 miles." They hit the Gulf Stream, February 19, and allowed 4, 3, 2 knots an hour for it on the next three days. Then they had a spell of weather: "Feb. 21, at 8 PM, weather looking bad at the NW, in topgallant sails, outer jib, mizzen topsail, spanker, furled ½ mainsail, double-reefed fore and main topsail. Midnight, heavy squalls, split main jib,

## Captain Abby and Captain John

sent it in, sent out new one. Ship laboring heavy and making much water." That was the story all the way towards Abby. The ocean was very rocky. It was bad all the way up to the "Roaring Forties," and when they got there, it was worse. It was all "threatening appearances at the NW," and "carried away fore topsail sheet," and "blowing a perfect gale." John even misspelled words in the confusion: "Midnight and a high eregular sea running." March came in like a sea lion. They were in the "Roaring Forties," with a vengeance! "March 1. This day comes with fresh gales and threatening looking weather. At 12 midnight furled gallants, furled manisail. At 3 PM made Nantucket lightship, bearing ENE, dist. 8 miles. At 4 Nantucket lightship bore north, dist. ½ mile. At 7 close-reefed fore and main topsails. At 8 heavy gales busted fore and main topsails. Clewed them up and furled them. Ship lay under foresail, double-reefed, 1¾ spanker, fore topmast staysail. Ends heavy gales. Lat. Obs. 41-08 N. Pumps well attended to. Var. 6° W." The crew practically lived in the yards. Next day, Smith, a Yankee seaman, froze his hands, and Peter Angulia, a Portugee, both his feet. They found 18 inches of water in the hold, but after twenty solid hours of back-breaking work, the pumps sucked. March 4 came in with a blizzard. At 7:30 PM the men were standing on an icy yard arm in the pitch dark and the howling snow, close-reefing the fore topsail, and James Martin fell from the port yard arm into the sea. It was like falling through a hole in the earth and out among the cold stars. They looked for him. But he never had a chance. A man couldn't live

## Captain Abby and Captain John

five minutes in such water. March 5, they made Highland light, 25 miles distant, by compass. It was like a window opened in heaven. They took on the pilot at 4:30 AM, worked up Boston Bay, took steam, furled all sails, and made fast at Battery Wharf. The log entries end. For John Pennell was bound for Middle Bays and Abby fast as the steamer could carry him. The bark *William Woodside* was ready for her other captain, John's mate.

# 8

# A Housewife Looks at a House 25,000 Miles Wide

"How happy I was that night to see my husband!" March 12, 1859.

So begins Abby Pennell's first diary. It is a black pocket diary, printed in Salem, for the year 1859. A very small book. A man could put it in his pants pocket and forget it was there. Yet there are enough words in it to make a book almost the length of a novel. Abby wrote fine. Like the flowers in the head of Queen Anne's lace. She has made me put on glasses for the first time in my life. The little book also has the wonder of a Yankee housewife at the wild and strange beauty of the world fresh as a daisy with dew on it at sunrise. And it holds enough sheer old-fashioned love of a woman for a husband to set any wife up housekeeping in happiness her life long.

John's words, in the log, are as a few pebbles on a wide pebbly beach to Abby's words. But then, a housewife faced with a new house to keep 25,000 miles around would be expected to have a good deal to say.

Abby welcomed her husband at his Brother Robert's house. She had no home of her own except the ocean before her. The second night the two drove over to

## Captain Abby and Captain John

Great Island, and slept at her mother's. There were trips to the village. John went to a Dunning party and "had a beautiful time." The two of them went to call, on March 17, on William Woodside, past master of the *William Woodside*, their ship now, and they found him "very low." The young captain saluted the old on the brink of the grave. It was goodbye for good. Both knew that. One boy to eternity gave the younger boy his best plaything, for he was going where he would not need it any more. The *William Woodside* changed hands, as the two of them shook hands.

Great Island again and company in the evening. More parties. The time was short. March 19 was "very fair sleighing." John borrowed Robert's sleigh and took Abby for a ride. A night at John's Sister Harriet's. On March 20 there was a reunion of the whole Pennell clan at Master James's—eleven brothers and sisters, with proper wives and husbands, answering the roll call. Then back to Great Island. Monday, Abby washed, packed up her things to go away, and ironed in the evening. And on March 22, there was the sleigh, and Abby said farewell to her childhood, to home, and to Maine: "I leave home this morning to go away with my husband for the first time, and it is hard to part. Went over to Middle Bays and from there to the depot, and went to Portland and took the boat for Boston. A storm tonight."

Abby was seasick on the Boston boat, inauspicious beginning, a taste of what was coming. And off and on for the next fifteen years. For Abby never entirely outgrew the habit of seasickness. But next noon she got a

## Captain Abby and Captain John

housekeeper's start, shopped in Boston and bought some curtains and carpet for the cabin. Charles, the ship's doctor, came. Next day came James Henry Pennell, blockade-runner-to-be, twenty, and full of the Old Nick, to sail as mate. He replaced Minot Dunning, Brunswick-bound. It was a family ship, sure enough. More parties, under Brother Charles's wing, in Boston, a lot of Brunswick people there. "Very sociable time," Abby wrote to Aunt Susan, of the Longfellow memories. Weather held them up. "Rained all day hard as it can pour." On March 30, they were off, headed for Havana, with a cargo of ice. Abby got her things all put away by ten o'clock, saw the sun set inside Cape Cod, and got seasick.

The ocean acted up for Abby on this her real honeymoon. They caught it heavy at the start. "Had to keep my berth today," writes Abby. "At 12 o'clock, night, squall with lightning. Lost some yards. Not much sleep." "At 10," writes John, "heavy squalls split mainsail and fore topsail, furled them. Close-reefed main topsail, furled foresail, outer jib, and spanker. Midnight, threatening looking weather. At 4 heavy sea on and ship rolling heavy. Set reefed foresail to steady her. Pumps attended. Ship rolling heavy, and a high and ugly sea often making breaches over the ship fore and aft. Ends heavy gales. Running ship under close-reefed main topsail, reefed foresail." For once John's entry outdistances Abby's. "April 1," writes Abby, "under close-reefed main topsail and reefed foresail." She was picking up the sea terms fast from her husband. And she goes on, "Sea sick all day today, and have not slept

## Captain Abby and Captain John

much tonight"—and adds, triumphantly, "John sick, too." John didn't put that down in *his* log! Good sea captains always did get seasick when the occasion demanded it! It was an axiom not necessary to set down.

It was "more moderate" according to both of them next day. Abby had caught her husband's habit of noting the weather first each day. She kept it up all through her diaries. And she didn't stop it when she was in port and the weather didn't matter, any more than John. Abby wrote that she felt "quite smart." Yet she was suffering that second and worse kind of seasickness, homesickness: "A lonesome Saturday night to me on the ocean." Not much like the recent night at James's with a score at the table! And next day, "My first Sabbath on the ocean, and a lonesome day it is." "Bent new mainsail and set it," said John. "Ends fresh gales." "It looks frightful tonight," answered his wife. But the going improved. It got warmer. "Light airs and fine," said John. "Warm enough to keep the windows up," answered Abby, and she saw a bark. That was something, for a Yankee woman used to company.

It was something indeed. And it was a comfort Abby was going to have all her sailing days, wherever she went. One of the things that strikes me most impressively when I read the old logs and sea journals is how populous the ocean was eighty years ago. No matter in what God-forsaken part of the Atlantic or Pacific a ship might be, almost every day there would be a ship to meet or "in company." The oceans were well peopled. The human race was all over them. Today, save on the narrow steamship lanes, it would be infinitely more

## Captain Abby and Captain John

lonely. Weeks might go by, years might go by, with not a ship, not a steamer, anywhere. This is a loneliness science and economic revolution have brought in. The two of them have emptied the oceans of life and made a desert of the greater part of the surface of the globe. It shows what progress and the art of having things easy can accomplish! Having things easy is one of the things that ail the world most today.

Abby was getting her sea legs. "Am smart enough to go to the table to my dinner and have been up on deck this afternoon and set awhile. Slept all night last night," and later, "Quite smart and appetite gaining some. Hope it will remain so." "All sail set," said John. "Beautiful morning," chimed Abby. "I have been smart enough to cook some today and sew some." When a Yankee woman is able to cook, she is pretty well on her feet! "It was delightful last evening, up on deck till 10 o'clock. Feel first-rate today, and good appetite." "Ends fine," wrote John. This was what the Gulf Stream could do for honeymooners. And Abby, on April 11, made some pies and finished a dress. "Done considerable work for me. Within 78 miles of Abaco." "Ends fine," reiterated John. Next day they passed Abaco and Great Stirrup Key. Abby washed and baked a pan of biscuits! "Ends fine," cried John. Abby started a muslin dress, saw a lot of ships, and did some cooking to celebrate John's birthday. "Light airs and fine." "Don't seem to get ahead very fast," wrote Abby. "Tacked ship," answered John. They made land at midnight, on the lee bow. He "supposed" it to be the Bahamas. They anchored on Bahama Banks next morn-

## Captain Abby and Captain John

ing. John counted ten ships anchored with them, in his log. Abby counted eleven, in the diary. She probably counted her own. All the vessels left at once, Providence letting them have a little wind, on April 17. Past Gun Key, Orange Key, Dog Banks, our old friend Double-Headed Shot Keys, past Matanzas, Havana at last. "Made Cuby," wrote John. "Furled all sails. Up awnings. So ends sea account." The first voyage together was over. Abby found a letter awaiting her from her mother.

Abby described Havana as looking very handsome. "Employed at various jobs," John wrote. But his wife did some cooking and rejoiced in the call five sea captains made on them, April 21, Captains Pinkham, May, Nicholas, Tyler, Harriman. All Yankees, by their names. Havana was full of Yankee sea captains.

That's another thing you notice about housekeeping on the sea eighty years ago. It doesn't make any difference what port it is on the globe, Yankee sea captains and their wives will be taking tea together. Men from the smallest hamlets on the Maine coast meet schoolmates in Canton or Liverpool. Neighboring farmers meet in mid-Pacific on a fine day, and their wives exchange calls! Home was every part of the sea.

The muslin dress was finished just in time. The social life Abby emerged into was a gay and brilliant one. John made not the slightest note of it in his log "while laying in Havana." He noted merely that he was discharging his ice, hay, sawdust, and empty hogsheads and taking on ballast hand over fist. But Abby set down calls, sings, sociables. There was a party on a Down

## Captain Abby and Captain John

East brig and "quite a company." Captains May and Pinkham called again. Abby combined business with the pleasure: "Done some cooking and went on board of Capt. Hare this evening. Had a pretty good time." Which is Yankee for a magnificent one! There was "beautiful music all around us," Abby noted one morning. Maybe Capt. Pinkham had a cornet with him and was serenading her. "Hackled into the hay," wrote John.

Abby and John went a-sailing with Capt. Pinkham. They went "on board of" another captain, on board the *Acacia*, too, and ashore to the hospital, "looked in and gathered some flowers." Abby fixed over John's dress shirt, for it was in great demand, ironed some, hemmed a table cloth, and entertained company, all on one day! "Had a fine time." Capt. May called again. Abby commenced on a skirt. Captains Pinkham, Nicholas, and Hay called and spent the evening. "Health never was better." Abby went to call on Capt. Pinkham next day, but found him out. He called on her the following day, though. And the next, he and Capt. Bachelder took tea with Abby and John. Tea is a little word, remember, for the old big supper of Maine. Then Abby and John went aboard Capt. Pinkham and took tea with him, right back! And spent the evening. Next day, Captains Pinkham and Nicholas visited them forenoon and night. "But the mosquitoes very thick." They went on board Capt. Loring, but, Abby wrote, "had no time at all." Capt. Means called, and Captains Pinkham and Nicholas. Then Capt. Pinkham "was aboard to dinner and aboard to tea," and spent the evening. But on May 5,

## Captain Abby and Captain John

Abby had to note the melancholy fact: "Capt. Pinkham has gone out."

Capt. Nicholas called, though, Abby caught up on her cooking—which she had been neglecting lately— and the crew finished discharging the cargo. Abby went on shore for the first time. (She had forgotten the Hospital, I guess.) They hauled off into the harbor. "The mosquitoes dreadful thick." It got "dreadful warm." The edge of the gaiety seemed blunted. On May 7, Abby solaced herself by doing some cooking and some letter-writing. "But a lonesome Saturday night it is to me," she wrote in the diary, "My thoughts are at home." Saturday is the Maine Yankee's day of joy. Abby often missed Saturdays terribly during her years at sea. It was the hardest day to get over in the week. Abby never got over missing Saturdays. "Passing clouds," noted John. Sunday, the Maine day of seriousness, was some better. For Capt. Bachelder and Capt. Nicholas were on board all day, "and," said Abby, "we had a sing and went a sail this evening." "Fine," is all John set down for this red-letter day.

The sociableness burst out again, in spite of mosquitoes. It cooled off. John chartered the *William Woodside* for Europe, to Abby's delight. Abby made a mosquito bar, did some cooking and sewing, and they went aboard Capt. Cole for the evening. Capt. Bachelder hauled alongside them, to take ballast in company. When Abby had hung her wash out to dry, she went over and visited. Capt. Bachelder entrusted to her the grave and ticklish business of picking out a dress for his wife, back home! Capt. Nicholas and his brother

## Captain Abby and Captain John

came. They came again, with Captain Angus Curtis and two others, and spent the evening. Abby took a walk up around the forts. Our Capt. Causland, teacher of swearing to young Pennells, blew in, fresh from a 68-day run from Europe. Captains Nicholas and Curtis, a Harpswell man, joined Abby and John on board, and they had a grand sing. Next day Abby made a lace cape, to keep up with the Havana whirl, ironed, and went aboard Capt. Nicholas for a good time. Next day she ironed and cooked and "went a sail this evening round an English frigate." She boarded Capt. Race next, and found Captains Nicholas, Curtis, and Emerson there. "Done a large washing today and went aboard of Capt. Thurlow and took tea. Then went aboard of Capt. Jasper Nicholas and spent the evening."

I don't suppose you could find such an entry as that anywhere in the world outside of the diary of an American sea captain's wife. American ladies seem to be the only ones in civilization, so far, who can do a big washing in the morning and then hold their own in laces and silks at tea in the evening! They still can. It is one of our greatest achievements as a nation.

Abby rose at five o'clock in the morning and sailed out a piece with Capt. Nicholas, who seemed to have taken Capt. Pinkham's place as her leading captain after John, past Morro Castle, to start him off properly for New York. The party was breaking up. The *Ben Bolt*—sweet shades of Alice!—pulled out for Trieste. Next morning, Abby did not feel smart, but managed to starch John's shirts, do some cooking and ironing,

## Captain Abby and Captain John

and go ashore after tea. The mosquitoes got thick again.—Don't they always when your friends are leaving you?—Capt. Race and some other captains sailed for Baltimore. And Abby made up a big batch of Maine molasses candy to surprise John, who was abed and asleep in broad daylight. They commenced loading. It was sugar, this time. They had started with ice and were rising in the scale. They took in 2725 boxes and 333 barrels of sugar. Abby was afraid of it. It was a cranky cargo, sugar, and held a ship back in the water by being mysteriously alive, some way. "Capt. Curtis," she wrote her mother, "says every ship is crank loaded with sugar, and will not sail so fast loaded with sugar as they will with anything else." Curtis was a Harpswell man, from Abby's own islands. He knew.

And Abby had no use for the Spaniards, who raised the sugar. They had held John up: "You can't do as you want to here. You have got to do as the Spaniards want you to, and they are forever doing everything, and cannot put any dependence in one word they say. Havana is the last of all places for a vessel to go, to make anything, I should think. Everything is so high, and their expenses are so much. John has just come off mad enough. Says he cannot go to sea until Tuesday morning. We have got to be patient and bear it, I suppose."

A newspaper arrived from home. John got a letter from Brother Charles. "All well." Steve, a new hand, went ashore without liberty. Mrs. Thurlow, first captain's wife to put in an appearance in the diary, came on and spent the day, her husband joined them for tea. Abby did lots of cooking and acres of dressmaking:

## Captain Abby and Captain John

nightdresses, a pink skirt, a white linen skirt. She knit some. She and Mrs. Thurlow went ashore for a shopping spree. Abby bought three dresses. "Took tea with Capt. Thurlow, John and I did." Capt. Hoyt of the bark *Pilot-Fish* hauled alongside, to take out ballast— Abby spells it "balace"—and they visited with him. John disappointed Abby, and she missed a trip ashore. Capt. Curtis visited with them. But Capt. Thurlow sailed for Laguia. A steamer arrived from New Orleans, and John got a newspaper. Abby noted that John was quite late getting home. On May 31, she set down the sobering fact that it was the last day of Spring, and asked, as she noted the flying of time, "Where shall we be a year from today?"

Sea captains' wives never knew. It might be Java, it might be a farmhouse on Potts' Point, Harpswell. It might be in 3500 fathoms of ocean. Life was uncertain for everybody. But especially for the people of the sea. That was probably why sea captains' wives stayed so young.

John was setting down a more realistic commentary on life: "Account of stores on board. Unbroached—5 bls. beef, 2 bls. pork, 4 bls. bread. Broached—$\frac{1}{4}$ bl. cracked corn, $\frac{1}{4}$ bl. beef tongues, 1 box fish, 4 bls. hard coal."

Bread here doesn't mean what we mean. No, indeed! Bread means the sort of unleavened cracker, christened "pilot bread," which, when he bit into it, even a strong man in his prime and blessed with two sets of flawless teeth might leave three of his best incisors in. If he wasn't careful. I cut my teeth on pilot bread when I was

## Captain Abby and Captain John

a baby. The effete babies of today would lie down beside it and die.

Capt. Doughty, another good man from Abby's own Great Island, blew in from Liverpool, June 1. "Perhaps you will be surprised," Abby wrote in her Havana letter to her mother, "to have me tell you that John and I have spent the forenoon with Capt. Doughty on board the ship *Marengo*."—Abby always did have a weakness for Napoleon. Her grandmother Orr, the old lion of Orr's Island, had been a fierce worshipper of the eagle of Austerlitz and Marengo, was well posted on all his campaigns, and had gotten Abby to read up on them.—"He arrived here last Tuesday from Liverpool. I was glad to see him. I never see him look so well in my life as he does now. He is very fleshy, almost as large as Uncle John Reed. I thought, when I see him come in, I would go aboard of him and surprise him. But Capt. Angus Curtis went aboard of him and told him I was here. So he came right aboard to see me. I had to tell him all the news I could think of. He says he wants to go home dreadfully and is in hopes to go north from here. . . . I have seen quite a number of Harpswell folks here." And Harpswell had, maybe, 300 inhabitants! Many of them apparently were in Havana. This Capt. Doughty, by the way, had the farm that bordered my Lost Paradise Farm and owned Misery Hill and the mountain lion on it.

John and Abby entertained five sea captains of Yankeedom at once: Hoyt, French, Erskine, Curtis, S———? It would be a party no mortal could duplicate today. Captains coming and going. Angus Curtis

## Captain Abby and Captain John

sailed for Matanzas. The ship *Clara Anne* for Falmouth. Abby shelled out nuts with another captain, after having got through a massive washing and ironing. Next day she starched, wrote letters, and ironed. Capt. Hoyt called. Doughty called.

In the midst of the social whirl and beauty of her first great foreign port, wearing fine silks and disporting herself in holiday, Abby Pennell's mind ran back to the little farm on Great Island and the plain and humble life going on there. Beside one of the world's loveliest southern islands, she thought of the sudden Summer coming over Maine. "Mid pleasures and palaces . . ." Her mind went home, with the song. Abby, like many other great Yankee ladies of the sea, was a farm woman, and would not outgrow plain and homely living as long as she lived. She wrote her mother: "I hear, by the way of Middle Bays folks, that you are having beautiful farming weather this spring and very warm, and that everything looked beautiful. I know just how pretty it looks. Those hard wood trees look so green, and apple trees and lilacs all in bloom. I long to be there sometimes, to go into the milk room and get some bread and milk, and some good brown bread. I have an awful appetite, and I am all the time thinking about your victuals. It will soon be gooseberry and strawberry time, and when you have some of them, I shall be on the ocean then, I suppose, tossing about." —In the midst of oranges and sugar cane, the Maine heart was among gooseberries!—"Tomorrow or next Monday, I suppose, school begins. Then poor little Sis will be trudging off to school with her dinner pail.

## Captain Abby and Captain John

Don't let her go to school too steady in the hot weather. She has so far to walk. Don't let her go alone. I dream of her often and of being at home. And I have dreamed of Caroline about every night since I left home, dream of living at the old place on Orr's Island, just the same as we used to be when she was living . . . I must leave off for tonight. I am going to make some biscuits for supper. If I could only have some hasty pudding and milk, I would give a good deal."—Let the Spaniards have their oranges!—"I don't sit down to supper Sunday nights without thinking of home. . . . I have done quite a washing today, and have got all ready for sea. Have to put everything up snug at sea. I do all my washing and starching and ironing for John. So it keeps me busy most of the time. Just enough for exercise. I suppose you have enough to do to exercise you! Mind and get some one to help you this summer. Don't do all the work alone. It is too much for one to do."

They finished loading June 4, and Abby cooked, wrote her mother-in-law and mother, received three letters, and packed up. "All ready for sea." Capt. Emerson called. They went aboard Capt. D——probably one of the far-flung Dunnings—and took dinner with him. (Dinner in Maine then, and now, among *honest* people, is at noon.) Abby came home and baked up a pan of biscuits for supper. And exercise. "My last Sunday in Havana. I am glad to say it." A Maine lady could stand the gay life only so long! Monday, Abby did a big washing, as a Maine housewife should—she never missed a Monday unless flat on her back or standing on her

## Captain Abby and Captain John

beam ends in a gale. A last sea captain called. They were for Falmouth. The last sea captain came with them out past the Morro—one day to see a battleship named for Abby's Maine sink at its foot and start a war—on June 7. Abby got seasick at once. "Out sight of land this afternoon at 3 o'clock, and I sea sick. So adieu to Havana."

"Now," Abby wrote her mother, "I am going to cross the pond for the first time!"

Though it was pleasant next day, Abby was flat in her berth, and her appetite at low ebb. She set it down that she had company in her misery: "John sea sick as I am. Not much comfort to be taken this way." Again no mention of this in John's log. Next day, Abby was a bit better, but she described the evening as "shivery." "June 10. Pleasant. The wind the same way this morning. Three vessels in sight. Smart enough to go to breakfast this morning, and went on deck this forenoon. The wind gone down some this afternoon. Done some. Spoke ship *Harrisburg* this afternoon, bound to Leghorn from New Orleans." The ocean was getting crowded with ships. They spoke a ship, and it walked right past them and was gone by sundown. Everything passed the *William Woodside*. The ship was the *E. Wilder Farley*, a dozen days out of New Orleans, bound for London, with "three ladies on board." All the same, Abby found Saturday and Sunday lonesome away from Maine. "How lonesome," she notes, "Saturday night is at sea." A German bark passed them. Abby was in hopes her appetite would improve soon. John set a hen,

*115*

## Captain Abby and Captain John

June 13, on nine eggs. Motherhood did not stop, for all the winds of ocean, among hens any more than it did among women!

A Yankee ship of the 50's, by the way, was a floating farm. Eggs fresh enough to set mean hens, of course, and plenty of them. There was usually a cow on the passenger list, as well as the flock of hens, often a pig, though he, poor creature, did not survive the voyage any more than the young lady from Niger, and sometimes geese and ducks and a goat. All the comforts and conveniences of home! Pigs were by far the poorest sailors. They were often unutterably seasick. Hens were the best and went about jaunty as ever though their coop might be at fearful angles.

Abby got smarter and smarter. She knit her way across the Atlantic. Wind from the south and the ship making eight knots, then ten. But the second Saturday was just as lonesome. A steam frigate passed them. "Not any sick at all. So ends this lonesome Sunday." Abby baked biscuits again. By John's log, I can see that she used up a whole barrel of flour in a month. For three people—James Henry included—this is about a record, even for those passionately fond of biscuits! Abby knit two pairs of stockings for John, made two nightcaps, lots of embroidery. She was famous for embroidery all over Great Island. Her pieces of needlepoint are still heirlooms in many families. It turned cold, and Abby had to put on her shawl. They were on the Banks, and passed icebergs in the night. Abby cleaned the cabin, "repaired" three pairs of John's pants, ironed, and made some mince pies. The flour

## Captain Abby and Captain John

barrel was getting low. No Maine woman could sail without her firkin of mincemeat any more than without her marriage certificate. Abby carried hers in a leather purse. The marriage certificate, not the mincemeat!

A sea boarded the bark and knocked the second mate galley west, crushing his head. But he got over it. Second mates had tough heads. Between knitting, embroidery, and pants, Abbey went to school to John: "Learnt the compass and am trying to learn navigation." John got "rehumatix." Abby always kept careful check on her health and John's, as a ship's wife should. The bark started leaking, 22 inches in three hours. Bad for sugar! But that didn't stop the Yankee shipmistress from making pies and preserving some peaches. The fourth Saturday night. Abby was getting more used to them. But the Fourth of July with no American clan around, no children, and no celebration was too much for her: "John and I has to spend our Fourth all alone on the ocean." But that evening she triumphantly set down her first latitude and longitude, the first fruits of the navigation lessons. And Abby goes on setting latitudes and longitudes down from this day on.

Abby made a pair of drawers and more mince pies. The cabin flour barrel going lower! She fixed her velvet headdress, saw pieces of a wreck, and two whales. The fifth Saturday found her feeling "rather slim," and Sunday was hard: "Don't seem much like Sunday at home." Abby finished a collar and the *Life of Napoleon*, Lat. 48-24, Long. 19-20. A lot of Americans besides Abby Pennell had a passion for Napoleon in those times. My father had. I remember his singing a song

## Captain Abby and Captain John

about soothing the Frenchmen's pain and bringing back to France the long-lost bones of Bonaparte. Though she made another collar, raided the flour barrel again, and made some nightcaps, Abby wrote, "I don't hurt myself with work." A sore mouth troubled her "considerable," in Lat. 48-54, Long. 12-32.

The ocean grew packed with ships. They were getting in. A bark and a brig astern. The ship *George F. Patten* passed them; a ship going west; more and more ships in company. They spoke the British brig *Ensign,* Capt. Sinnett, five days out of Newport, England, for Buenos Aires, and the Britisher boarded them to send mail back to England, and paid them in cabbages and potatoes for the favor! Trust a British ship to have cabbages! No Englishman could survive a day without them. Green vegetables were always welcome on a ship a long ways out from home. July 19, the Scilly Islands, and the Lizard at noon. England unfolded her trim patchwork. Abby wrote that it looked beautiful, and her health was "more than common good." Into Falmouth harbor. Just six weeks from Havana. Abby celebrated by doing some cooking, house-cleaning the cabin, and writing to her mother. And she got a letter from her mother and brother Elias. The second lap was done, of a life that would crisscross the world with lines on charts and seas. And Abby was happy in her knowledge of navigation and her husband. She hadn't really known John before. It took being alone on the ocean to bring out a husband. From all she had learned, she knew now that John Pennell was all wool and a yard wide.

Next day John got his orders. It was Abby's life-

## Captain Abby and Captain John

long dream come true. They were for Venice! Abby celebrated that news with a batch of biscuits. The following day it was custard pies. Still more cooking, then, letters from Charles the Great, Robert, and old Deborah Pennell. Abby went ashore, and the social flurry began again. She met Yankee Capt. Fisk and his wife and niece, another seagoing family. They called on a Mr. Warren, and he showed them a Cornish garden in full cry. "A fine time." Then a lovely Sunday, and aboard Capt. Fisk. They all went ashore for a walk around the habor. The Pennells took dinner with the Fisks, but John was taken ill, and they had to come "home." The bark meant home to Abby now. The Fisks came for tea. Next day, Abby did some shopping in town, visited gardens with Mr. Magg and his wife. "Had a number of little presents given me," she wrote. Dinner and tea with the Warrens. "Did not go to bed till 2 o'clock." That was the Everest of frivolity for a Yankee housewife. And who should come blowing in but their Havana and Maine friends, Captains Curtis and Erskine. The captains both came right aboard. But it was the Pennells' day of departure. Abby had got up at 6 o'clock to go ashore with John. They paid the Fisks a farewell call on their ship. By 9 o'clock Abby had put all her fine clothes away until she should burst upon Venice in them. She was a good Yankee wife, and did not dream of wearing her best clothes every day! Calico was for most days. They sailed at 2 PM. "Farewell to Falmouth."

Once off again, Abby, in her common clothes, flew for the sofa and gave it a new cover, flew to the carpet

## Captain Abby and Captain John

and gave it a good beating. New England parlor carpets did not stop at the New England shore. They stretched right out over the sea and covered cabin floors on all ships. Abby also fixed her calico dress. Next night John wrote in his log: "The cook very sick. Cook died at 10 PM. At 4:30 AM buried cook. Lat. 49-36, Long. 5-28." Such were the cook's headstone and footstone in the Bay of Biscay! By this time Abby had learned matter-of-factness, as well as navigation, from her husband. For she was even more brief and curt: "Cook died last night. Buried him early this morning. I cleaned out the pantry today, and John cleaned the storeroom." As if losses of cooks were everyday matters! A few months ago, the death of a man as close as a cook would have cast a shadow on Abby's whole day. "Very pleasant and moderate," added Abby. "Calms and fine weather," added John.

The poor cook died in a fit. The cabin boy came in handy, for he could cook. For the forecastle, not Abby's cabin! The cabin boy took over. Abby wrote to her mother that she did a good deal of the cabin cooking from then on, "just enough work for exercise." She didn't mind work. She was a Great Islander. But she took pains to insist, to her friend, the elegant Susan Chase, in her letter to her, that the work *was* exercise: "The cook died on the passage, so we had to let the cabin boy take his place. And I helped do the cooking for the cabin. I made all the bread and pies, cake and pudding..It was just work enough for exercise. I really took comfort in it."—And you couldn't have pried

## Captain Abby and Captain John

Abby Pennell away from the dough-dish with a cantdog! She knew, and elegant Susan Chase knew it, too.

Abby was up at five in the morning and baked a pan of biscuits and three mince pies for breakfast! She cleaned the caster and teaspoons and cut out a calico dress, and did a little sewing. Next day it was doughnuts she fried, and the stateroom and cabin she cleaned. Next day, a batch of raised bread. John had to broach another bl. of flour in the Bay of Biscay-O! Sewing galore. John got the supper himself on August 1. John didn't enter this in his log. I suppose if that had happened on a British ship, by a British captain, the British lion would have gone right out and looked for a lamb to lie down with! The following day, the Bay of Biscay recovered its reputation. It kicked up. It was too rough for Abby to take many stitches on the new dress on the ways. But the Bay of Biscay did not keep her from making "riz" bread for supper. It may, though, have sent her mind back to Brunswick and Bowdoin College. She set down a pang of homesickness: "Commencement Day at Home, and how much I think about it!" She wished she were under the Thorndike Oak that Thursday, hearing the Seniors declaim.

The New England housewife was a bit under the weather, the next days, but not too much to be unable to do considerable work. And she and John picked over some dried apples. Dried apples were as essential on shipboard as the ship's papers. One string of that Yankee leis made at least three reasons for a captain's going right through a gale smiling, browned reasons,

## Captain Abby and Captain John

hot from the oven, and marked with the featherbone pattern that let the savor of New England orchards erupt.

They sighted the British bark *Yarm* (what a name! Leave it to a Britisher to think up such an underdone one)—of Hartlepool, John added in the log—and the British schooner *Aerial*. Land, August 7: "See land all day long, the coast of Portugal. Looks rocky and mountainous, distance 18 miles." There were several ships, and a steamer. A day followed that was squally. Abby made a pudding for dinner and sewed edging on her nightdress and nightcaps. She made capital of the showers that fell by catching water enough to do "a large washing, and all dried and in tonight"—which was more. Next, Abby commenced "a pair of shoes for John, worsted work." Then she ironed and darned some stockings. Then took a rest by working some more on the shoes and making a cake for supper.

In the midst of all this, Cape St. Vincent went by. A host of vessels rocked by, a steamer passed close to. Africa lifted her wild, blood-red mountains into the sky. Beaches as lonely as craters on the moon opened out. The dark blue fan of the water in the Straits of Hercules opened under the bark. The legs of Hercules stood up, the southern one with clouds passing it halfway down. Two boats boarded the Yankee ship, and outlandish men sold Abby fruit like the apples of the Hesperides, melons like Winter moons or something out of the *Arabian Nights* tales. Moonlight swept over the mountains of Spain and turned them to unearthly silver. Abby was going through a gateway built out of his-

## Captain Abby and Captain John

tory, sheer poetry, and romance. She was sailing between mountains that were like something dreamt long ago and never again. And Abby was admiring it all, but she also had her two hands in her biscuits, her husband's shoes, and her wash, where a good New England housewife's hands should be! This part of her sailing might be called New England days off the coast of Spain, or Yankee housekeeping under the legs of Hercules! It would be the same story all this woman's life. "Off Gibraltar, passed the Rock at 9 o'clock, six miles off. Current set us off on Africa side. Two boats boarded us again today with fruit, etc. We got a lot of all kinds. And got some pumpkins, and I made some pies this afternoon." The Spanish gold of vegetables and fruits Abby changed right into the gold of honest New England pies!

Abby Pennell mixed the Rock of Gibraltar in with the Skolfields of her native Harpswell as well as her pumpkin pies.

"We passed the Rock of Gibraltar the 15 of August," she wrote her mother, "Monday morning about 9 o'clock. It was clear and pleasant, so I had a good chance to see the Rock, which is 1400 feet above the sea. It looked like a mountain, and I thought of Grandmother when we was passing, how much she used to talk about Sam Skolfield being to the Rock of Gibraltar. How little I thought of seeing it then! We got lots of fruit from there, boats come long side loaded, and could get it very cheap. We had grapes, lemons, pears, peaches, plums, apples, and some beautiful pumpkins. I made lots of pumpkin pies. And good ones, too. John said they tasted the most like home of anything that he had ever eat at sea."

Abby hadn't had any milk to do with. But she had made out: "I of course made the pies with water, and the pumpkins was so rich that they tasted nicer and richer than ours does with milk."

And she made the most of everything, as always. "I saved all the seeds."

Trust a Yankee wife to save everything down to the last seeds! The attic of my boyhood had whole flour bags full of pumpkin seeds, hung up out of the rats' reach.

Cape Sacratif, "some little villages that looks pretty," forty sailing vessels around them. And Abby's hands were on John's shoes. They were nearly done. A head wind forced them to reef the topsails. It blew so hard, it blew one of Abby's best Plymouth Rock hens, and a laying one, right off the deck into the sea. A Yankee sacrifice to wild Spain! Cape De Soto, and another small boat with pears and grapes and peaches. Abby got out her saucepan and preserved them. They began painting the *William Woodside*. Abby gleefully set down the fact that they passed the bark *James Cruickshank*, "the first vessel we have passed." Sunday, August 21, was lonesome, being a Sunday away from Maine folks. Next day, Abby celebrated her twenty-fifth birthday by working on John's shoes and preserving pears that James Henry had bought. She also opened a tub of butter on her birthday. She went on with the shoes. August 24, they made Pithyusae Islands, bearing NE by E, distant 15 miles, and tacked

## Captain Abby and Captain John

to the north. Abby copied this right out of John's log! She finished one of John's slippers and started right in on the other. She "worked over" some butter. "Found a little bird in the pantry this morning. But we could not keep him long. He soon left us." Abby was a great one for pets, always. She consoled herself by making some pumpkin pies. Sunday, August 28, seemed like Sunday, it was so lonesome. "Today is the last Sunday in this Summer. Not a vessel to be seen."

They sighted Africa, and Abby worked on the slippers and preserved some pumpkins. "Caught a shark today and have him in a cage." But he was no good as a pet. They got a bad thunderstorm, the worst Abby ever saw on the ocean. The fore topmast staysail was carried away. "I was up most all night," writes Abby, "and don't feel very smart today, but have kept up all day and made some pumpkin pies and worked on the shoes." She worked over some more of the butter. "The last day of Summer." The first day of Fall, Abby ironed and starched and worked on the shoes. An American schooner passed them going west. They sighted Africa again, Cape Bougarina. They saw it two nights, being becalmed. "Enough to make anyone sick, to have such weather as this," ejaculated Abby. They sighted another American schooner.

Abby "learnt to take the sun." She was very proud of this achievement, and crowed about it to her mother in a letter. She was just as good a sailor as John or anybody now: "I take great interest in learning. I can take the sun, and can tell where she is on the chart as well as he can, and work Longitude and Latitude. I

## Captain Abby and Captain John

believe I could sail a vessel now as well as anybody." A sailing life agreed with her. She had been won over. "It suits me exactly, going to sea. I never thought I should have enjoyed it so well."

The new sailor was even more sprightly about her sea legs to Susan Chase, Bunganuc friend of Longfellow's: "I guess you would laugh if you could have seen me sometimes when the vessel was down on her side. I have got so used to her now, I can walk as well as I can in a house. You will see me walking the ceilings in the house when I get home, same as the circus play actors! James Henry thinks I am quite a sailor."

A breeze came up at last. But Abby was sarcastic about it, "I am in hopes it will last so we shall get to Venice sometime this Fall." Cape Gardi, Tunis, and Abby ran up on deck to see it, and "spraint" her knee. "I met with a little accident," she broke the news of her fall gently to her mother in a letter, "on the passage. I suppose I must tell you. . . I went up on deck one day to see land, and went to turn round quick to get the spy glass, and spraint my knee. Something slipped out of place. It hurt me very bad, so that I fell, and John had to carry me into the cabin. I could not bear my weight on it for a week, and am lame yet. My knee swelled bad. I put on wormwood and rum. It helped some, I think. It plagues me considerable, and I have to be careful. There is just one way that I move it will make it slip out again. It seems as though there is a bone that slips out of place. I have to keep a tight bandage on it all the time, and go limping about. It is getting better slowly."

## Captain Abby and Captain John

They saw the land of Pantelleria, with some little houses on it. They sighted Sicily at last, and Abby celebrated that by finishing the long-drawn-out bedroom slippers for John. She didn't rest, though. She started right in on embroidery for her drawers. They met an American bark, *Elois*, of Boston, and said howdy with their ensign. September 10, Abby cooked and embroidered and looked at Sicily. It looked beautiful, but lonesome. It was Saturday night again, that was why. The swelling went down in Abby's knee. Abby saw a big city on Sicily, and made some sugar candy. Mt. Etna hove into view, Abby was making over her candy, and John, she writes, was mending his pants "in his shirt." There was no work for Abby next day, for there was a heavy sea, and she got seasick. John did, too, she adds. Abby got another pet, September 14. A dove lit in the rigging, and they caught it.

Next day looked bad. Something had come over the ocean. But Abby finished the embroidery on her drawers and started off on hemstitching a pocket handkerchief, as they were passing Cape Otranto, the Heel of Italy. At night it looked very bad. Sure enough, heavy gales hit them next morning. They went under reefed topsails only. The Gulf of Venice rose up on its haunches and came at them. "The worst tonight I have seen on the ocean," cried Abby. "Gales and very wild," said John. Abby waxed eloquent about this blow in her letter to her mother from Venice: "We come the whole length of the Gulf of Venice under reefed topsails the most of the time. It was fun to run before it when it was fair weather and steady wind, and see land all the

## Captain Abby and Captain John

way. But the wind would strike off the mountains in gusts and cause a tremendous sea. It would look frightful sometimes, and specially nights. We had thunder, tempests, and squalls every night. I never see lightning before, the worst lightning that I ever see at home was nothing to this here. I thought a number of times the Bark was on fire. I did not sleep much nights in the Gulf of Venice. It is a dangerous place to be in, full of islands and sunken rocks, and gales of wind all the time. If we get out of it as well as we come in, I shall be thankful. . . . We had heavy weather and was near the land, which made us feel some uneasy. Thick and rainy, but before night it lifted up a little, and we was close under the land, and the weather looked very bad and squally. So we run for a harbor. The wind was off shore, but there was a strong current setting us in. We was in hopes to get a pilot that day, but the weather was so bad, there was none off, and we knew would not be that night, it was so rough." They got to a port sixty miles from Venice. "It was lucky we did, for it was an awful night at sea, so the pilot told us."

They came out, shook off their troubles, and went up along the coast of Italy, through many islands. More and more islands. The sun came out. But Abby's knee was acting up again. It was rather chilly. It felt like Fall. Abby had to put on her bonnet and shawl. It was a dismal Sunday to her. But the land looked pretty after all that storm. The pilot came on at Port Pola. His name was like a flower, Rosigno. Things began to look brighter. Abby admired the view: "The country looks beautiful all along the coast, and a number of

## Captain Abby and Captain John

pretty villages, a delightful looking place . . . Shall not get to Venice tonight, but we feel at rest with pilot on board." Abby went into more detail on the view in her letter to her mother: "We sailed up long shore, so I had a good view of the country. It was delightful. It is a beautiful country. The land is low and level and thickly settled. As far as I could see was villages and gardens and orchards. I cannot tell you how beautiful it looked." Abby was sure such a lovely land was a Christian place. It couldn't help being: "I think it must be Christian people here, for they have a great church with a steeple high as a monument to every two or three houses."—If only life were that simple and plain! It was, to a Yankee captain's wife in 1859. She would have agreed with Tom in the *Water Babies* that the young lady in the great house must be a very dirty young lady because she had so much soap around in her room. "Soon as we hove in sight of Rovigno," Abby went on to her mother, "we hoisted the colors for pilot, and one come off to us. We took pilot at nine o'clock in the morning. Then we felt safe, for all was in his hands. Then we stood across to the western side of the Gulf of Venice."

They got to Venice next day, September 20, and came to anchor at noon in Beulah Land.

Life's first lap was done! Abby had reached her dream.

# 9

## The Carnival of Venice

I SUPPOSE, if you had asked any Yankee wife in the middle of the nineteenth century what her idea of heaven was—after Saturday night, baked beans, and the whole family gathered around them—she would have answered Venice. Abby Pennell would have, anyway. Now Venice was not a regular port in the Yankee sea captains' lexicon. It was all the more romantic for that. It was a fairly hard place to get a vessel into and out of again, if she drew much water. It was off the worn track of sea commerce. But Yankees knew about it. Especially Yankee wives. Poets and artists had made it a nineteenth century Carcassonne for folks all over the world. Because of its inaccessibility, Venice was more glamorous than even shining Cadiz or Leghorn or smart, up-and-coming, Yankee-like Trieste. It meant music to the Yankee mind, music of carnival and romance. It was a place the robust husbands thought of when they made love. Love-making was something that could go on in public, there. The only city in all the world, for Yankees, where that was so.

Abby was all edged for Venice. She had gloried in their going there from the time they had got their sail-

## Captain Abby and Captain John

ing orders in Falmouth. It was really the center of her honeymoon. There would be other peaks to life after this, but no peak quite up to this particular one ever again. Abby had been revamping stays and binding hoops and sewing on flowers across two seas all for this moment. The beautiful views of Italy's shores, after the blow, had been ushering her up to this glory. Now she was there!

There had been an awkward moment or two getting into it. They had almost been quarantined, Abby wrote her mother: "The inhabitants was dreadful afraid of us because we come from Havana, a sickly port. When John went on shore, he said they would run from him like a fox." But John had got a "clean bill of health" from the officers at the Customs after they had come on board *en masse*, and with a doctor, to look Abby and the crew over. It was a ticklish job getting the bark up to the city, too. Everybody lent a hand, though. "The American consul sent down four boats and about a million Italians to tow us up to the city," wrote Abby. "They have no steam tow boats here. Had to go up a channel just wide enough for the vessel to go in, and very crooked and 8 miles long, all fenced off with stakes." But the approach to Beulah Land ought to be difficult. They got there finally and hove anchor. "Looks very pretty," noted Abby, "all around us."

The Yankee mistress of the *Woodside* would be glad to get ashore. "I have not been out of the Bark for a meal's victuals," she wrote, "since I went aboard of her, except in Falmouth. I spent one day on shore there, but always went ashore when John did and come off when

## Captain Abby and Captain John

he did. And I have been aboard six months steady. I think," she added, "I have done pretty well." She deserved a holiday, and in Paradise, or as close to it as it is proper for a Yankee wife to come while she still has her breath and wears her apron. Abby was still on the sunny side of twenty-six.

Abby had arrived. She put her apron by. She put on carnival dress for the carnival that was Venice. She got out her hoops and set all her stays. "Looking over my basque today," she set down in her diary. "Ironed my collar and undersleeves. Had a grand gent to dinner today." The carnival was beginning. She put down the carpets in both cabins, did up John's shirts, and finished her basque. She had started a washing, Venice or no Venice, but the coming of the Customs officers broke it up. "Mr. Lloyd and son aboard this afternoon. Very pleasant people here."

Abby descended in her basque at last, on September 24, into Beulah Land. She and John put up at the best hotel, the *Vittoria*. "Got a nice room, furnished nice." She settled herself and breathed deep. She and John stepped out into the streets that evening. "Everything looks delightful," wrote Abby, "and rich." It was so wonderful she forgot to miss home even though it was Saturday night. She feasted on fine food and on throngs of elegant people moving about the *Hotel Vittoria* on marble floors that reflected their magnificence. Women like swans on a glassy pond. And such hoops! Boston had nothing to compare with these. They were big as an ox-cart wheel! The silk dresses whistled! Abby's Middle Bays gown seemed suddenly sleazy. But

## Captain Abby and Captain John

Abby held her chin up and took no backwater on the marble floors. "Sunday morning in Italy in the city of Venice!" she wrote with a flourish in her diary. Not many American women ever wrote that! That day it was St. Mark's lions, carved out of dreams, winged with awe. Pigeons came down like clouds from the sky. The pillars were right out of the *Book of Revelation.* There was St. Mark himself, lying right in the middle of a palace. Abby had never dreamed the apostles were such high-toned and well-dressed people! "Everything looks rich and ancient." The bride of cold Middle Bays breathed the southern loveliness in through her skin. She went out again that evening, "on the square to hear the band play." Life was good. It was complete. The captain, who was her lover, beside her!

Capt. John's wife was in Venice three weeks. And every night but three or four she went to hear the band. "It was beautiful," she cried in the diary. "Enjoy myself very much." Abby lived on music every hour. "Oh, Susan," she wrote to the elegant lady of Bunganuc, who may have known so intimately the music of Longfellow, "I hear music enough to charm you. There is delightful music here all the time. I don't know what kind it is. But I hear it every afternoon. It plays on the bridges and in the streets. It is enough to do anybody's soul good!" . . . "This isle is full of noises." . . . But the band remained the peak of pleasure, every night.

The lady of the *William Woodside* walked through a dream. She sat down and told Susan Chase all about it, in a long letter with a colored engraving of the

## Captain Abby and Captain John

Bridge of the Rialto at its head. The bridge where the merchants of Venice shone and hoary Shylocks nursed their hate. "I wish I could give you a description of this beautiful city, but it is impossible for me to describe a place that is so curious. However will try and do the best I can. The city is on 72 islands, and bridges goes from one island to the other. No horses or carriages to be seen. But they go in little boats called Gondolas that are fixed very nice for the ladies to go in. The water goes all through the city, and it looks as though the buildings was setting on top the water. There is one wide canal that is very wide runs through the city, and there is a bridge built"—somebody has cut out the engraving of the Rialto as a keepsake and removed some of Abby's ecstasies with it.—"Then there is a place called the square that is very pretty, about as big as the Mall at Brunswick."—I, too, once measured all things by the Brunswick Mall, a piece of the Twelve-Rod Road to the sea that our town fathers kept cleared that wide of trees, so an Indian's arrow would not be sure of killing the ox-teer walking in its middle.—"At the head of the square is St. Mark's Church, built of clear marble and gold and silver, set in mosaic work. It is splendid. No language can describe the rich work there is on that building. It was built in the year 1500, and St. Mark's body is buried in it." The saint lay next to the joys of the dance, as Abby went on to tell: "At the foot of the square is a large building with a beautiful dance hall. On one side there is a palace of marble built for the Prince of Austria to live in when he comes here. On the other side is a palace for theatres and coffee rooms, and underneath is splendid shops of all kinds. And it is all light with gas, and the bands playing in the square every evening!"

It was heaven descended on earth. "It is a beautiful place to walk. We take a walk there every evening. The buildings I speak of are clear white marble all round the square, and are five or six story high and all carved work, and when lit up with gas it is the most picture-like looking place that I ever saw! I have not seen a building of wood or brick, all stone and marble. The city looks ancient and rich, and some of the marble palaces are so old they are dropping down. We have been in five churches that are magnificent, and one is called the richest church in the world, so our interpreter told us. I cannot think there could be anything go beyond it. I cannot describe it, for I shall not have room to tell you all I have seen. But if I live to see you again, I shall have a lot to tell you. We are stopping on shore awhile, at the *Hotel Vittoria.* Have been here two weeks . . . It is a beautiful building and very large and furnished splendid. The floors are all marble, except the sleeping rooms. We dine by ourselves, and such hour as we like. . . . Oh, Susan!"

The woman of Great Island described Paradise in more simple words to her mother in Harpswell: "I wish Elias was with us to see the curiosities here. The city is built on seventy-two islands, and the water goes all through the city. They go through the streets in boats. No horses nor carriages here. It looks queer to see the ladies step out of the houses into the boats. There is bridges built in some places."

## Captain Abby and Captain John

Abby cut out a silk dress, lower in the neck.

She made new dresses. She went shopping. She walked the Rialto. She bought pictures of the city. She took a steamer and went over to Trieste for a day, took a carriage up the Mount, and dined in a sumptuous hotel equipped for the Austrian Empress. She came back again at midnight by boat to Venice. Abby climbed up a tower in Venice 360 feet high and looked down on her dream. And on the last day of September, in the Year of Our Lord 1859, this Yankee housewife stepped out of centuries of stern repressions into a gondola, and lay down! ... It was the peak of the peak. Life, in many ways, would be downhill after this ride. She reclined like Cleopatra and floated down the watery streets of heaven. John was by her side. They went, she wrote in her diary, "to see the railroad bridges and the church of Scalina, which was the most magnificent building that ever was seen. Built of solid marble." They floated back home. The band closed the day like a benediction. Abby bought a basket for two shillings, and John got the pair of shoes being built for him. "They look nice." And next morning Abby wrote in the diary that she was living in Canaan now: "I am seated in a beautiful room at the *Hotel Vittoria,* in Venice, Italy, taking all the comfort that can be taken in this world! Fixed my pink skirt today." It was the top of the carnival. Mince pies, and even pumpkin ones, were a whole universe away. Cold Maine October was forgot. Abby had even forgotten that it was Saturday and that she should by all rights have been lonesome!

Abby liked the Italian people. "I like the appearance

## Captain Abby and Captain John

of the Italians a great deal better than I do the Spaniards," she wrote her mother. "They are very pleasant appearing. Not so impudent and saucy as the Spaniards. We are the only Americans there is here, or has been for a long time." Americans were quite a curiosity. "There is a great many Italians that speak English well," Abby wrote Susan. A gentleman from Leghorn came. But that was to see John on business. An Italian lady, Mrs. Gestolini, made up to Abby. She could talk a little English and tried it out on Abby on a walk with her to the Prince's gardens. She brought her husband and child and her brother on board Abby's vessel. John and Abby showed them what Yankee housekeeping was like. They were much impressed. "Very pleasant folks," wrote the sea captain's wife. "Liked them very much."

Being a dressmaker herself, and a first-class one, Abby was interested in the fashions of the capital of romance. She was at home in her hoops, of course, for hoopskirts had rolled around the world. She wrote Susan Chase about the Venetian styles: "The ladies dress here about the same as at home. Wear very large hoops, larger I expect than they do at home. They are very pleasant appearing people."

There was not, of course, the gaiety of Havana. But there were some nice Americans around. They called and entertained. There were Mr. Lloyd and his son. He showed them St. Mark's. Mrs. Wing, of New York, called. But Abby wasn't taken with her. "Don't like her appearance very much." They entertained the Lloyds at dinner, and made plans for Mr. Lloyd's going with them to Trieste. But the American consul was the gem

## Captain Abby and Captain John

of all the folks from home. He was young. He was good-looking. He was a perfect fit for Venice. If we had to depend on the diary solely, we might not know how much Abby was taken with *him:* "Had a call from the American consul this afternoon. He is a very pleasant young gentleman and good company. Like his appearance very much." The letter to Abby's mother was only a bit more expansive: "The American consul was glad to see John, and is coming to see me tomorrow. He is a young man. John likes him very much." But it is in her letter to Susan that Abby expanded most on this high light of Venice and carnival: "The American consul calls to see me. He seems just like some one from home. He is young, about 20, and very lively and good company. I believe I should set my cap for him, as Harriet Eliza says, if I wasn't married!"

But holidays cannot last forever, even in Venice. One can have only so much romance. Among marble palaces and rich churches, Abby began to be lonesome. Even in her palace of a hotel. "Have been here two weeks," she wrote Susan. "It is very quiet and still. Don't seem much like the hotels at home. I have no one to speak to when John is gone. So it is lonesome." The dream was wearing thin. "I shall go on board in a day or two."

The truth was Abby was beginning to miss the gossip and bustle she had been used to all her life. She missed the Topsham Fair. Anybody would. Venice is Venice. But it isn't any substitute for that climax of the Brunswick and Harpswell year, golden with prize pumpkins and bright with the sunflower eyes of matched oxen, with gules of apple jelly and the azure of crisp

## Captain Abby and Captain John

Maine sky, called Topsham Fair! It was the mark by which I measured all time in my boyhood. So many weeks before or after the Fair. All the farmers reckoned even their sons' births that way. It was coming on fairtime now, a quarter of the globe away. Abby was thinking of that sobering fact, in the midst of carnival. And it was coming on time for the Pennells to be launching their annual ship. She was thinking of that, too: "I suppose," she wrote plaintively to Susan Chase, "it is about launching time and Fair time, too. I would give all my old shoes to be there. John often speaks of the launching and how he would like to be at home." *Lusisti satis.* The play was breaking up, the dancers unmasking.

Venice was not so perfect a place, when you really came right down to it. Shopping, for instance. Things were awfully expensive. To be sure, she found bargains in kid gloves: "They are quite cheap and very good, get them for five dollars a dozen. John and I got a dozen. I find them to be strong and good." This to Susan, and she wrote Susan she was going to advise James Henry, the young scapegrace-to-be, to invest in kid gloves, too, to give his lady friends when he got back home. But gloves were only one item in the life of a Yankee woman fond of good clothes. Other things were not cheap. Abby's whole sense of New England thrift was beginning to waken from the dream of Venice, just as her conscience had begun to, about Topsham Fair and the launching.

The postage was high, she wrote her mother. So high she could write her only two letters from Venice. Other

## Captain Abby and Captain John

things were costly: "Went into a shop to see about some picture frames, but did not get any." Abby finally bought some little pictures of the city, but she had to go back two days after and change them. And dress goods were out of sight. "Walk this afternoon," she set down in the diary, "to look at some silks, but they was too dear to buy, so I shall not buy any here." And she wrote Susan of her deep disappointment. It would be Susan's, too, for she figured in it: "Went into some stores and priced some articles of clothing. I have been out a number of times with an interpreter to see about getting some dresses for James Henry that he was going to get for Augusta and for you and his mother. You all have an idea at home that everything is cheap here. But you are greatly mistaken. Everything is very high. I was very much disappointed. There is no silks here, under 30 or 40 dollars, that you would wear, and not pretty at all. Very large figure and bright colors." —Like the souvenir embroidery the French seamstresses made for the American soldiers of the A. E. F. in my war. They believed Yankees were half Indians and wanted barbaric colors. "I don't know," added Abby, "but what James may have got the dresses, for I have not seen him for two weeks."—James was on his own carnival.—"But if he has not, I shall advise him not to get any here, as we are going to Trieste. I think he could do better there. I have been over to Trieste with John. Went one day and back the next in a steamer. It is a very pretty place, I think. It seems more like Portland or Boston. Has wide streets and horses and carriages. It seems the most like home of any place I have

## Captain Abby and Captain John

been in since I left home. It is surrounded with high mountains, and thickly settled on the side of the mountains, so it looks very pretty at a distance. I went into some of the shops while I was there, and saw some quite pretty silks and great deal cheaper than they are here. And everything in the dress line is cheaper than it is here." Thrift should be resumed in Trieste!

More than dress bargains even, Abby was missing the excitements and the homely news of home. Home was breaking through the haze of Beulah Land. Things were going on in Maine, and she was missing them. Her heart turned away from Venice and carnival to Middle Bays. She was hungry to hear what her friends were all doing. Some were marrying, and some were dying, and she not there to know it and see it! "I was very much pleased to receive two letters from you and Elias, this afternoon," Abbey wrote her mother on Great Island, "and to hear that you was all well. For I have thought a great deal about you all. We got 6 letters from Middle Bays, so I guess we have got all the news for awhile. I was surprised to hear of Lettice Reed's marriage so soon. And also Harriet Orr's. I think she has done great things. There seems to be a great many sudden deaths, all around. I know Rufus Dunning will be missed on Harpswell Neck." Little events of home loomed over St. Mark's.

But big American events, too, were in the air. Abby touched on them: "We had some English papers sent us today, and I see by them that the *Great Eastern* has made a start and will leave the 29th of this month for Portland." The national events ran out and touched the

## Captain Abby and Captain John

local. For Abby was of a seafaring family, and Maine seafaring families bordered on the great world. She resumed her talk to her mother on the angel of the new epoch, the transatlantic cable-ship. "I suppose you will all go to see her. I wish I could be at home to see her. She must be a sight worth seeing. I suppose Elias will believe that she is built when he sees her." Brother Elias was a doubting Thomas to anything that did not run by sails.

Then Abby returned to family revolutions: "I think my going away," she wrote her mother, "is a good thing for you. For I believe you have gone round more since I have been away from home than you ever have before. I am glad to hear it, and was glad to hear that you had your teeth taken out. You will not suffer so much with the toothache now." Abby knows what Summers mean on a Maine farm.—I know I dreaded them. But they were pleasant to look back on from the rest of the year, which was sheer vacation beside the heroic task we had on Great Island, keeping our old New Warrior mowing-machine—built in Springfield, Massachusetts, about Abby's time—and the horse alive in the hayfields, next farm to Abby's father's!—"I suppose," Abby wrote, "you have all had to work hard this Summer, and too hard. You had such good haying weather"—I used to pray each night for a fog!—"that Father and Elias liked to kill themselves with work. I am glad it is over with." And I know Abby Pennell would have given more than her old shoes to be there in the bosom of her family even in haying time, when stories and sentiment are short and boys find life a burden. Abby, being a woman,

## Captain Abby and Captain John

would have had it easy, anyway. All she would have had to do would be to cook a few meals of victuals a day for the haymakers and rake scatterings, to rest in between. Abby was worried about her father's having had to go to see the doctor. She sent them all her love and her caution not to work too hard, which all Maine people always give to all Maine people and which nobody ever pays the slightest attention to.

Abby wrote Susan that she was sorry to think of leaving because she dreaded the trip home in Winter time, for all her new sea legs: "The weather is very pleasant and warm. There has not been an unpleasant day since we have been here. I am sorry to leave the place so soon. We shall leave here in a few days for Trieste, to load for New York. I am sorry that we have to go home in the Winter time. I dread cold weather. I shall be likely to see some rough weather on the passage home."

In her lonesomeness for home, Abby had tried to mother young James Henry Pennell, twenty years old, the mate. "We have high times," she wrote Susan, "talking about home sometimes, generally at supper." When Maine folks get lonesomest. "I wanted him to let me mend his shirts and stockings. But he would not let me touch them." It would have been a major New England revolution if a bachelor had allowed a young matron to look after so intimate clothes as his stockings and shirts. I don't know what on earth Abby was thinking of. But maybe it was Venice and carnival.

Abby and James Henry, in one of their high old times, talked over the news of a new arrival at Middle Bays. "I hear Elizabeth Giveen has another child,"

## Captain Abby and Captain John

Abby writes Susan. "I think her and Tom believes in multiplying the earth." Abby, who was married to the youngest in a family of eleven, was properly shocked. "If I was in her place, I would go into the pigsty and have them by the litter. For if she goes on this way, the town of Brunswick will be run over." James Henry, being a man, and not having more than a single man's momentary interest in the matter of multiplying the earth, was not shocked at all. "James Henry says, 'Go it while you're young!'" So Abby tells Susan, and adds, "I guess they mean to."

And Abby closes this letter to Susan with apologies and love to everybody. "I must soon close, for the want of room, I think."—(On her last page she has got almost 1000 words in letters about the size of a pin point, and has shaken the foundations of what sight I have left!)—"I have written you a long letter, such as it is. You must excuse poor composition and writing and nonsense. Wish I could get as long a letter from you while here, but don't suppose I shall. Give my love to Julia and Hannah and Augusta and all in the neighborhood. I will send Willie and Ella"—Aunt Nell, who annihilated the Longfellow letters, now seven years old and as yet uniconoclastic!—"a little picture of a boat they call a Gondola, such as John and I goes in. John sends his respects to you and all the family. I hope to see you all by New Year's, if we are spared to reach home again. It seems a long ways to go. . . . This paper is not ruled, and you will see that I have written very straight."—Straight as the bees fly in Middle Bays!—"Yours with affection. Good bye."

## Captain Abby and Captain John

The exile from Great Island also promises her own family some presents: "I shall get a picture here of the city, if I can, and some ornaments, and something for Sis. Tell her she must eat a good lot, so to grow fat by the time I get home. I don't want to see her looking poor. I think a great deal about her. I don't know where we shall go from here, nor how long we shall be here. I expect a fortnight or three weeks. . . . I must close, hoping this will find you all well and enjoying good health as I am. You must excuse the writing and mistakes, for there is so many in and out and such a noise, it gets me excited so I hardly know what I am doing sometimes. Your daughter, Abby J."

Promises of presents, gossip, news of deaths, births, and marriages. Middle Bays is lifting up above the three-hundred-foot towers of Venice and the winged lions of St. Mark's. Maine is growing clearer as the dream fades. The holiday is almost over.

Yet Abby plunges again into what hours of carnival are left. She writes her mother boastfully that her husband John "is sitting up here eating a peach as big as his head. The peaches here," adds she, "are very large, as large as the cups. I wish I could send you some of the fruit." But Middle Bays looms even bigger than the Venetian peaches. "John says you must all go to the launching."—It was the ship *John O. Baker*, this Fall, and the model of it is by me now as I write.—"Give my love to all the folks, after taking a good share for your selves. So good bye." The dream was thinning almost all away.

But there was still the band. Abby clung to that,

every evening. She added three or four more churches to her list of sights seen, bound to get her money's worth. "They were splendid beyond description." She went to the glassworks and bought some glass bosses at fifty cents each. She bought some spoons for the *William Woodside*. She also cut herself out a pair of stays and cut John out six shirts and "commenced on some embroidery for drawers"—enough work to last her home across the Atlantic! Two bits of the fairy gold of the carnival she bought also: two canary birds and a cage thrown in, for two dollars and a half. She carefully noted down the cost. She named one of the birds Dixie, not foreseeing how bitter a name that would be to her Yankee people and her calling in a few years.

One more hour in the Prince's gardens. And one more strand in the bright dream fading so fast before New England thrift and conscience—she and John rode once more in a gondola. They went down to Napoleon's garden. It was heavenly. That is what Abby meant when she wrote in the diary, "Looked very pretty." Once more Abby Pennell paid idolatrous tribute to Napoleon. She was to pay it once more, still more passionately, as we shall see, at St. Helena. And the bark *William Woodside* sat for her portrait. John and Abby were having it painted for John's nearest brother, Robert, whom they made their home with when at Middle Bays. And there were the Venetian sunsets. Sunset after sunset. Abby drank them in. A few last churches. "Went to see some churches this forenoon, Jesuartz Church. That was fine. Barnabas Church. Had a great feast in this church, and splendid music. Then went to see the Acad-

## Captain Abby and Captain John

emy. That was splendid, full of paintings." The bloom seems to have gone off the sights, though, and Abby seems to be getting in as many as she can crowd into a day. "Then come home. The last Sunday in Venice. Went to hear the band play."

But next day the shadow of departure fell on the diary. Abby was putting slots in her new stays and packing up her things to go on board. She changed two pairs of gloves that had imperfections in them, and succumbed to one of the vast Venetian hoopskirts she had written friend Susan about. Middle Bays would stick out their eyes at that! A last trip "to the Prince's garden and got an ice cream." It was a last act of carnival. Ice cream was moonlight and romance, then. Being rarer. Next morning the rain veiled the city as Abby went aboard. Maybe her eyes were in the same condition.

Abby had no time for tears, though, once she was on board. She had never seen the cabin in such a state. It was all dirty. Nothing was cooked. She put her apron on her and sailed in. She made the dust and fuzz fly. The painter had done the cabin over in white. Like all painters, he had left a day's work of cleaning behind him. Abby did her duty. She knocked out a pan of biscuits or so. She finished by six o'clock, all petered out. But the cabin was a New England room again. In the heart of Venice. A scrubbed Yankee heart. Abby was stiff in her joints next morning. But she flew to the pantry and turned that out, washed the dishes and "put things to rights." It was better to work when tears were close to one's eyelids. They hauled out of the dock.

## Captain Abby and Captain John

The domes of Venice began to sink under the earth.

It was some comfort that they anchored off Napoleon's gardens for the night. "The last night in Venice," Abby penciled elegiacally. And added, "I suppose"—which is the Yankee for I am sure—"am sorry to leave so soon." They had hard work getting out by the backwater. They had to be towed by row boats. Then when they were on the sea, there was no wind. Abby made a sheet and pillow case for the berth. They were still off the city at night. Abby sat down and wrote, October 14 —it was one of the days of Topsham Fair at home— "Adieu to Venice forever! I never expect to see it again."

And she never did. One does not go twice to Carcassonne. Or on honeymoons. Before she fell asleep that night, Abby wrote once more, in the margin of the little black diary, "So farewell to Venice!"

# 10

# The Long Way Home

THE ROAD HOME from Venice was four months long. It was bound to be downhill. There is only one Venice in a lifetime.

In spite of her brave words to Susan, Abby was good and seasick crossing the Adriatic to Trieste. John was seasick, too, as usual. "In company." But Abby spruced up after they got there, and cooked some. And by Monday, October 17, Abby was her Yankee self again and observed the day as a Yankee should: "Done a very large washing to day. Did not get through till night and feel tired and almost sick." Washings are big, after carnival. But Abby was still on her feet: "Made some bread for supper and just changed my dress." Next day, as the vessel began loading, Abby flew to work, healer of holidays, in earnest; starched and ironed and cooked. "Work all the time, health good tonight, but feel very tired." The ironing was a two-day one. John's shirts and vests on top of her chemises. Abby began to tack a comforter in her odd moments. In case you are too young or too far from New England to know what tacking a comforter means, it is tying bow knots of yarn through the six-inch layer of wool which is the

## Captain Abby and Captain John

regulation blanket of Maine. The knots are to keep the wool from drifting to the bed's edges and leaving your knees exposed to the Arctic night. I could throw a pretty fair tack once. The comforter Abby tackled was a two-day job, too. But Abby took her black silk dress apart in the midst of it, for a rest.

The weather had turned bad since Venice. It was thick. It was rainy. The sea was ugly, even right in Trieste harbor. The bark broke her moorings astern. Abby had to stay in all day. And it came on to pour. It rained cats and dogs. But the Yankee housewife got some comfort out of fixing up a Maine Sunday supper of baked apples and milk. The second Monday rolled around. Abby did another Homeric wash. But it poured, and she could not get it dry. "Had to put my clothes in soak. It came on to rain again at noon, so I could not hang them out." Abby made some squash pies. She sat up doing embroidery beside her sleeping captain: "John is to bed and asleep. 9 o'clock in the evening." Abby got her clothes dried out next day, ironed and starched, sewed on her black dress, and embroidered her drawers in the evening while thinking of the launching she had attended at New Meadows a year ago this very night.

John's wife got ashore at last, in the town that reminded her so of clean, smart Portland. She got weighed at a Mr. Carroll's. She weighed 141 pounds. She went shopping, but did not actually buy anything. Often there is more New England sheer joy in that kind of shopping than in any other. Next day, Abby cooked John up an Indian suet pudding "that was very good"

## Captain Abby and Captain John

—if she did say so as shouldn't—and sewed on her black dress. Next day, it was heavy squalls. They drove the *Woodside* "onto a Spanish bark and done some damage to us and to the other bark." Abby made some blancmange for supper. And John bought her a new patent flatiron!

Thick still, the following day. Abby got the flowers back on her silk dress and set up the stove in the cabin. "Rained all day hard as it could pour." The Saturday lonesomeness had returned. John was ashore in the evening, and that may have accounted for part of it. Sunday dinner was roast turkey, and supper, pudding and milk. Still raining. Mr. King and his son called. The stove came in handy next day, it was very cold, and they had a fire. The black dress was finished and looked like new. Abby received, through James Henry, a gift of a jar of preserved ginger from an English sea captain in from Bombay. The first day of November, Abby rigged up her big Venetian hoop, made an Indian pudding, and took a walk all round the harbor, to a small village, then back 'longside the water "clear up to the depot." Next thing, she cut out shirt bosoms for John and two pairs of drawers for herself. It was some kind of a holiday and shindig on shore, Abby couldn't make out just what. "No work done in this place today nor yesterday." She went to bed still hearing bells a-ringing. Then it was collars for John, and another walk, this time in a lovely garden. Night again and a moon, more silvery than the Maine moon. "A beautiful moonlight evening tonight and splendid music on shore." A ghost of Venice. John was sound asleep, though, in his

## Captain Abby and Captain John

bed at nine o'clock. Abby had her moon to herself.

Shirt collars again, and another shopping trip without buying anything. A visit at a Mr. Sagarovich's office, and sewing on the drawers at night. Sunday was a lonesome one again. Abby hoped it was the last one in Trieste. "A year ago this time we was at Robert's having high times. Now in Italy." Lonesome. But Abby soothed herself on roast duckling and milk for supper. Wash day again, and this time Abby got the clothes dry. She fixed over a merino skirt. She almost finished her drawers. Then starching and ironing with her new patent iron. She went to bed feeling tired and sick, the proper way to feel a Monday night in New England.

Abby was good and sick next day. She was coming down with a cold she would remember all her life. She did her best, though, and tried to shake it off by sewing, Yankee panacea. But this cold was one to be respected. "Severe pain in my head and back and distress all over me." Next day Abby was worse. But she had to drag herself ashore and keep a dinner engagement with the Trieste nabob, Mr. Sagarovich. "Don't feel much like it, though."

If Abby had been well, she might have recaptured something of Venice. For she was entertained in a palace five stories high, halls of marble, "furnished beautiful." Maybe Mr. Sagarovich was a Shylock of Trieste. Anyway, the Prince of Austria was one of his tenants. That was the kind of man he was. The Adriatic Croesus did things up in style. They were two hours dining. A Yankee woman must have found that almost immoral. John and Abby met the man's handsome family. Abby

## Captain Abby and Captain John

wrote her mother all about it, later, when she had got on her feet again: "Last Thursday we was invited to dine on shore to Mr. Sagarovich, the man that John does his business with. He is one of the richest men in Trieste. The Prince of Austria lives in one of his houses. They don't look much like houses. They look about like the great hotel in Portland. Palaces, they call them. He sent his clerk after us in a splendid carriage at 2 o'clock. So we dressed in our best and went and had a beautiful time. He had a teacher in his family that talked good English, and one of his daughters could talk some. He has a very handsome family of seven children, all grown up, and are very pleasant. They could not do enough for us. We was two hours dining. They had everything that could be thought of. Their house was splendid, built of stone and marble, and five story high. I have not time to describe the inside. I must let that go till I get home. Mr. Sagarovich was educated in New York, and he said we were the first Americans that he ever had to dine with him. He is a whole gentleman and a fine looking man. They were quite old folks, about sixty. We stopped till six in the evening."

But Abby's head was like an augur hole all the time, and everything slipped through it. "We left at 6 o'clock, and glad enough was I to leave. All the time I was there with the cold and pain in my back. Am very sick tonight." In her mother's letter Abby used a significant phrase, "We went home. Home I call it, for it seems more like home to me aboard the bark than it does any wheres else, and I take more comfort on board than I do on shore."

## Captain Abby and Captain John

Abby went to bed. She was flat on her back for a week. High fever, no sleep at night. "Poor John doctors me day and night," she writes in the diary, "and is almost sick himself. . . . Never was sicker in my life. Have done everything and taken all kinds of herb teas but no better tonight. Blowing a hurricane." But hurricanes and high fevers did not stop Abby Pennell from writing each night in her diary. Like John Donne, seventeenth century Dean of St. Paul's, she followed all the stages of her illness with appropriate commentary. John got a doctor out. John finally got Abby to sleep with laudanum. Abby "sweat dreadfully nights." The doctor came two more times. She was able to sit up a bit, November 17. By November 20, she was sitting up all day and writing to her mother.

She wrote her mother that they were all ready for sea and that she was glad enough to leave Trieste. Five weeks of hurricane and rain, and she with a cold. She did not let on to her mother, New England daughter that she was, that she had been deathly sick. Instead, she wrote how "hearty" she was and how much she weighed—"142 dressed," the most she had ever weighed. Carnival had agreed with her. "Poor John," though, "is nothing but skin and bones. I never saw him so thin before. It worries him so to have to be here so long that it makes him poor. He weighs only six pounds more than I do. . . . I am in hopes John will flesh up some after we get to sea, for I hate to see him so poor." Abby's ideal of beauty and health is stoutness. She is constantly wanting people to flesh up.

In her letter, Abby hopes her mother will have good

sleighing in the Winter and will save some of it for her when she gets home, though it may be February before she gets to Great Island. She is sorry to hear of three deaths, and writes that John says Henry Pennell will be missed and doesn't know "what his old father will do, for he was all the son he had that he could depend upon." Abby speaks of being sorry to miss the launching of the new ship and wishes John had the *John O. Baker* instead of the *Woodside*, which everything on the sea passes, apparently. "They say she is a beautiful ship. I wish it was John's luck to have her to go in. I think he thinks a great deal about her. I hope he will not have to go in this vessel much longer, for I think that he ought to have a better one, anybody that takes so much interest and does so well for the owners as he does, I think, ought to have a good vessel to go in. But must hope for the best. Perhaps everything works for the best." Abby sends her love to everybody, and wonders if Elias, her brother, is in school, tells Sis that she wants to buy her something to please her in New York, and declares she dreams of them all at home every night.

The *Woodside* had taken on a cargo of fruit and rags and steel. Not a great one, but it was better than going "to Orleans in ballast," wrote Abby.

Abby was still in bed when they left Trieste, November 21. They were in for it. The winds took a notion to be all contrary ones. That is the way of the world after holidays. It took them forty-eight days to get through the Mediterranean to Gibraltar! Abby did more sewing and cooking than she had ever done in her life before at one stretch. She mended John's pants and overcoat and

## Captain Abby and Captain John

sewed on an apron off Venice, city of dreams. She finished her drawers and the apron. She sewed on her stays off Meleda. Sewed on her stays and made a cake off Point Austria. She mended all John's stockings and knit "a heels" to one pair off the mountains of Italy. Finished John's stockings and finished some drawers and knit some off the same mountains. She made pies and sewed on her nightdress off Otranto. Finished her nightdress and commenced on some embroidery for her pantalets off Mt. Etna. Commenced on John's shirts off Sicily. Kept on with the shirts, still off Sicily. Finished a shirt and made some gingerbread for supper off Cape Bon. Began another shirt off Golita. Sewed on the shirt off Cape Bangorani. She worked on the pantalets and made more gingerbread. More embroidery. Made a lot of mincemeat. Sewed on the shirts. Finished a shirt and stitched part of a bosom off the Pithyusae Islands. Made John some handkerchiefs and stockings and some mince pies still off the Pithyusae Islands. Took up another pair of stockings for John and embroidery, still there. More work on the shirts, and a bosom sewed, off Cape Palos, Spain. Finished the third shirt and did some cooking, still there. Made some mince pies and puffs, preserved some prunes, and worked on shirts and bosoms, still off Spain. More shirts. A lull during some hurricanes. Then finished a shirt off Cape Legata and made some currant and raspberry pies and put up some damsons. Then Gibraltar at last, and no more sewing for a bit. For the gale of a century hit them, and stopped Abby's needle for a few days.—This is the log of a New England housewife's sewing and cooking

## Captain Abby and Captain John

across the Mediterranean Sea! And Abby never took a stitch or lifted a pie plate on any of the six Sundays! That is a kind of test for a New England conscience!

There was plenty going on for Abby besides sewing and cooking during this month and a half, even though the *William Woodside* wasn't going on much. There were scores of barks, brigs, ships, and other craft to see. The Mediterranean was chock full of them. Many of them were lucky and going east, taking what wind there was with them in their sails. Most of the others passed them, even in no wind at all. "A bark in company, supposed to be the *Margaret* from Trieste for New York, sailed after we did." And the *Margaret* was hull down over the horizon ahead of them next day. There were twenty sail off Cape Palos, Spain, mostly brigs, it was so still. The vessels clustered thicker around them as they finally got into the bottle neck of the Mediterranean. "40 vessels in sight with studding sails set." Abby saw one brig piled up high and dry on shore. The vessels crowded in like scared pigeons into Gibraltar Bay ahead of a sky like red hell and a gale coming up. And a lot of the vessels never came out of that death trap under the mountain when the great wind came in after them.

Abby saw a lot of scenery. She saw a good lot of it two or three times. "Right off the island of Lagosta tonight, just where we was last night." And again, "Off the island of Meleda, the same that we were last night. Discouraging." And "the wind the same old way, ahead!" "Passed Cape Legata again this morning," wrote Abby sarcastically. It was getting to be a habit,

## Captain Abby and Captain John

passing Legata. They had gone backward. "32 miles to the eastward of where we was yesterday, off Cape Legata." "Have to beat all the time," moaned Abby. "Don't get ahead one mite." Abby saw the high cliffs of Curzola with red spots of sand. She saw Austria, "very high and mountainous." She saw Italy with high mountains white with snow, then Italy lower down, with "little huts built round all over the country." She saw the little villages along the Toe of the Boot. She saw Etna, "that is 10,874 feet high. It is up into the sky, the highest mountain in the world!" She saw Augusta and Syracuse and three lighthouses along the Sicilian coast with gales off Sicily making her eyeballs jingle. "Turned everything upside down in the cabin." Wicked-looking fiery red clouds rose out of the west, "a tremendous sea running." The ship rolled through an evil twilight with nothing but close-reefed topsails and reefed spanker. It was like sailing along the edge of Inferno. There was another gale, and reefed topsails, for Christmas. Abby had never spent such an unsteady Christmas in all her born days. "Last year I was at home Christmas, and John was in Havana. And this year in the Mediterranean Sea. Where shall we be another year?" The sea was acting up enough to make even a Yankee sea wife wonder. The rolling made her think how five years ago she went down to High Head, Harpswell, to a singing school and how the dead Caroline was still with them.

But it was calm New Year's Eve. Too calm. Abby was becalmed with a huge fleet of vessels off Spain, thinking of home and mother. New Year's Day, 1860,

## Captain Abby and Captain John

was a Sunday, and a "long and lonesome" one. The homesick Saturdays and Sundays had returned. Abby saw two whales on January 2, and three windmills going it in a village on Almeria Bay, on January 3, and a big man-of-war. It was reefed topsails again on January 4, for another gale hit them. Again the universe ran red with a wicked light, and a dreadful night rushed down upon the little bark. "Oh God," pleaded Abby in her diary, "watch over us this gloomy, stormy night. Looks frightful. A sea just came over her and came into the cabin. First time I have seen that. Hope I shall not see any more, but must trust in him who does all things well." Abby was to have more seas come in and call on her in the cabin, this voyage and others. But this blow let up, and they got a fair wind at last. Abby thought of home on January 6, and how seven years ago, this night, was the night before little Sis had been born and how she was at a spelling school on Orr's Island enjoying herself. And then Abby headed into the worst gale of her life.

Abby had had other things to think of besides gales, too, crossing the Mediterranean. The wedding anniversary had come and gone. Two years. And very happy ones. She could say it with all her heart. She did so in her diary: "I always shall remember the day we were married, the commencement of a happy and pleasant life so far to me, and I trust always will be as long as we live . . . And may God spare our lives for many years to come."

And John had been deathly ill almost all the way, with an abscessed ear. Abby had not been able to take

## Captain Abby and Captain John

her clothes off some nights, nursing him, the two weeks before Christmas. John was in terrible agony. Abby gave him laudanum, she made an Indian meal poultice and put it on his ear. She was frightfully worried, to have John so sick, with those fiery clouds sowing the first hurricane over the sea. There are few such hours in life. When they come, their fiery radiance lights up the faces of husband and wife, and they see themselves as never before or after. It takes a good husband or wife to stand that light. John stood it. Abby stood it. But Abby was at her wits' end: "Such a heavy sea I could not sleep in the berth. It was a frightful night, and poor John did not sleep at all, his ear pained him so bad, and pains him all the time. I have done all I can do. It don't relieve him any. I can't bear to see him so sick. I had rather be sick myself." Abby fell back on the best old Maine remedy for anything that ails you. She put a mustard plaster on John's neck. John began to get better at once! And Abby took up the embroidery which she had laid by to nurse John. That was a sure sign John was on the mend.

The gale of gales came on them of a Sunday, January 8. The sea piled itself up into mountains like the Sierras on their starboard. Abby rolled so she got no sleep. They scooted for dear life, with scores of other winged travellers, for the Rock of Gibraltar. The wind was screaming like a million banshees, the bark nearly standing on her beam ends, plunging up a mountain and then burying herself part way up the masts as she came down. They got into Gibraltar, behind the Rock, and anchored. But gales tore down on them from the

## Captain Abby and Captain John

Rock, and the harbor ran with livid green mountains. A hundred vessels, some of them Americans, pitched bare-poled like a forest in a storm. Night came on. It was a night of hell, and the harbor was a seething cauldron of death by morning. The *William Woodside* pulled her anchor and ran foul of a brig. It may have saved their lives. Captain John was up all night. When dawn came, many vessels were lying shattered on the shore. A British bark which had been anchored beside Abby and John had broken away and crashed on the back side of the Rock, and all upon her had been lost. A steamer and a schooner also had broken up. The bay was full of drowned men and the beach strewn with them. "I am thankful we are safe," Abby wrote. The gale was going on around them as she put down the words, and more men were going to death. "Tonight a great many vessels getting smashed up all around us." It was so bad that Abby forgot to do her regular Monday washing!

Abby found the time to write her mother a letter about what they had been through:

"I expect you think we are near by New York by this time. But I guess you would think different if you knew what kind of weather we have had to get along with.... Waves running mountains high and breaking all over us, and come into the cabin! I stood in the cabin door the most of the time, looking out when I dared to. I thought a number of times, if you could see us and know just where we was, on the back side of Gibraltar and the wind blowing us on, you would not rest very easy. I could not help thinking how comfortable you

## Captain Abby and Captain John

was at home, sitting 'longside your stove, and nothing to disturb you, and we tossing about cold and wet and feeling so anxious to make the land or the Rock of Gibraltar. For it was so thick that we could not see but a short distance. But we got in safe, and we was thankful to get in before night. For it kept coming on worse, and danger of being driven on the backside of the Rock. There was five vessels and one steamer lost there last night, not but a little ways from us. I can see the masts of one from where we lay. There was a great many lives lost. It is an awful place in bad weather. We was so thankful to be here. For if we had been out last night, we should have been lost. There was a great many vessels in company with us Saturday, and some was lost, and they are coming in here all the time in distress and stove most all to pieces. It was a dreadful night. They say they have not had such a blow here for a long time. There is quite a number of American vessels here, and most all of them have got damaged in the harbor but us. It blew so heavy that they dragged their anchors and got foul of each other, and some got smashed up dreadfully, and some went ashore close by us. And we expected that we should get smashed up by the other vessels. But we escaped, and that's all. We may yet. It is very disagreeable weather here today. It has been thundering and lightning, with heavy squalls, all day."

Sickness and death, Capt. Abby and Capt. John had looked both in the face, and had come off with flying colors and more in love than ever.

Abby did her washing, Tuesday, January 10, while

## Captain Abby and Captain John

people were cleaning up Gibraltar harbor and collecting shattered ships and shattered men. She got it done in time enough to go ashore and do some shopping in Gibraltar. A small boy from Portland, Maine, who was living there, squired Abby round. Things were too high, though, for a thrifty Maine housewife. She came home early. She went again next day, after she had had to dry her clothes in the cabin, and found the town very muddy going. This time she brought some things: 3 spools of cotton for 15 cents, a shirt bosom for 40 cents, a bosom pin for 37 cents, a yard of cambric for 12 cents, some other dress goods, a paper of needles for 6 cents, and 12-cents' worth of oranges. A Mr. Garese sent her a present of two boxes of raisins and two of figs. Abby washed again but did not put her clothes out on her line from the cabin to the mizzenmast. It took Abby four days to dry them in the cabin.

Abby put another installment on her letter and told her mother about going on shore and described the British Navy's eyrie of a century ago: "I have been onshore twice and took a walk through the city. But I had to go in the rain and through mud ankle deep almost. So it was not very pleasant. It is a curious looking place. The city lays on one side of the Rock. And the side next to the water is walled in, and there is only one entrance into the city, and that is through gates, and they are shut before dark. So if you are not out of the city before the gates are closed, you have to stay there all night. They are very strict. The place is inhabited by all nations, mostly by Spanish and some English. It is owned by the English. It is a small place, not handsome at all. I have a picture of the Rock and city, and something for Sis."

Abby is proud of having weathered the rough time they have been through. She boasts to her mother in the letter that she has not been seasick one mite for all the gales. She tells how she nursed John when his ear kicked up. She had her sea legs on and got around in spite of the bark's standing up on her hind legs: "I managed to get about and wait upon him. It was a case sometimes, there was such a heavy sea for me to get round in the cabin. I run most of the time from one place to the other. I thought a great many times that you would laugh if you could have seen me, for I could not help laughing at myself sometimes. I had to go all ways and sometimes got knocked over backwards." Abby tells how worried she got over John but is glad to write he is well now.

She tells how much she thinks of them all at home, and dreams about them a good deal. She also wonders how the sleighing is. "I suppose," she writes enviously, "Elias is sleighriding about every chance he can get. I am afraid I will lose all my sleighrides this Winter if we are as long going to New York from here as we was coming from Trieste here. But I hope a bad beginning makes a good ending. And I think we ought to end well." Abby hopes it is not so cold a Winter as it was a year ago. She is in hopes John and she have escaped the worst of it, for it will probably be March before they get home, "if we live to reach there." The worst two months are past: "December and January are the worst

## Captain Abby and Captain John

months to make a passage to the westward in, so they say." Abby says John had prophesied ninety days for the voyage from Trieste to New York, and Abby thinks he is in a fair way to be proven a good prophet, the way their bark is making it and the way the winds are always coming at their nose!

"Tell Sis," writes Abby, "to be a good little girl. I thought of her on her birthday, and how plain I could see how she looked! I think of her often and want to see her." Abby has missed them all so at home that she is bound to take them all with her to look at, in the small, next voyage: "I shall not go away again without all of your miniatures. I thought a great many times I would give a good deal if I could have them to look at. We thought of home Christmas and New Year's. Christmas we had a heavy blow, had to take in sail. And New Year's we was becalmed close into the land of Spain, called Cape Palos, a large fleet of vessels in company. It was very pleasant that day."

One thing Abby Pennell has made her mind up on: her young brother must never, never be a sailor. She knows Elias and his hankerings. But he must drop them all and settle right down to plowing and haying for good. Any fate would be better than seafaring. Abby has been through enough to know what being a sailor means. Elias needn't think he is going to graduate from his smart dory to a brig: "You must tell Elias that he must not think of going to sea for a living. Leave off thinking of that, and think of something else. For it is no life to live. I shall discourage him from that idea if I can. And tell Father not to let him. Tie him first."

## Captain Abby and Captain John

And Abby adds, out of her hard-won wisdom, "I guess if he should go one voyage, it would sicken him of it. It is a miserable life for a man to live!"

You can put Abby's vehemence down to that shaking up she has just been through under the Rock of Gibraltar. And to the fine long men she has seen floating backside up in the waves, or face up with staring eyes and stiffened fingers done forever with sail and gale. This was only a momentary mood. Abby didn't really mean all she said. She got over it, as we shall see.

And his father couldn't tie Elias to Great Island. A dozen ox-chains couldn't have tied him. Elias went on that voyage his sister said would cure him. It tempered him as water does red hot iron. It set his soul forever on the sea. You cannot change the chemistry of the stars. There was no chance of driving the sea out of the marrow of a Maine coast boy's marrowbones in the Year of Our Lord 1860! Elias Reed grew up to be one of the finest of Brunswick's fine captains. He followed in his brother-in-law's footsteps. He even wore his shoes. He took over the *Deborah Pennell* when John graduated from that flagship of the Pennell fleet to the finest Pennell ship of them all, the *Benjamin Sewall*. He grew up to be one of the stoutest and last of the Yankee princes of the Atlantic and Pacific oceans!

Abby might just as well have dropped her letter into the sea.

On January 13—a Friday, too, but it was the first fair breeze they had had—John and Abby Pennell sailed out of Gibraltar with a hundred sail bearing them company. There were broken bones of oak behind

## Captain Abby and Captain John

under the Rock, but no gale could wipe out all these shining children of the winds. The sea had blossomed out white with them once more, the moment the sun showed his face. Abby was at the center of a vast lily of amazing white life such as the world will not see again.

"So I take my last look at the Mediterranean Sea, and think I shall always remember it."

So Abby would. For she had been tried by fire and wind and water and holiday within it. And she had come tempered for life out of them all.

The Atlantic was a mill pond after the Mediterranean. It was John's shirts falling finished regularly one by one from Abby's hands, pumpkin pies, and singing all the way!

Abby finished a shirt, got through another lonesome Sunday, repaired a pair of John's pants, read and sang through another Sunday. They passed the Madeiras. Abby celebrated with a pumpkin pie. More shirts. A pair of stays. They signalled a French bark.

Across the Atlantic, in Middle Bays, Gussie Pennell, eighteen, was writing her Brother James Henry aboard the *Woodside* that there had just been a spelling school at the little yellow schoolhouse, where Capt. John had once sat with a smarting tail and past which Nell had carried the ten-quart pail of molasses: "Had about forty schollars. Had a real good time. We are going to have another next week." Alva Giveen had also had a spar fall on him and "got hurt quite bad." And Gussie was busy with poetry, as well as spelling, and putting verses into her little red-backed memory book full of the sentiment and fatalism of her day. There is quite a

## Captain Abby and Captain John

lot of both in a single poem in the little red book of her thoughts:

> Each on his own strict line we move,
> And some find death ere they find love.
> So far apart their lives are thrown
> From the twin soul that halves their own.
>
> And sometimes, by still harder fate,
> The lovers meet, but meet too late.
> "Thy heart is mine!" "True, true, ah true,"
> "Then, Love, thy hand!" "Ah no! adieu."

Abby made John a cotton undershirt and six pumpkin pies. Then she made herself Malta-lace undersleeves and tape trimming. It rained hard, and blew. But the wind was fair, "so let it blow," cried Abby. She made a pair of drawers. John killed three rats in the cabin. The last day of January. "We are going over the road fast!" Abby cried. Husband and wife were back in the bloom of health. John was shirted for a decade! Pumpkin pie every night, and the canary bird singing!

Abby finished her drawers and did an enormous washing. "Washed a lot of new cloth and nine shirts for John." The shirts were not soiled ones, they were the new ones. But like all Yankees Abby washed things always before wearing. "Could not hang them out today. . . . Quite moderate. Am sorry to see it." For Abby was stretching her heart out ahead towards home and wanted to get there fast. She cut out chemises. Kept the fifth anniversary of her Grandmother Reed's death.

## Captain Abby and Captain John

Grandmother Reed had been blind for years before she died, but her mind had been alive as a fish-hawk's. She had told stories of Napoleon and her Orr ancestors, the pioneers of the island. And Abby had sung to her by the hour, sitting on the arm of her chair. And grandmother had sung with her. And Abby's best friend among her cousins, Lettice Orr—whose marriage Abby had just heard of back in Venice—namesake of grandma's, had sung the older Lettice, with silver hair and blind eyes, *The Rose of Annandale*, grandma's favorite song. The young Lettice's new husband would put the scene in a poem of his one day:

> "Come, Letty, sing *The Rose of Annandale*,"
> Said grandma, gray and old and blind,
> But young in heart, and crystal-clear in mind
> As in her happy girlhood far away.
> The loitering sea-breeze, rippling Casco Bay,
> Played with her silver hair that distant day,
> And fair Orr's Island smiled 'mid summer green.

"I always shall remember it," wrote Abby in her diary. "I trust she is happy in another world." Brighter than Orr's Island, and hearing a lovelier song than *The Rose of Annandale*.

A lovely moon came up full and silvered the sails of the *Woodside*. Abby walked under the cloths of silver. The light ran over the waves and came up to her. "It is a beautiful moonlight evening. Warm and pleasant. Have just been on deck to walk awhile. I do enjoy myself finely such weather as this! It is delightful." And

## Captain Abby and Captain John

Abby was tremendously excited. One of her canary birds had laid an egg today! At this rate, who knew but what the cabin would soon swarm with bits of the carnival of Venice. "John and I eating oranges tonight." Silver of moon and gold of oranges. The world was running with joy. There was only one small shadow. One of the canaries was sick. Maybe parenthood had been too much for it.

"Beautiful weather all the time," wrote Abby. She took the sun all by herself with the chronometer on February 5, and was only four miles out of the way by John's reading! Abby scalloped a skirt. Grandma Reed had been buried five years ago this day, and John had sailed as mate on his first voyage as an officer on that brand-new Pennell paragon, the ship *United States*. The studding sail broke in a squall. But Abby made a lot of cakes. The fore topsail gave way and ripped apart. But Abby sewed up a long rip in John's pants. So it all balanced up in the end!

And on February 11, 1860, in mid-Atlantic, the pig breathed his last. The second mate butchered him. It seems rather elegiac, at this distance of eighty years! And he almost home. But he was one Great Island pig who could say he had been in Havana, had crossed two seas, and breathed in the heart of Venice! Maybe he died happy in that knowledge. It was spare-ribs and fresh shoulder for Abby and John.

Abby was reading a good deal. She was reading the *Bible* straight through, for one thing. A Bremen bark passed them. They had a blow, enough to make them take in sail, but not enough to make Abby furl her em-

## Captain Abby and Captain John

broidery. "Health good," so it runs day after day. But the canaries weren't doing so well. Possibly the effort of producing progeny and adjusting new matrimonial problems had affected both in health. Abby separated them on St. Valentine's Day, 1860. Again, that seems rather hard, at this distance. "Appetite good." Abby was a fine sailor for life now. Head winds discouraged her, though, the latter part of this voyage. They passed a Spaniard going east and got his longitude. It wasn't very close to theirs. Abby ran up a cake and finished her fourth pair of cotton stockings for John. John speared a dolphin with his harpoon, and they had fresh dolphin cutlets for supper. A fair wind came at last, and they bounced along at 9 knots. Abby ran up a chemise and repaired a shirt for John. "Done other little jobs, too." They passed Bermuda, three months out from Trieste. They met a brig and a schooner. Abby made a cake and a pair of undersleeves. But she lost her rosettes from Venice. She was standing on deck, and a sudden squall wrenched them from her hair. . . . Another strand of carnival gone!

They entered the Gulf Stream and passed Hatteras, seventy miles off. There was lightning, and it made Abby's head ache. Abby washed the cabin woodwork and that in the sink room. "It took me all day." She saw some cordwood floating. Nearing New York! Abby mended John's pants and fixed her hoop skirt and otherwise prepared for Broadway and its gaslights. Vessels gathered thick about them, all headed north. Sunday, February 26, Abby finished the *Bible*, begats and all. They bid the Gulf Stream goodbye. The next

## Captain Abby and Captain John

day came the pilot, and they made Barnegat light at noon. Abby did a washing and cleaned the staterooms and front cabin. "And happy I am," cried she in the diary, "to see the land of America again!" Nearly a year away. "At anchor off Sandy Hook . . . Shall go up to the city tomorrow." But she didn't, she cleaned the carpets instead and "fixed things up a little and finished my chemise."

A tug took them up to the city through the fog, and they anchored off New York at noon, February 29, 1860. There were letters and letters—maybe the shadow in them!—All well at home, thank goodness! Abby sat down at her diary and wrote: "This ends my first voyage to sea, which has been very pleasant. The last night of Winter. Where shall we be next year at this time?"

In these simple words Capt. Abby summed up the most exciting and memorable year of her life, her sojourn in Beulah Land, and the year she really got acquainted with her husband. She had a dozen ocean voyages ahead of her. But none would ever be quite up to this first one. She was a veteran sea woman. From now on, she would take gales and sails and adventure for granted. She would keep on with her sewing and cooking, and her piety. She would keep other diaries. Three more. But she would never open her eyes so wide or her heart so wide again. Nor would she ever again set down what she saw and felt, and the homely details of living, so naturally, so untouched by "literary" conventions, in so simple and beautiful a way.

# 11

## Reunion at Middle Bays and Harpswell

AFTER THE BARK *William Woodside* had been towed into dock and more letters had come, Capt. John Pennell sat down and played to Abby on his accordion. It was John's relief at hearing good news from home and his love of his wife that made him do so. He set the mood of the whole next fortnight of their life.

It was the kind of fortnight only Yankee sea captains and their wives, who lived upon the great love of family and friends, ever could know. John and Abby, like other Yankee sea couples a hundred years ago, had to crowd all their families and friends and talk into a few days. Before the long silence fell again. Though they grew to love the sea and their calling, they lived years of anticipation of these few hours of quickened life and accelerated joy, so few and far between.

Abby's first act, once she got her eager feet on Broadway's brick walks, was to get a watch chain made out of her own hair for John. That was how happy she was to have solid land, that did not tilt up and slide off, under her feet after a year of water. She also prepared for the joy ahead by buying herself a dress for $4.13. She wrote in her diary that she did not like going a-

## Captain Abby and Captain John

shopping in New York very well. But she went ahead and got a dress skirt and lining for herself—$2.72; two more yards of lining—$0.24; still more linings—$2.10; undersleeves and hairpins—$1.25; collar and undersleeves—$1.25; thread and silk—$0.13; three picture books for the children—$0.62; toys for the children—$0.50; neck handkerchief—$0.30; two cards of hooks and eyes—$0.08; a small leather work-bag—$0.50; a bonnet for herself—$6.00; a velvet dress for her own mother—$4.88; and a gorgeous black silk dress for Mother Deborah Pennell, who had urged John on to become a sea captain with a birch switch—$12.00! The dresses were in ascending order of importance. Abby paid more for her two mothers' dresses than for her own. That was like Abby Pennell, to her dying day.

The homecoming wife also bought Charles the Great a cap. And in another day, fast as the cars and steamer could carry him once he got the word of their arrival, came the great Charles himself, ship's doctor, to take over the *William Woodside* and to wear the cap. I sincerely hope it did not contribute to the baldness which Abby's youngest son later on surprised his Uncle Charles in as he sat in his office at the side door of his house at Pennells' shipyard!

Now that she could see the whole past year in the light of Broadway and in the perspective of her whole life, Abby Pennell recanted that letter she had written her mother while rocking under the Rock of Gibraltar. She sang a different tune, now. The sea life wasn't so bad. It was a hard one, but it was also John's and her new home. She had made her bed. Even if it was a hard

## Captain Abby and Captain John

one, she would lie in it. She would go where her husband went. *Whither thou goest, I will go; and where thou lodgest, I will lodge; thy people shall be my people, and thy God my God.*

Abby's mother, probably overpowered by the Gibraltar letter, had more than hinted to Abby in her letter to her in New York that it would be nice if her daughter stayed home on Great Island for a long vacation from the deep. But Abby flared up at the suggestion: "You seem to think that we ought to stay home awhile to get recruited." Recruited indeed! there was no need of *her* being recruited. "I don't think we need recruiting. For I have lived very easy this past year. I wish you could live as easy as I have." Horses couldn't drag her away from the easy ocean life. Not *her!* Of course, there had been a little wind and a few ships' masts sticking above the Mediterranean. But these were trifles. "We have had very pleasant warm weather all the time," Abby declared in her letter to her mother from New York. "Had some squalls and thunder showers off Cape Hatteras, but nothing to hurt us. We have," said she, forgetting her Trieste influenza and John's ear, "been well all the time. I have not been sick an hour since we left Trieste. And never enjoyed myself better. My first voyage to sea has been very pleasant all round. And I have enjoyed it very much. So you see, it will encourage me to go again." Recruiting?—Sho! sho!—There was no pulling her away from sea life. She was a captain, for good and all.

It was warmer on the sea, too. There was *that*. "I think, by what you write," wrote Abby, "that you have

## Captain Abby and Captain John

had a harder time this Winter than we have had, although we have spent the whole Winter on the ocean. For we have not suffered any with the cold. It has been as warm as June ever since we left Trieste." Hard life on the sea?—Sho!

Her mother had also hinted, apparently, that Abby might slip away home to Brunswick early and let John take care of the bark. She would have all those extra days. Really, her mother had hurt John's feelings by suggesting any such thing! John was vexed, and it took a lot to vex John. Abby told her mother how John felt: "John says he thinks you don't care anything about him, whether you see him or not!" No, Abby's place was New York, as long as her husband was there. "I think I shall wait till he comes. It will not be but a few days. And I want to look round here a little, to see how New York looks."

Though she is committed to the sea life for life, Abby, of course, wouldn't mind staying home for a little stretch. "I don't think I should object to staying home awhile, if I had the opportunity." But only for a brief stay, mind.

Abby commented on the news from home. She was sorry to hear of her friend Elizabeth's having had the typhoid fever and of Mrs. Sinnett's death: "Mrs. Sinnett is done with this world. I trust she is better off in a world that is free from sin. She has been a hard-working woman. The family must miss her. And the neighbors."

I don't think you could ever better that for a typical, and beautiful, New England epitaph.

## Captain Abby and Captain John

And Abby comments on Sis and Elias: "Tell poor little Sis that Abby wants to see her dreadfully. You must let her go up to the depot with Elias if it is pleasant, when I come home. I should not know Elias, to see him with a black horse. I am very sorry to hear that they have swopped that good horse away. But I suppose Elias has got a two-forty now, that will go so fast you can't see him!"

Deaths and illnesses and horse trades pile up when a person has not heard from home for three months. Much life goes by when one is a sea lady and rolling on the waters of the world with only a husband to love and talk to!

Abby flew to her sewing basket and kept the next three days in New York full of dressmaking, against her emerging, trailing clouds of glory of Venice, plus Broadway, in Middle Bays. The cabin was her lodging still, no hotel. Charles came to dine. Abby took a cold, naturally, and had a sore throat, but that did not stop her dressmaking. She went up to town in a snowstorm on March 9, and loaded herself down with presents for the children, Sis and the young Pennells. And at five o'clock she boarded the steamer for Stonington, Connecticut. She reached there at the chilly hour of two in the morning, and she and John got at once on the steam cars for Boston. And in a mere five hours more, she was at the Hub! "Very pleasant night and pleasant this morning in the cars." She was going home. Being up at all hours was sheer joy. Abby got to Portland at half-past twelve o'clock and took the Kennebec and Port-

## Captain Abby and Captain John

land RR to Brunswick, arriving at two in the afternoon.

All Middle Bays and half of Great Island were there to meet the two homecoming captains. The boy Elias was there, with the Old Boy in him bigger than a woodchuck and the new black roader. It was a Maine welcome. They all adjourned from the depot to Brother Joseph's house in town and ate him, probably, out of house and home. Then the whole doubled clan moved by horse and sleigh to Middle Bays. All the Pennells were greeted in rotation. Then Abby's clan moved on to Great Island, and more jubilation. "Found them looking just the same as ever," wrote Abby, her heart running over. And she tumbled into bed and "had a good night's sleep."

She needed it. For next day, March 12, it was reunions and visits and parties and reunions again. After doing Great and Orr's, Abby and John returned to Mother Deborah's in Middle Bays. All the Pennell brothers and sisters were there. A vast snowstorm descended. Sleighs flew up and down the road. A call at Charles's, at Ben's, tea—supper—with Mrs. James Pennell, and then the evening spent at Jacob's—where I sit writing this—and, last, a ten-o'clock visit with the bright-eyed, eighty-year-old matriarch of all the Pennells, Deborah, in her little house on the hill from which she had sent them all out into the world and fortune. And the black silk was delivered, and Deborah almost let her neck fall and her eyes mist up, but didn't, and sat up calm and proud as if she was used to having gowns from Broadway every year in her life, and

## Captain Abby and Captain John

thanked her daughter-in-law quietly.... The dress was fine enough to be buried in.... Then to Robert's house, and to bed. So John and Abby were divided up among the Pennells. It had been a full day. Abby had distributed herself over it and among the Pennell families with fine impartiality. She had described the palace she had dined in, the churches she had seen and the towers she had climbed, the gondolas she had reclined in. She had left a wake of excited youngsters revelling in gifts from Venice and Trieste and New York. "Had a fine time and am happy to be home again."

Next day was the same. Only there was also a trip to town and longer rides over the Brunswick roads. The sleighbells tingled, and the white breath of horses flew. "Quite decent sleighing," Abby jots down. Which means, translated out of Yankee, a hundred silver bells ringing, two horses curvetting with plumes at each nostril, the runners whistling over the snow and leaving silver trails, the Maine sun a-blazing in a turquoise sky, a thousand fir trees sparkling with snow on every last twig, and Abby's heart in her mouth as she slid through the bright world under fur, with John by her side. But Abby was able to crowd in a little sewing on her black dress's waist between sleighbells and demonstrations of affection and happiness.

The following day, more hilarity at Abby's house, with Sis and the others. Then a party in the evening at Joseph's, on the Twelve-Rod street of Brunswick. All the big-wigs of the town and township played cards and talked and put on airs and graces as only hard-working Yankees can put them on when they get into their best

## Captain Abby and Captain John

bib and tucker. And there was singing, too. The Woodsides were there and the Skolfields and the Curtises. Every sea captain's wife in the place. John and Abby, the latest homecomers, were the center of all. It was a late party, for Brunswick in 1860. "Sung and played cards," writes Abby, "till 11 o'clock."

John and Abby slept in town. And they shopped in Brunswick in the morning. Then they drove down and over Gurnet Bridge through a sparkling day and found Mr. and Mrs. Jacob Pennell at Abby's father's. They spent the day.

But the crown of all and the peak of happiness was that night. John took down the fiddle of the house and played. And Abby's father got up on his pins and did a dance! He did a dance such as only a Great Islander can do when his smart daughter has come home in silks from Venice. Sis laughed and mother laughed, Elias clapped his hands and kept time. A high-toned Pennell coming down to the more robust and carefree level of Great Island, and being one of the jovial crew! It was a fine and warming sight. And John sang as he fiddled, and his handsome father-in-law danced until he nearly brought the house down. And Abby laughed till her tears came down her cheeks. "Quite funny," she wrote in the diary. Which is the Yankee way for saying you laughed till you cried.

The goings and comings quickened. For the time was growing short already. Dinners at the different Dunnings', at Mother Pennell's, and she in the new black dress that creaked. Trips to the village. Calls on Pennells and Woodsides and Bowkers. Supper at Jacob's.

## Captain Abby and Captain John

Another dash to town. Back to Mother Pennell's. But the sleighing was all gone now. Spring was in the air, and departure. Abby went to church in Brunswick. "Enjoyed it very much." Parson Adams at his best. Abby was the lady who had been in Venice now, and the whole congregation eyed her admiringly. Then down to Deborah's, and a great host of brothers and sisters there as usual. Home at night to Great Island. The pussy-willows were out, the roads were deepening with the muds of Spring. Smell of life in the air. The time was short.

When John went to Middle Bays on business next day, Abby, as the proper beginning of her two days in the bosom of her own family, washed. But callers broke in on her washing. Angelina and Henry Doughty and Tristram Scott. Abby's hands were damp with suds. Talk and laughter and songs. Still Abby managed to cut herself out a pair of stays and get her clothes dry. Next morning John came. He kissed her. He was off, ahead of her, for New York. The joy was breaking up. Aunt Susan of the Longfellow glory came all the way over from Portland to bid hail and farewell, and to thank Abby for her fashion news from Venice. Goodbye and goodbyes. Abby finished her dress.

And on March 21, first day of Spring, Abby packed up her things. "Must leave home again to go away on my second voyage. Hard to leave my home. But I must."

And Abby really wanted to go. She was eager to go. For she had been converted. The sea had won her over. The lonely companionship of a husband, with all the rest of the world shut outside, with time shut outside, was her delight now. The life at sea was the real life. The other was only shadows. Lovely shadows, hard to leave, but shadows, involved by time and by one another. It was good to come home, but it was tiring. It was an artificial existence. Abby told how things stood with her now in a letter she wrote to her cousin, Lettice, who had moved up away from the ocean on the Kennebec with her new husband: "We have enjoyed ourselves very much since we have been at home, but I often think I enjoy myself as well at sea. For I feel more settled. I have to go so much when I am at home, from one place to another, that I soon get tired of living that way, and wish myself away off at sea."

Brother Elias, feeling big as a man but also sad as a young stay-at-home brother can get, drove Abby round to Middle Bays, "with Joseph's horse." The last dinner with all the Pennells. Then to town and the cars. Adieu to all. Abby had Mr. King, the new mate, in tow. John had left him to her to fetch along. They reached Boston at eight o'clock in the evening. Abby put up at the *New England House* there. In a snowstorm next morning, at eight o'clock, they took the cars for New York. New York at five that afternoon. Abby went to the *United States Hotel* to lodge. "Found my husband and Charles." Next day, Abby went shopping. She found the streets of New York frightfully muddy. Mud to the ankles. James Henry, about to leave them and the city for Middle Bays and the beginning of his own meteoric and ill-starred career, escorted Abby around. Abby got dress patterns for Angelina and old Deborah.

## Captain Abby and Captain John

And John?—"John went to Barnum's Museum. Saw some wonderful sights!"

The fortnight they had lived a year for and crowded a year into was over. Ahead of Abby and John lay the seas, the hard and lonesome days. Yet ahead, too, lay their great and quiet love there, under the gales.

Abby would never leave her husband and the sea. She had tried, her first year of marriage, to stay home and wait. But she never would care to do it again. She loved him too much. She said as much to her Cousin Lettice, to whom she so often bared her naked heart, in a letter she wrote her some years later: "I think you must be lonely to have Amos gone. I know what it is. You think it is bad enough to have him gone a few weeks. But how would you feel to have him go on a voyage to sea without you? I often think of my feelings when John went away, when we were first married, and left me at home. I said then, if he lived to get back again, he never would go without me again. And he never has so far. And I don't think he ever will. For it would be harder than ever, for us to separate now."

It is not given to every woman to love her husband in the simple and whole, and even naïve, way Abby did John Pennell. Or to confess her love so simply and directly as Abby does hers to her Cousin Letty: "We take a great deal of comfort together, and always have, and live and think as husband and wife ought to, that is, pleasantly and happy, and without any unpleasant words at all." The sea, Abby thinks, has made John and her love each other that way: "I sometimes think that folks that go to sea think more of each other than others do, because they are together so much. And have no other company."

The two of them are so happy that it seems something must happen. Maybe they will not have a chance to be happy very long. "Sometimes I cannot help feeling," Abby writes Lettice Orr Hinds, "as though we should not live a long life together, we think so much of each other."

It was as if Abby had lifted that heavy curtain none of us dares to lift, or could lift if we dared, and looked into a harbor almost too lovely for earth, and had seen the end of all things there for her, in such a small handful of years.

## Farewell, Deborah! Hail, Elias!

IT WAS THE SAME OLD *William Woodside* waiting for John and Abby. No new ship. They hove anchor and left New York, March 27, towards New Orleans. They were twenty-two days on the voyage. The weather behaved, and about all Capt. John had to set down were family birthdays—Brother Joseph's, Brother Robert's, and his own. He kept them all in mind. It was a proof of the family solidarity.

It was cotton, back to the mills of the North. The mills of New England were humming. But there was another humming in the land. Human voices, South and North, were drowning out the sound of the mills, fierce words ran under the sky like thunder. Words that could never be taken back. Words that nothing could heal. A nation was about to break asunder, and scatter and shatter the American merchant marine, and the life and prosperity of the Pennells, to the four winds. But Abby and John foresaw nothing of that.

Back in Middle Bays, a new vessel was building, that Summer of 1860. The stout bark grew out of the white trees of the Brunswick forests, dwindling now at last— 599 tons of them. It grew through the days of dande-

## Captain Abby and Captain John

lions, days of buttercups and daisies, days of Queen Anne's lace and fringed blue gentians. Deborah Pennell, for all her eighty Summers, was interested in it. She walked down every day to see the ox teams sweat. The sound of the double-faced broadaxe on oak was music to her ears. And Deborah always took home an apronful of oak chips to get her supper on. But when October blew golden and red over the world, and the maples turned, her smart boys wouldn't let Deborah go down there any more to the shipyard. They said it was getting too cold for her to risk rheumatics.

But on December 1, 1860, John took her, in her Broadway black silk gown and all, by carriage to the yard. Then they walked down and aboard the ship. John had her arm, and Abby had her arm. Abby on one side and her smartest, youngest boy on the other! Deborah was very proud. There was a great crowd of Brunswick people there. Deborah couldn't make out what all this hullabaloo was about. There was great cheering when the bark ran down the bank and into high water under Deborah's old feet. She was quite pleased and giddy. And when she was being taken off, John pointed for her to look up. She was sitting under the stern of the vessel, under the golden letters of her own name! There it was spelled out for all the ports of Christendom to read. She had had many surprise parties in her life. But none like this. She put her proud old head down on John's shoulder and wept like a little girl with her first doll in her lap. The old mother of ships went home seeing nothing through her tears. The rest of her life—the six weeks of it—would be, in spite of the pain, a continuous and

## Captain Abby and Captain John

beautiful dream. Time slipped in its cogs for Deborah under the *Deborah Pennell's* stern, its inexorable meshes no longer held. Years flowed and melted into one another backward after that moment. She lived a dream. And in the dream, her husband was somehow back from his place under the white pines and the roses, back at her side, talking to her at the same time her sons talked to her, and strange new sons of sons. She heard Jacob through all their words.

And John Pennell had a surprise party, too, that December day. Charles the Great handed the bark *Deborah Pennell* to him to sail! The *William Woodside* was all right for carnivals and honeymoons, but an expert captain like John deserved better things. The *Woodside* should go to James Henry Pennell, youngest Pennell captain, as his first rung up the ladder. Charles handed the *Deborah* to Abby as her home for the next fourteen years. John did not weep, at least outside. But Abby did, looking at the fine mastless vessel on the bay. It reminded her, somehow, of a great cradle. She could not see into the years ahead. Time slipped no cogs for her as it had done for the dying Deborah. But she felt something very solemn. And if Abby could have looked ahead and seen what burden that cradle would rock, even then, I am sure, she would have gone bravely on into the years to come. For Abby was a woman built to take life just as it came into her wide arms.

Up on the banks of the Kennebec, at Benton above Waterville, Abby's best cousin and the girl she had grown up with, Lettice Reed Hinds, wrote Abby how she and her new husband, Amos, were dreadfully sorry

## Captain Abby and Captain John

they had not been able to come down and take in the launching of the *Deborah*. Their new house had been too much for them. Lettice was busy with planning. There had been literary and studious distractions, too. Professor Foster of Waterville College had given them a splendid discourse in their church, and Professor Smith was giving them others every Sunday. Amos, who was a poet already as well as a schoolteacher, had gathered quite a library together. They were buried in books. And they nourished their souls, too, on *The Atlantic Monthly*. They also took two weekly newspapers, *The New York Tribune* and *The Independent*. "I should think," she wrote, "you would miss the papers very much at sea." Abby really ought to subscribe to *The Independent*. It had "the best writers for its contributors." Why, even the great Mrs. Stowe, author of *Uncle Tom's Cabin*, having got a war nearly off to a magnificent start, was going to have a new story in this periodical, beginning in January, 1861. And it was all about the coast of Maine, and Abby's part of that coast! What did Abby think of that? The title of Mrs. Stowe's serial was *The Pearl of Orr's Island*. Wasn't that exciting? "I am almost impatient," cried Lettice in her letter, "for it to commence! If you were going to be at home where you could get the paper, I should urge you to subscribe for it—the terms are two dollars a year, payable in advance. Perhaps your mother would like to take it. I do not know what the story will be."
—Mrs. Stowe didn't, for she wrote each installment as it came due, and lived in continual surprise with her characters and events.—"She probably received some

ideas in connexion with it while residing at Brunswick." Little did Letty guess it was to be crammed full of Pennells and her own Orr's Islanders, her own and Abby's folks, as well as acres of local color and unimpeachable sentiment.

Of course, Lettice had done other things as well as improve her mind. She had been to a party: "It passed off as parties usually do—there was a good deal of nonsense said, and much kissing." A good Yankee description of a party, I think!

Lettice sends news of Orr's Island friends. Alice's "beau" is still in California. But Charlotte Richardson has got hers to the altar. No gold of California and fairyland for him! Lettice had a lovely house at Benton, with a "rather limited, though quite pretty, view." Letty looks out on the Academy and her church's steeple and apple trees. Religion mixed with fruit, as it should be. "Occasionally, I reach up my hand," writes Lettice, "and take an apple from our fruit dish— Won't you have one, Abby?" she teases. But Abby is going away as usual. "Soon you will be bounding away from me on the ocean again." Lettice wonders when Abby and John are going to be rich enough so they can leave the sea and settle down near her and be one big happy family.

The very literary Lettice remembers the happy days with Abby on Orr's. She slips the bridle on Fancy and lets her loose: "I have been there in imagination a great many times, and have lived over again those happy days I used to spend there when you lived in the old homestead, and dear old Grandmother and Caroline were

## Captain Abby and Captain John

with you. Oh! I love to think and live over again all the sunny spots in memory!"

Abby had no chance to begin Mrs. Stowe's new story in *The Independent*. She sailed from Bath, Maine, January 16, 1861, for New Orleans, on the maiden voyage of the new bark *Deborah*.

John said goodbye to the old Deborah his last day at Middle Bays. His mother was in her bed. The smart young captain saluted the stern old captain about to heave up anchor forever for a port too far for sails. John knew it was goodbye for good. He did not kiss his mother. Nobody had ever kissed Deborah Pennell, except, maybe, her husband, years ago. John shook her by the hand. It was the way sea captains said farewell. It was thanks for the birch rod which had set him on his watery road around the world. Thanks for the rod that had made him a man. Deborah's eyes kindled. She had fought a good fight and kept the faith. She had her own ship, and her youngest son captained it. Things had turned out well. She could not see what lay ahead for her country. She was fortunate in that. While she was still gazing at John, it was Jacob whose hand she was holding, and great voices were round her out of the past.

The day after John sailed in the vessel named for her, Deborah Pennell died.

Deborah was buried in the black silk dress.

Down in New Orleans, on February 24, year of fateful beginnings, 1861, Captain John D. Pennell sat down and penned a letter about the beginnings of a new sea captain. He flourished his hand about and put

THE BARK *DEBORAH PENNELL*.

## Captain Abby and Captain John

his finest scrollwork into his words. He was writing to his wife's father, Arthur Reed, of Great Island, Harpswell, Maine. He began in formal style, as a son should, to a father: "Dear Sir: I take the opportunity to inform you of the good health of Elias. Abby and all on board thinking you would be anxious to hear about Elias, thought I would write to you." It was all right. The stars had worked out their pattern. Arthur Reed had lost a boy for good, and his only one. But he had gained a sea captain.

Elias had gone for a sailor a few months after his sister had told her father to tie him up rather than let him go. He had sailed with his sister, on his sister's vessel. And he had not been sickened, as she had promised he would. He had devoured the hard life and come up tall, like a man, for more. He was the sea's forever now. Nothing could change him. He had gained in weight, too: "Elias is well, stout and rugged. Has fleshed up since he left home and is getting along finely. He is the smartest boy I ever saw on board a vessel, for a new beginner. He seems to like very well, and wants to stick by. So I don't feel much like parting with him, although I suppose you would like to see him come home, as all Parents are always anxious to have their children always round them."

In these few plain words, John Pennell writes the history of Elias, himself, a thousand other Maine males, the history of Maine itself in the golden day of sail, as well as a brief history of all men everywhere and in all times. There is no staying at home under parents' wings, for men. There is no easy way in life. Only a man's way. To get out and build his future himself.

"He shall have the best of my care and attention," John Pennell goes on, "and I hope you will rest easier than heretofore, as I hear you have been so anxious you cannot content yourself in any way. When he wants to come Home, I will find some way to get him on his way. But as long as he is contented, I want him to stop, as I think he will make a smart man."

Men like to make men. It is their business. It is one of the greatest joys they have. Their own sons, but other men's, too. John was making a man. He wasn't going to be turned aside. He had a fine man on his hands.

And the other captain of the *Deborah* stamped her approval on the same matter, and in the same letter to Arthur Reed. John did not use the last page, so Abby used her pen on it. It was the stars' work. Elias and the sea had wed. "I am glad to see him stay by. He is perfectly contented and wants to go, he says, if we will have him." And it's no use their not taking her brother. He will go with somebody else: "If not, he will get a chance to go with Capt. Orr." Harm' Orr happened to be in New Orleans, too, as Orr's Island men always happened to be in all ports of the world in those days. Harm' was as surprised to see Elias, Abby wrote, as he would have been to see his own mother.—Maybe he would meet *her* there, next trip!—Harmon was looking fine also, by the way. "Looks the best I ever saw him, and is very fleshy."

Yes, her father and mother would have to resign themselves to having a sea captain instead of a farmer

## Captain Abby and Captain John

as their son: "It is not worth while for you to worry so much about him. He is just as well off as though he was with you. I know you need his help. But it is just as cheap for you to hire help. Which you must do. For I think he will follow the sea. I thought it would be just so with him. I am glad to see him take an interest, and be smart. I expect you and Mother are lonesome to have no one with you but poor little Sis. But she is a good deal of company for you." So the one who had sworn Elias should never be a sailor recanted. It was the way the world is made. No changing it. The men will go, forever, and the girls stay. Sometimes even the Maine girls went also. For the Reeds had lost Abby to the sea.

Not all the boys of the Maine coast, though, even then, passed the test that Elias Reed had just passed. There were two playmates of his with him on that voyage. Evidently Captain John had taken a whole nursery school of possible sea captains with him, to test out. David Rich had passed. He was going with Harmon Orr as second mate. But a boy named William had not passed. He had tried the sea out but was going home from it. "William has killed the sailor and is coming home." That was the way Captain John put the tragedy. And with him on the same vessel were coming home Charles Orr and Thomas Skolfield, two with the sea written in their very names! Maybe they might have another try. But not William. He was done. The nursery school was breaking up. Elias stood top of the class. He would be all by his lonesome now, and would probably be lonesome. But he'd get over that.

## Captain Abby and Captain John

And both Abby and John wrote that they had taken Elias into the cabin with them. He was a coming sea captain, and it would be better for him not to lie with the common men any longer. And he would be less lonesome, too. "Don't worry about Elias," John wound up. "Take it easy and live happy. Capt. H. Orr is loading for Havre, at 1½ ct. Tell Sis her miniature is lying on the table. Looks as though it was going to speak."— Abby had kept her word about taking the family with her!—"Should think she would be lonesome. From Your Friend and well Wisher. John D. Pennell."

Captain John is for Queenstown, Ireland, with cotton, 2161 bales of it, there to await orders for his next move. Cotton is the money cargo now. The mills of England are roaring for more and more. John is going in for the big money. "This is a good freight." He quotes the prices in different places: Havre or Bremen, 1⅝ cents per pound; Antwerp or Hamburg, 1¾; Glasgow or Liverpool $1\frac{3}{16}$ pennies; St. Petersburg, 1 penny. John wishes he had been at Orleans a week sooner so that he could have got more for his Maine lumber before "the large arrivals" put the rates down. All Brunswick, Harpswell, and Maine were there, apparently. But John is still in hopes to make something pretty on this voyage. He is pleased with the new bark's maiden showing. She works well and is "a good sailer."

Abby wrote to her Cousin Letty that she was glad to be sailing; New Orleans was hot, and it was dirty: "You cannot imagine how glad I am to leave this place. It is so warm here. I never saw any warm weather before! The warmest day I ever saw at home is nothing to what

## Captain Abby and Captain John

it has been here all the time since we arrived. I don't think much of the place. It is a very large city but is full of dirt and filth. It is the dirtiest place that ever I was in. But it is quite pretty out in the country. We rode out a number of times. And have been round considerable, and got acquainted with a great many captains and wives and with some of the folks onshore. So we have enjoyed ourselves very well. We met with Capt. John Bishop and his wife from Harpswell, here in a ship from Liverpool. They have been going to sea a long time. I was pleased to see them, and we have been together all the time." Abby wrote Lettice also that she and John expected to have a good deal of happiness that Summer. She was surprised to hear that Letty and Amos, a Waterville College graduate, had turned farmers and wished she could see them: "I should like to go and see you and see how you look keeping house and farming. I did not think that you and Amos would ever go into the farming business, although I think it is a good idea. For you can have a home of your own to go to whenever you wish, and it is a sure way of a good living."

Before he finished his letter home here on the edge of a land rankling with hate like chain lightning, John Pennell, between making young sea captains and feathering his nest with cotton, said a wise word on the national situation. He was a conservative, as always. But conservatives had no place in the United States of 1861. No one was listening to them. If their words, and John's, had been hearkened to, Captain James Henry Pennell need never have been ruined and two

## Captain Abby and Captain John

million young men, including some Pennells, need never have made the red clay of the South redder with their young blood: "There is a great excitement here on our political affairs, and I think, if the People could call a convention and choose some good conservative men to agree on some plan of adjustment, that the Union might be preserved. But as long as it is in the hands of the hot politicians, I don't think there is any hope of being United very soon." Jefferson Davis had already been inaugurated as President of the Confederate States of America.

And John Pennell sailed away across the Atlantic with the guns of Charleston booming on Sumter behind him.

The *Deborah Pennell* pulled out of New Orleans on March 9, and made Le Havre in seventy-eight days. There was not much out of the ordinary on the voyage. The log is as good logs should be: brief and conventional. The *Deborah* started out cranky, got down on her beam ends once, but she settled down nicely after a bit. There was some heavy going, with topsails only, and seas boarding, around the first of April. They had lots of company. They were near mid-ocean when the Civil War exploded and Brother Ben died, the first of the Pennell brothers to go. The first break in the family chain! His unfinished house fell to others. The first house of the Pennells to go into alien hands. John took pilot from the *Petrel*, sixty days out of New Orleans, and made fast at Havre—the port where I entered my war and heard the opera *Mignon* in 1918—May 26, and heard that his country had split in two. The port

## Captain Abby and Captain John

of New Orleans had sunk behind John, below his life's horizon for years to come, as though it had never been. It had taken a fortune for John, and for many another Yankee captain, with it as it sank. And the Atlantic had become a sea of peril overnight. Captain John discharged his cotton. He did not go to Queenstown. No one knew on which side countries would stand next day. The war had cut across everybody's fortunes.

John went, in 325 tons of ballast, bee-line for Buctouche, New Brunswick. At mid-Atlantic, in company with the ship *Atlantic* of Bath, Maine, and another ship with painted portholes—ominous sign!—John celebrated the Fourth of July by flying the Stars and Stripes of his halved country. The two other ships did, too. He was among friends. John varnished the decks. He made the Magdalena Islands in the Gulf of St. Lawrence, July 17, and came to anchor at Buctouche, the 21st. First voyage on the war-struck Atlantic over! John had come home by the back door. Back doors are safer in wartime. Confederate privateers had already begun to destroy millions of dollars' worth of Yankee ships. The news of the Union disaster at Bull Run came to John's ears here in New Brunswick.

John wasn't in New Brunswick long. He sailed for Sharpness, England, on August 27. The second day out, he ran into a fleet of fishermen, and stopped and did some fishing himself. He even caught a codfish in a pail! They were that thick. On the last day of August, off Cape Breton, he caught forty cod. On September 8, John was nearly run down by a large ship. There were the usual September gales. They saw two or

*197*

## Captain Abby and Captain John

three vessels a day, the ship *Persia* of Bath among them. September 24, John anchored off Cardiff. He discharged his lumber at Sharpness, was towed to Cardiff —where a hundred of my fellow officers went AWOL to London after my war—and loaded Welsh coal for New York, and got under way, November 15.

They had some weather. There were gales. John observed the first birthday of the *Deborah*, December 1, and his fourth wedding anniversary the 3rd, in a gale of wind, with foresail and spanker furled and a tremendous sea. It snowed and blew harder. The jib was split, sails were carried away, the fore topsail yard went. December 12, John bent and set a new jib, and set the flying jib. Elias Reed was very busy. The next day, the fore topmast was carried away, the next, "All hands employed getting down fore topgallant yard, topsail mast, upper topsail yard, and gear." It grew worse. They rigged in the jib-boom. It looked like the end of the year-old *Deborah*, and boats and God knew what after for Abby and the crew. The gale howled louder around them, waiting to get in the last telling blow. They tried two days to get the fore topmast down. They did it at last. John fitted a new one. It took two days to get it up. They "signalized" an English steamer bound east. The gale wore out. They breathed again. December 20, a ship with the ominous painted ports. They sent up the fore topmast. More snow again. It grew wicked cold.

Christmas Day, John "tried to catch a fish, did not get a bite." Another steamer. They killed the hog, and ate him instead of Banks codfish. One less soul to go

## Captain Abby and Captain John

through what lay ahead! Bad weather again New Year's Day. The upper main topsail yard was carried away again, and the topsail split, and a bit after that, "the wind struck with great violence and blowed away the mainsail." Seemed to Abby that she would have that boat ride, after all. She put on double red underflannels, and made John do so, too. She packed up the miniatures in a little parcel. She was ready to take her chance on the waves. But John wasn't, yet. He took in all but the hurricane sails, and hove the bark to, shipping tons of water. He saved her. The *Deborah's* day was not yet. The Atlantic was not to be her grave. Her grave was awaiting her in the North Sea, off Holland. And on a day when another hand than John Pennell's would be on her helm.

Wild weather continued. Other vessels were catching it. On January 4, they sighted a vessel with colors half-mast. While they were looking at her, her mainmast went. They bore down on her and found her in a sinking condition. She was the schooner *Teaser*, Bangor. They took her captain and mate and crew aboard. They left her for the bottom. Her pig-iron would never mow gray soldiers down. John bent a spare foresail for a mainsail. January 6, he worked all day on the main topsail yard and got a terribly lame back. Fine weather at last, the 7th. The topsail yard went up the next day. Then thick fog shut down. At three in the morning, the 10th, John heard heavy breakers going on a beach somewhere along Long Island. He tacked at once to the southwest. A close shave! Fire Island light. Next day the pilot aboard, and the anchor went out at the Narrows in a

## Captain Abby and Captain John

blinding blizzard. There were three days of snow before the tug came. John put up at Pier 27, East River, January 16, to discharge. "Hayden and French settled with the crew." One more voyage across an ocean full of gales and war, 57 days. And John wrote in his entry next day: "Elias Reed went home."

Elias went home seasoned by Winter gales, hard, bitter work, hard knocks, a rescue at sea, and a good look at death straight in the eye. He went home a sea captain in all but name. He would soon have that. Elias went home a man.

## The Cradle at the Mainmast

AFTER THEY HAD VISITED Barnum's Museum and seen the sights, Abby and John went home, too.

But they did not stay long. After a Pennell reunion, without old Deborah, the keystone of the whole arch, and without Ben, and after visits with the Skolfields and Jordans and Orrs, and a photographic afternoon at Mr. Perry's, in Brunswick, and a spell of road-breaking through the snowdrifts by John and Abby's father, on March 14, 1862, Abby and John left Middle Bays to be gone for over three and a half years. The oceans of the world would become their wide home during that time, friends and relatives would die, family circles would be broken, before they returned. For time rushes on, and there are many ruins made in three years. The Civil War would burn itself out to ashes, and the blood-stained flags would come home. A thousand Yankee ships would go to the ocean's bottom. Lincoln would go down into the shadows, with Socrates and Charlemagne. Whole chapters of American history would be closed. Master James would fall into his ship's hold and die. His James Henry be disgraced and exiled. The Pennell Brothers would begin to break up. Steam-

## Captain Abby and Captain John

ers would be coming upon the Atlantic more and more, and wooden sailing ships be hearing the sound of change and coming doom.

And John and Abby Pennell would have their first baby and carry him at the mainmast for more than a year. Through gales and sunshiny days, the baby's crib would rock there. But the little son would never cry out delighted or afraid. For his cradle would be a double one, and he would lie with closed eyes in brine.

Time can do a great deal to people in their maturity and working hard for happiness.

John and Abby had to make two starts on that long voyage, both from Philadelphia. Abby had a tooth pulled and a shipwreck. The tooth came first. Abby had it extracted "with considerable pain." But she salved her sufferings with sightseeing in Philadelphia. She wrote to Lettice, her cousin, about it: "I like," she wrote, "to go to new places and see something different every voyage. I like here very much. Philadelphia is a delightful city. I never were in a prettier place in America. The streets are very broad and clean, and laid out very pretty. I had a pleasant ride Sunday all through the city, rode across the Schuylkill River and to Girard Colleges, and went to church part of the day, and dined onshore, to the gentleman's house that loads the ship. . . . The people are very pleasant and agreeable and so cosy in their appearance that I feel at home when in their company. I never enjoyed strangers' company so well before anywheres as I have here. It is a lovely place, I think. Hope I shall like Dublin as well. I wish

## Captain Abby and Captain John

you and Amos were going with us. How much I should enjoy your company in the passage!"

The *Deborah* finally got under way on April 8. But a sudden gale swooped down on them as they were going down the bay. There was no managing the bark in such close quarters. They went ashore on the Delaware Capes, ground their keel into the dunes, and felt the whole universe of water come over them. It was Abby's first shipwreck. She didn't like it one bit. John thought the *Deborah* was gone, the breakers pounded her so like hammers. The cabin door was stove in, and all Abby's treasures were awash. She seized the miniatures and poor little Dixie, the canary. She saved what she could. John cut away the main- and mizzenmasts to ease her. It was like cutting into his heart. That did some good. They took to the boats after a while. The waves were easing off, and they made dry land. But Abby swallowed more salt water than ever before in her life. They hurried to Philadelphia, and Brother Charles was still there to take them in and console and comfort them. The *Deborah* was saved. But they had to unload her cargo and take her back to the city to be repaired. And John came down with the diphtheria, and worried Abby most to death till he got well. It seemed as if an unlucky star was warning them not to go this voyage.

On May 20, Abby and John made their second start, "with all the sailors drunk," as Abby noted bitterly in the second diary she had just begun to keep. They sailed out of the Delaware just as the blue army, with

## Captain Abby and Captain John

my father in it, entered the swamps of the Chickahominy to face the hell of the Seven Days' Battles before Richmond. They had a fine crossing, after the bad start, 33 days. Elias was with them once more. He had been a great help in the shipwreck. On the way over the Atlantic, Abby caught a bird that flew on board and put him in Dixie's cage. The dog a friend had given them in Philadelphia had fits, and John had to shoot him. Abby saw Fastnet lighthouse first of anybody on board. They were towed up to Dublin and landed just as the battle smoke rose thickest around Richmond, the Sunday church bells of the city filled the ears of Union soldiers dying by the thousands there. The Atlantic crossed safely the third time in war.

In Ireland, Abby and John got the news of the loss of the first vessel they had sailed together, the bark *William Woodside*. It was like hearing that Venice had sunk into the Adriatic! The Confederate pirates had got her. Abby played whist and ate Irish strawberries and cherries, saw fireworks, and went through Trinity College, but she did not take to the Irish people, Dublin, or the weather. Dublin was a great come-down after Philadelphia. It rained most of the time, too. "Dublin," Abby wrote in the diary, "is the most ancient looking city I ever saw, and the people look the same." And Abby wrote Lettice that she liked "the learnt Irish" all right. They were "polite in their manners and pleasant." But she had no use for the other kind of Irishmen: "I believe the low Irish are the most indolent, drunken, lazy set of human beings on earth. Are surrounded by beggars every time we go into the street, so

## Captain Abby and Captain John

lazy they will not work, and get their living by begging. It is pleasing to see what way they will take to make you give them something." Dublin itself was all right, if it hadn't been for the weather: "Dublin is a large city and very ancient looking, has broad, clean streets, and very pretty parks and public gardens. The River Liffey runs through the city, is about as wide as the Sebasticook River. There is a number of bridges to cross on. And all the shipping lays in this river, and little steamers are passing up and down all the time. It would be a pleasant place if the weather was decent. It is very cool and rains every day. It seems more like November than Summer. I should enjoy myself very much, if the weather was comfortable, if we go to walk or ride, we are sure to be caught in the rain."

Abby was glad when they took the steamer and went over to Liverpool. Liverpool was fine. It was full of Yankee sea folks: "A very lively place," she wrote Cousin Letty, "more shipping there than any other port in England. I enjoyed myself very much while there. I saw so many captains there from Brunswick and Bath that we were acquainted with, it seemed quite like home."

From Liverpool John and Abby went by train to London. Abby liked the ride and saw "castles that looked to be hundreds of years old" on the way. But London was the apex of delight. Abby went sightseeing every day there. John went with her when he could. But some days he was tied up with business. "Business before pleasure," was John's motto, as Abby wrote Letty. So she joined up with "a gentleman and wife" at their hotel and went with them on the round of wonders. She runs out of breath describing them to Letty, and she fills the diary full with the sights of that week she was there. Abby took in the great Exhibition. "Saw the works of the whole world and magnificent sights too numerous to mention," she wrote in the diary. "No tongue," she cried to Lettice in her letter, "could describe the splendor of the buildings and the things that were in them! The works of the whole world were to be seen. I didn't think what was there from the United States"—Abby forgets that a war is on—"was represented very well, but I understand they have taken a great many premiums."

Abby ran into Capt. Snow of Brunswick, and felt more at home at once. Then she did the Houses of Parliament, Westminster Abbey, and the Thames tunnel. And she went out to Hyde Park and "saw the nobility and the fashions, and that," she cried in the diary, "was worth seeing!" And to Letty: "Went to ride in Hyde Park to see the nobility promenading, and they looked brilliant, if they were Englishmen. But they all have that English look to me, let them be dressed in what they will." Abby liked the country even if she didn't think the English people were so much. "It seems like a garden," she wrote Lettice, "they take more pains in cultivating their land than we do."

But the Crystal Palace topped all. Abby crowned her London visit by going through that. "It was the most delightful place I ever saw," she set down in the diary, "a perfect Paradise!" She went into ecstasies in describing it to Lettice: "Seemed to me more like Para-

dise than anything on earth. I wish I could give you an idea how it looked. The buildings are all glass, and the grounds around them are laid out magnificently. Nothing but trees and flowers to be seen as far as the eye could extend. And fountains of water playing gave everything a silvery appearance and dazzling to the eyes. I could not think of anything else but Paradise!"
—So a Great Island housewife sums up that last word in Victorian elegance, that wonder of the world of sideburns and hoopskirts, and monument to Britain's greatest Queen. The Crystal Palace staggered Abby. Let her comment in the diary sum up all she had seen in the capital of the earth, London: "Have seen considerable!"

John, meantime, had chartered for Singapore. So they quitted London, July 22. "Liked to have got jammed to death in the depot," Abby jotted down in her diary, as they left. She was in no condition to be jostled, and dreaming still of the Victorian dream in glass and water. Back to Liverpool, and then by the steamer *Prince* to Dublin. They got the *Deborah*, and sailed to Cardiff, arriving July 31. And there was Capt. Pinkham with memories of Havana three years ago! And other American sea captains were there. There were grand reunions. But Brother Elias went home, to sea-captain for himself from now on, and his going left a lonesomeness in Abby. She had a row with the sailors, August 10. She sewed pillow cases and entertained Capt. Pinkham. The *Deborah* went under the coal tips at last. The coal started coming, and Abby and everything were covered with dust.

Something had been missing these happy five years

## Captain Abby and Captain John

John and Abby had been living together. Something that made them still think of Maine as home, being wanting. But on September 5, 1862, that something came to them on board the *Deborah*. And their vessel would be home now, forever. Their first son was born.

"A darling little son!" Abby set the day down in her diary as one she would never forget. There wasn't a prouder mother in the world. He was a large, healthy baby, and it was like putting her hands in a rose jar to touch him. It didn't seem to be true. Yet there he was. Now she and John were really married. Abby had sewed right up to the day the baby came, and she was smart enough to bathe him and dress him when he was one week old. Now they could sail away in peace, through all the years and all the oceans.

The bark *Deborah Pennell* went down the Bristol Channel in mid-September. She was headed for the Indian Ocean, safe sea for a Yankee baby in 1862, and Singapore. John and Abby were as easy in their minds as they had ever been in their lives as they passed Lundy Island. England went down below the sea. New waters all ahead. They made good time. "Pleasant weather," September 20. The new boy was a fine stout boy. "Calms and light airs," September 21. "My darling baby slept in my arms most all day," Abby wrote in the diary. They were well off Spain, Lat. 40-07. But John Pennell did not fill in the latitude next day. Instead he penned in frightened black: "Our dear little boy taken very sick in the evening with convulsions." And the following day, September 22, the calms had given way to fresh gales, and John Pennell wrote in

## Captain Abby and Captain John

heaviest black ink: "At 6 o'clock AM this morning, our dear little boy died."

"We done all we could do," Abby set down in her book. "But all of no use. We had to give him up to God who gave him. But Oh, my grief was too great to be borne when I found he was dead. All my anticipations of the future were cut short, and it seemed as though there was no comfort for me. But we have got to bear with all that is put upon us and submit to God's will. But it was so hard to part with our dear baby, just brought into the world for us to look at, and then taken away." Abby put down the latitude and longitude, for John: Lat. 39-18, Long. 14-11. She also put in verses to comfort her heart. Trite, threadbare verses. But they were sunlight and sweet, fresh wind to a mother mourning for her first-born son:

> Short was thy stay on earth, sweet flower,
> Thou never knew'st a thorny smart,
> Lived but to bud and gain the power
> To twine around a parent's heart.
>
> But oh, sweet flower of tender birth,
> Thou'rt taken from a parent's love,
> Pluck'd from the fading flowers of earth,
> Transplanted to the fields above.
>
> There in a rich and fruitful soil
> Thou'lt ever bloom without decay,
> There grief ne'er comes nor heavy toil,
> There flowers never fade away.

## Captain Abby and Captain John

They were headed away from Middle Bays, for the other side of the world. Hereabouts lay the cook who had been buried their first voyage together past these coasts. It was for Abby to say. Abby said the word. John got his hammer and saw, and rock salt. His log entry for September 24 reads: "Put our little boy in the first coffin this evening, filled with salt pickle." And next day: "This PM put our little boy in the second coffin and filled with pickle ¾ of inch all round. And put the little body away to be kept and sent home." And Abby's diary: "We put his little body in liquor and shall keep him until we go home, if we live to reach there." John put him away at the first step of the main-mast, lashed on against the gales and seas. Abby wanted the snug cradle John had made so beautifully put up there, to know it was safe. She said she would be less lonely if she could see the cradle up there.

The only change in the log thereafter is that John takes more care in scrolling his fine capitals. As though he sat long at making them, just past meridian each day, when he wrote up the log. He reported himself as "quite sick," October 2, off the Madeiras. And next day it was Abby's illness he set down: "Violent pain in her right side." Abby said she would have died if it had not been for John. He sat up with her, night by night. She said that in her diary. The rest of her pages for October are blank. Abby was "some better," two days later. Abby got up at last and about. John caught a shark. The old calm and sure life came flooding back slowly wave by wave. October 17, "squalls from every point of the compass." They were in waters they had never sailed

## Captain Abby and Captain John

before. New winds and currents. A strange, heavy swell. And rain. And healing. And the baby rocked away in his high cradle.

Many ships began to be around them every day. They crossed the Line, October 30, their first time. Abby began her diary again in a new hemisphere. Sweet work, the comforter, in sails and sewing. The two captains stood up tall and brave on their deck. "Fine weather," so John. "Another delightful evening," echoed Abby. The boy was safe. Abby could see. A new half to the world. Abby left the iron bedstead and went back to her old berth at last, November 13. John caught a spotted pigeon on a hook and line. But Abby let him go again. Its feathers were soft as a baby.

And November 20, a new great bird, white as snow on his wings, came to meet them, a bird of a new hemisphere came with outstretched wings. Wings wide as two tall men together. He settled on their deck with friendly blue eyes. He made himself at home. They fed him and measured his wings. Nine feet from one wing tip to the other. It was an albatross. He was like a symbol of peace ahead. After some days, they put him overboard. For he could not get into the air from a deck. He needed all the ocean to clap with his feet as he started up. He flew around the bark once and away. Goodbye and good luck.

November 24, Abby made some molasses candy. November 26, John caught another albatross and two seagulls. The seas grew higher. Some came aboard. They were making as much as 175 miles some days. They rounded Africa as December came in. Two whales in

## Captain Abby and Captain John

company. And ships Abby "supposed" to be whalers. A mysterious look came upon the sea: "Very green about 2 PM. Suddenly changed to deep blue," wrote John. Around Good Hope. And their unnamed son rocked at peace at the mainmast.

They slanted north again, their wedding anniversary. John noted it: five happy years. And Abby noted it: "We have lived a happy life together and never have had trouble until we lost our darling child." Into heavy gales. The topmast studding boom blown overboard. They were used to storms, these two, by now. They fairly flew, 210 miles one day. Mountains in place of waves. Glass falling. More gales. St. Paul's Island, December 17. December 20, John caught an albatross measuring ten feet at his wings. Fine weather Christmas Day. And heat beginning. "Begins to feel like Summer," Abby wrote. It was the warmest Christmas Day Abby had ever seen.

They were becalmed New Year's Day, 1863, 88 degrees on the thermometer. There was bright moonlight that night, and "nothing to be seen but the vast ocean." It made Abby feel solemn, this New Year's: "Year after year is rolling on," she wrote, "and our lives are growing shorter, and we no more prepared for our eternal home than ever. And are spending the best part of our lives on the ocean, away from all that is near and dear to us. But we are thankful to the all-seeing God that we are permitted to spend our days together, and share each other's joys and sorrows. For we have experienced both this year. It was joy to us when our dear baby was born. And Oh, what sorrow to part with it! But such is

## Captain Abby and Captain John

life." There was the finest sunset Abby had ever seen. The Indian Ocean was like turquoise and gold, like the pavements of heaven. The sky was solid amber. Abby set it down as a good omen in her diary. She dreamt of her baby that night.

Abby killed a rat in the cabin, after "quite a jubilee." British ships were passing them. John painted the quarter-boat inside and out. Abby did a vast ironing with the thermometer at 88. They crossed the Equator, January 15, with the Dutch *Undine* in company. Into the Northeast Monsoon. "All hands at work cleaning insects out of the provisions," Abby observed, the 21st. John caught a shark the 22nd. Abby saw wood and coconuts floating in the water. Nicoba Islands, January 28. Then many islands, multitudes of them.

The first day of February, a boat came alongside filled with coconuts, plantains, bananas, chickens. And John and Abby filled themselves with fresh fruit and meat. Abby's first Malays grinned up at her. Feet like hands and faces old as Methuselah. The two men and two women in the boat were stark naked. Abby put the shocking fact down in the diary. But she added that she was glad to get the fruit! They went between Merro and Track Islands. The tide was so strong it sent up breakers around them. Abby saw a snake on the water, swimming. It all reminded her of the beginning of the *Bible*, Adam and Eve and snakes! The Malay mainland loomed up. Greener than green. It steamed with beauty. Scents came off it upon them so deep and full that their heads ached. They were going past islands and land like opened flowers. Greener than fairyland. Dutch ves-

## Captain Abby and Captain John

sels everywhere. Pleasant on deck here, with Maine under snow! Abby took out her embroidery and sat in her rocker on deck. Her baby rocked gently overhead.

Abby saw her first Chinese junk. They hove anchor in Singapore Roads, February 19, 157 days from Cardiff. And death seemed farther away than that. The boats swarmed round them in an instant. They were loaded down with birds like wisps of the rainbow and fruit like baskets of jewels. Seashells like clouds at dawn. Abby bought some shells. Then the mosquitoes arrived. The *Deborah's* decks were crowded with brown Malays. Naked bodies jostled Abby. Malays, "chattering like so many monkeys and covered with coal dust." They had started to unload the cargo. The sharp contrasts of the East: leprosy and lapis lazuli together.

John's wife went up to Singapore and shopped. She walked on green earth after a half year of decks. She loaded herself down with pineapples, and came home. A Portland captain arrived. Abby went to church and "had a good meeting." Capt. Merriman of Harpswell Neck came in with the *Lorenzo*. If it had been a port on the back side of the moon, a Harpswell captain would have hove in! They took dinner with Capt. Merriman, neighbor to them at Middle Bays. Abby went for a walk each day. The Portland captain, Loring, and his wife and two children and Capt. Merriman took dinner with the Pennells. The whole Yankee colony went up to Singapore shopping. John picked up a stray dog swimming in the bay, and Abby made a pet of him. The Maine captains swopped some second mates. Second mates had a quick turnover! John finished discharging

## Captain Abby and Captain John

his coal, March 3. Capt. Merriman came again to dinner.

John weighed anchor and headed for Akyab, Burma, the 7th. Capt. Merriman went along with him. There was a thunderstorm that set the world on fire, cascades of flame poured down. John painted the poop. He made Little Andaman Island, March 21. "Very hot at work painting." Still sleighriding at Middle Bays! The new second mate turned out to be "a miserable scamp." They had a rumpus with him. John and Abby had got the worst of the swop! Akyab, April 4. John took out ballast and loaded cargo. There were letters from home. But they were full of the lost baby. They renewed Abby's sorrow. Abby found Akyab a dirty city. She took tea with an old "bacheldor" on shore and had a fine time. April 2, Abby was on shore again and took a ride into the country. She "went to see the natives burn their priest." Abby does not mention if he was alive or dead. Anyway, "it was a curious sight."

Akyab was full of American sea captains. All of them called, and Abby and John called aboard of them. All the Yankee wives got together by themselves for an evening, and their husbands went ashore together by themselves. They did not get back till three o'clock in the morning. Their wives waited up for them. I imagine there were some curtain lectures. I hope there were no Kipling Burma girls a-sitting and thinking of the white men after they left! But I know there would be none such waiting for John D. Pennell. And Sunday, April 26, was a red-letter day. For all the captains of the American fleet and all their wives and children went on

## Captain Abby and Captain John

an American picnic over on Bolongo Island. The temple idols must have stared and wondered hearing *Home, Sweet Home* and *Kitty Wells* ringing out under the banyan trees, and the pythons must have trembled in the canes! And to wind up, the whole band came home and spent the evening with the Pennells on the *Deborah*. "Enjoyed it very much," wrote Abby.

John and Abby took a New England horse-and-buggy ride out to see Malay rice being put up. Fifteen ships arrived or left. John left Singapore himself, May 2, for Falmouth, England, with 12,675 bags of rice, 1071 tons.

Through the thickness of the world, Master James Pennell had just sent off, April 3, a letter to his son, James Henry, to thank him for the fine gold watch and chain his son had sent him from England, engraved from the youngest Pennell captain to the master builder of Pennell ships at Middle Bays. He addressed the *Anglo Saxon's* master as "Capt. James H. Pennell, Dear Son. . . . I will acknowledge to you the receipt of your splendid Watch and Chain. I feel very thankful to you for so fine a Present and accept it with much Pleasure, and hope it may be a lasting token to each one of us while here on earth, and that we may yet both live and prosper in all the Duties of this life, and at last meet in Heaven. May God bless and protect you through all the trying scenes of life, is the best wishes of your Father." James had two more years to live, and his first-born was still undisgraced. James advised his son to get his ship out of the dangerous American waters as soon as ever he could and make his base England.

## Captain Abby and Captain John

"I think the Privateers will drive all American ships out of the Atlantic by the captives they are making in a short time, or that we cannot get any business for them." And even as he wrote, James Henry was beginning to play with the idea of running cotton past the Union blockade!

John Pennell had fair weather going back. Hot; 96 degrees on the sea, one day. Abby tended her hens and tidied up the cabin. Some wind. Split a jib and bent a new. Some calms. A large school of sharks chased them. The English bark *Futty Allum* in company two days. But as they crossed the Line, June 12, she was hull down on the horizon ahead. John caught seven Indian Ocean fish and a dolphin. He lost his hat overboard. But he carried two tall beavers for just such accidents. On July 2 and 3, 1863, John was lowering his and Abby's berth, and Abby was making a bead pin-cushion. It was a lovely day. And on the other side of the globe, blue men and gray men were sending lead the size of a man's thumb tearing through one another's bodies, and blood was running through the wheat at Gettysburg, Pennsylvania. The fiercest battle in history was roaring on at home, and double canister was ripping furrows through great armies. The South ran yelling up to tip-top highwater mark, broke, and began to ebb away towards the end.

The Pennell rooster blew overboard on the Fourth. They hove to and tried to get him, for future chickens' sake, but no use. John made 198 miles, July 8, with the lee rail under most of the time and a merry wind in the full sails. Abby commenced one of those head-baskets she had seen in London, now all the rage, for beauty's sake. The crows were thick over the Round Tops. Abby's canary Dixie died, as the South died back across Maryland and deep into Virginia. Abby and John buried the bird at sea. John noted the loss in his log. 200 miles, July 19. The second mate took sick. They made the African coast, July 25. A squall tore the mizzen staysail to rags. The next to the last day of July, the bark listed to port in the gale. John set fore topsails, but had hard work bringing her up on her bottom. They pumped a lot of water out of her "and a good deal of rice." John topped the hard-luck day off with a spell of colic. Vessels began to fall in with them. A ship with the sinister painted ports. John noted that she looked like an American, and he was shyer of her for that reason. She minded her own business, though. A "Morphrodite" brig.

John took a vast sweep, a hundred miles farther south than usual as he rounded Good Hope. He had his reasons. Each day he combed the sea with anxious eyes. He expected to see, any day, the horizon smoking in a tall pillar of wicked yellow. For the shadow of the fearfullest privateer in history was like a hawk's shadow on these waters. The *Alabama* was down here, plying the trade for which her builder England should later pay dear. John had had word. The sea hereabouts was full of death. But the shadow did not darken John's horizon.

Two ships, two barks in company. Two ships, three barks. Land was seen once. August 9, John caught ten fish "from the bottom." After two days with the British ship *Channing*, they parted company with her. John

## Captain Abby and Captain John

had beaten a vessel at last! He noted Abby's birthday in his log.

And Abby's dream for years came true, August 30. John shortened sail, and stood in for a bleak lonely mountain of an island that morning. At nine o'clock, they hove anchor at George Town, St. Helena. That afternoon, John and Abby and Mr. Dunning, mate and brother-in-law, of the myriad Dunnings of Brunswick, and Elizabeth Pound, Abby's English assistant, went to Longwood and visited Napoleon's tomb! Abby's heart must have beat very fast, and not altogether on account of the mountains she had climbed. For her grandmother's hero's bones were still there, then. She stood at the feet of the great. Life could hold only a few such moments! Abby plucked a little flower from Napoleon's grave. She stuck it on the letter she wrote with bated breath that Sabbath eve to her mother. "A sheaf from Napoleon's grave," she wrote beside it. The little flower and its leaves are as green now as they were seventy-six years ago. And Abby is dust under the Bowdoin pines.

Abby had climbed all sorts of mountains to get her flower. She guessed her mother would be surprised: "If you could see the mountains that we had to climb to go there, I think it would frighten you. It brought to mind many things that poor old Grandmother used to tell me about Napoleon and St. Helena. I little thought then of ever going there!" Abby had done all she could to preserve the day in memory: "We gathered flowers and leaves of everything we could reach. I don't think I shall forget this visit to St. Helena." Probably the landscape

## Captain Abby and Captain John

wouldn't, either, for some years to come. Abby described the island to her mother: "It is a gloomy looking place. ... The island is 9 miles in length and is 2700 feet high in some parts. It is mostly rock and a lonely looking place. Jamestown, a sort of village, is in a valley between two high mountains. A very unhealthy place, I should think. I hope this will find you all well." The shadow of the lonely great man and his lonely island was on Abby's mind.

They had got a lot of other green things from the island, though. "Went on shore to get some vegetables," wrote John in the log. "Vegetables and potatoes," wrote Abby, "which we are almost suffering for." They ate themselves out of the reach of scurvy. To her dying day, Abby would always associate Napoleon with new potatoes!

Abby described their voyage to her parent. Long and tedious was the word. Four months getting this far. "How much longer we shall be making the rest, God alone knows." They had had a hard time in the Bay of Bengal. Forty-seven days to cover twenty degrees and get to the Equator. Wind a head wind all the time, and currents always against them. "It was trying to the patience." But they had had "a fair chance" to Good Hope, but were off there twenty days in calms or gales. Abby told about the shifting of the cargo and how the *Deborah* "made some water. It made her very crank for a while, but she is all right now." The *Deborah* is slow as cold molasses, but they are getting used to it: "She sails very slow, worse than ever. It is discouraging to be so long getting about as we are. But we cannot help it,

## Captain Abby and Captain John

as I see. John says he has got used to it now, so he don't mind it at all."

But more than slow going and green vegetables and flowers from Napoleon's bones is on Abby's mind. The Civil War is on it. That is what is keeping them on the world's other side. "I long to be with you once more," writes Abby, "but I hardly know when to look for that time to come now. We don't feel safe to go home in this war. If times were good, we should go home this voyage and go to housekeeping. But the prospect looks so poor now I don't hardly dare to think of it. But we must hope for the best and be thankful to the Almighty if we cross the ocean in safety this time and escape the Pirates."

Pirates is the word for the Confederate privateers. And as Abby writes the word, her nephew, who saw Venice with her at carnival, is becoming something rather like them. Abby goes on: "We feel very uneasy and anxious about them. I hardly think they would take us, for our cargo is in foreign account. But they could rob us of provisions and many other things. We must trust to Providence, I suppose, for that. We have been very fortunate to keep clear of them as long as we have." Abby tells of four privateers cruising off the Cape of Good Hope. "And the *Alabama* is one of them, and seized two vessels from Akyab that left the week before we did, and has captured a number of others. So I think we were lucky to keep clear of them. We did not make the Cape when we passed, and kept well to the southward. So I expect that was how we happened to steer clear of their clutches." But Commodore Vander-

## Captain Abby and Captain John

bilt to the rescue! His namesake is on the *Alabama's* trail now. But Abby thinks the *Vanderbilt* may be the one taken herself. "The steamer *Vanderbilt* left here last week for Cape Good Hope"—probably with a British ship ahead of her to warn the British-built Confederate pirate—"in pursuit of the *Alabama*, and if she falls in with all the privateers, they will take her. That will be the next news you will hear!"

This Yankee wife, worshipper at the feet of the greatest war-maker of them all and maker of a million widows, is sick and tired of the American war. "What work this is! We felt in hopes to hear that this wicked war was ended and the privateers out of the way, but was sadly disappointed. It seems as though it is no nearer ending now than it was when it first began. I thought the North could do more than they have. But it seems that everything went against them. It is dreadful to think of." Abby, looking at the war from a sister's angle, hopes Elias "will keep out of the way while it lasts." She longs to meet him somewhere and trusts he will keep away from home and danger. "Kiss poor little Sis for me," Abby winds up. "She will be a young woman before we get back, I expect."

The years were slipping by. Friends were growing old and dying. Yankee ships were being swept from the seas. A nation's agony went on and on.

A baby was rocking serene in his small cradle.

John paid his port dues to the British and sailed from Napoleon's isle the last day of August, in company with two English vessels, one for London and one for New York. The New York one had Abby's letter

## Captain Abby and Captain John

with the flower from the grave of the sun of Austerlitz. They made Ascension Island, September 6. On the 9th, they "sprung fore topmast studding-sail boom by the hellyards parting and getting the sail in the water." Friday, the 11th, John planed the main deck, and crossed the Line the 14th. He celebrated next day by drawing an American flag in the log and under it the motto, "United We Live." His nephew had just gone over to the enemy. September 18, John drew the same flag falling. Who knows what hand was on his hand then, and he not knowing it at all! Next day, they had a scare. A large British steamer passed them. John set it down that he thought she was a privateer for sure, at first. On September 21, Mr. Dunning, the mate, had a "fuss" with the scallywag second mate. John had to straighten them out. I bet Mr. Dunning got the best of it! John noted the black anniversary: the baby had been in his cradle a year now. John swopped longitudes with a Norwegian. Ships almost every day, some with painted ports. Gales began, October 17, Topsham Fair time. English vessels poured past them day after day. But the *Deborah* succeeded in overtaking one British bark. The little boy rocked calmly in his high cradle.

But another boy left them on October 29. It was near the end of a gloomy day, a blow brewing, and they were reefing the mainsail. Abby was watching the men do it. They were having a hard time, and hanging on by the skin of their teeth. They were so high up she couldn't make out who was who. One seemed to be having quite a time keeping his balance. And as she looked at him, he swayed, flung out his arms, and went down headlong

## Captain Abby and Captain John

into the evil-looking waves right past her cabin door. Man overboard! It was the ship's boy. He had been with them two years. Abby had never seen death so close to, but once . . . a year ago.

The bark was going seven knots. But John hove her to, nearly going over with them all. The boy had been like his own boy. They put the quarter-boat off. A great wave reared and swamped her. The men clung on and were pulled back from boiling death. They lowered the forward boat, they got it upright into the sea. The second mate leapt in. The boy was like his boy, too. Four other men went over. They pulled away, the boat standing bow almost straight up, then down and out of sight, gone over a wave's side. They came up again. The mate and the four men rolled away into the evil crevasses with living, changing sides. It was growing dark in the chasms between the long steep waves. No John Henry to be seen. They rowed about for hours, it seemed. Night came on over the wild sea. They rowed hours before they gave up. All the men loved the boy. It was no use. They had to leave him.

They had to leave him "to seek a Watery Grave." That was how John wrote it in his log. "A nice good Boy, John was, always willing and obedient to all calls, and we feel and deeply lament his loss." John added that he was lost in Lat. 44-27 West, that he was sixteen years and two months old, and had a sister, a brother, and an aunt living in Cardiff, "his native home." Captain Pennell drew a mourning band in dark ink around his entry that day for four o'clock, "sivel time." And John put another cartouche in heavy black around his entry under sea time and wrote a more literary obituary: "At 4 PM while reefing the mainsail, John Henry Ottagan, Boy, fell from the main yard overboard, and was lost. A native of Cardiff, England. In Launching Quarter Boat, swamped her. Got one of the Forward Boats over safe and sent 2nd mate and 4 men in search for him. But Blowing heavy and thick weather and Night coming on, all our Efforts to save him were Vain, and the Boat returned without him. And he would soon be obliged from the cold to Sink and Sleep his Ever Lasting Sleep Beneath the Foaming Billow."

John Pennell never had much to say in his log unless it was something absolutely essential. When he uses such phrases and capitals, you can tell that he is dipping his pen into his heart.

Abby dipped her pen in the same place when she described their new loss to her mother: "It is with sad feelings that I write you of the loss of our poor little boy Johnny, that we thought so much of. I think you heard me speak of him when at home. We lost him in a gale on the 29th of October. He fell from the main yard while reefing the mainsail, at 4 o'clock in the afternoon. They hove the bark to and soon got out a boat. There was such a sea, she filled alongside. But they succeeded in getting out another and sent the second mate and 4 men in search of him, but could not see anything of him. It was thick and rainy and blowing heavy, and a very heavy sea, and coming on night. It was nearly dark when the boat returned. They kept the bark to, for two hours. But all in vain. Poor boy perished, no doubt. It was a gloomy night to us all, and we lament

## Captain Abby and Captain John

his loss. He has been with us two years and was a most excellent boy. So respectful in his manners, always willing and ready to our calling, and was beloved by all. Was 16 years of age, and always would, if he was allowed to, go onto the yards, the first one, to take in sail. But John never would let him go in rough weather, and did not know that he was on the yard at the time. But it seems as though it was ordered to be. And I do sincerely hope that I never shall witness the like again."

It was not far from the place where their son had died a year ago.

Two had left the bark in a year. It was a year of gloom, with a war going on and on over home. And news of another boy gone awaiting the mate.

They saved the swamped quarter-boat, and sailed on, one boy short. But their own boy was safe at the main-mast, no matter how the gales blew.

They plowed through many gales, from the looks of the log, with sadness heavy upon them, carrying news of death to people in Cardiff. They made the Lizard on November 5, took a pilot into Falmouth, and found news of death awaiting them. The family circle had been broken again. Andrew Dunning, Sister Harriet's husband, in the little house next to my big one. And next day came news of two more breaks in the family chain of love. Their brother-in-law and mate, Jacob Dunning, heard of the death of his little boy. Two of John's nephews, Reed Dunning and Frankie, Brother Joseph's little boy, were gone. When you are out of hearing of a large family for a year, you must expect

## Captain Abby and Captain John

to hear sad tidings when word comes from home again. The mate looked like a dead man.

Abby had to set down more laments in her letter to her mother: "The news of Andrew Dunning's death came very unexpected to us. I should have thought of everyone in Middle Bays before him. He always seemed so well. It is sad news. Poor Harriet and them little children will feel his loss. And they must miss him very much in Middle Bays. But he has gone only a little while before us, and it shows us the necessity of being prepared for death." Abby had been sure she was going to have bad news on her arrival. She hadn't been dreaming about her home folks for nothing night after night. That was a sure sign, as all Maine folks knew.

John's wife went on to her other lamentations, "the sad news of poor little Reed Dunning's death and Joseph's little boy. It is very hard for Mr. Dunning and Paulina to part with such a boy, for he was all the company they had. But what consolation it must be to them to see him die so happy! I trust he is happier than to be in this world. Poor Jacob took his death very hard for a while. But today he is calm and pale as a ghost. It is the first trouble he ever knew, and he thought a great deal of Reed, was always talking about him. I pity them all. Poor Joseph and Arabella have had to part with their little boy. But it seems they have a little girl that will fill its place. Still they will miss him very much."

Abby thinks of her own little boy at the mainmast. "John says it would have been much harder for us if our baby had lived to that age and then been taken

## Captain Abby and Captain John

from us. I know it is true. But it is hard to part with them, at any time. They are little angels now, and we ought not wish them back."

Deaths and sorrows. Changes are coming in. Time is passing. Children departing. Husbands and wives bereaved. Jacob Dunning has only five years before he will drown, and his wife go queer. The world is growing older and sadder. John and Abby are growing old. It is the way life goes.

Abby ends up by saying that it seems to be "quite sickly" in Brunswick, and hopes her mother and little Sis will take care of themselves.

The only bright spots in Abby's letter are Mr. Dunning, the mate, Sis's and Elias's being well, and Capt. Winchell's visit. "Mr. Dunning is a good mate," she writes of the man who has just lost his son, "and a good fellow. I think a great deal of him. And it is a blessing to us to have some one with us from home. And I often think if we were alone with strangers, we should not feel quite so easy, as we do to have him with us." Abby is pleased as can be to have Sis's letter. It read just the way Sis talked, "and if she wrote it, I think she done remarkable well." Abby is sorry to hear Sis has been under the weather. She tells her mother not to let her go to school too steadily. Let her write some more letters, though, for "it will learn her to write letters and to compose." Abby is glad to hear that Elias is a full-fledged mate now. The man John made is going up tall in the world. "He has done well." Abby would write to her brother if she knew where to reach him. He must be thankful to be out of "this drafting" of the war. Abby

## Captain Abby and Captain John

hopes he will stay away from home "till this war is at an end, if it ever does end. They seem to be at it yet as hard as ever." Abby thinks of her father and mother there on Great Island, "sitting in the dining room, father in the corner smoking and you on the other side of the stove in the rocking-chair, sewing and knitting, and Sis in front of you, and so on. My thoughts are at home day and night." Abby would like to be there if only Winter weren't coming on. And home has come to her, for Captain Winchell, of Brunswick, of the ship *John Watts*, from the East Indies, has been visiting with Abby and John, and they have had "quite a sociable time."

Some consolations there were, in a year of gloom and war.

Abby saw the cradle come down, which John had made for their baby. The baby was safe in it, sound asleep. She saw the cradle put aboard a home-bound ship. She had had the baby for more than a year. That was longer than some mothers had theirs. That was something, in this life. Now his chance had come, and he was going home. He would not float around in the ocean. He would be safe and dry. Of course, he was really playing in heaven now, with his cousin Frankie Pennell. But he was still here, too, in his cradle. He was going to Brunswick now to have a proper funeral and all. He was too young to own a name. He would be simply "Baby" on his gravestone and for all eternity to come. But she would know the little nameless Pennell in heaven among all the thousands of babies there. Abby would not bring her sewing out and sit under the mainmast any more. There would be no need. For the long lullaby was over. The lullaby that had been sung over half the surface of the globe.

The day after the baby started home, as they were heading out of the harbor, a mighty gale came upon them, the greatest Abby had ever seen. The whole world trembled. They could not get back into the harbor, try as they would. So they headed for the open sea. Perhaps it was nature bidding their baby a solemn farewell.

## 14

## A New Ocean and a New Son

THE *Deborah* WAS BLOWN by the southwest wind right past Falmouth up the Channel. "Finding we could not get in, bore away from Plymouth, the glass falling very fast." Then suddenly the wind changed, and blew them the other way. "Blew a perfect hurricane." John Pennell had never seen such weather before in his life: "The barometer down to 28 and $\frac{8}{10}$, the lowest I ever saw it. The bark under fore topsails and fore topmast staysail." They would probably have gone down if it had not been for the high coast of England on their port bow. As it was, John's eyeteeth rattled in the gale. He hove to and faced it, standing on his hind legs and then his front. The bark was like a cork bouncing under the wall of England. Then the second hurricane let up as quickly as it had come. Quiet. Except for the Andes the opposing gales had left, great waves running uncertainly back and forth. Abby came on deck with her eyes big as saucers. John put his arm over her shoulder. They were still in the world of the living.

John headed her for Liverpool. He made the Irish coast, November 14, Holyhead—where I nearly got blown off Wales to Ireland one January day—next day,

## Captain Abby and Captain John

and the next, John was in Stanley Dock, unloading rice enough to feed the whole west of England for a year.

Abby and John loaded coal next. On February 24, they sailed out of Liverpool. They were for a new ocean, the Pacific. Abby was going to round the Horn, and she would have a chance to do half a year's sewing before she would set a foot on land again. They gave America of the North a wide berth, for the war was still blazing there. The ocean was fairly crowded with vessels. Seven a day sometimes, with a steamer or two besides. It was mostly reefed sails down the length of the Atlantic. They rolled about in the Bay of Biscay for two weeks, to Abby's disgust. On March 7, the day John broached a new keg of butter, a heavy sea hove the *Deborah* on her beam ends and shifted her cargo. John had to go about and keep her before the wind for two hours while the crew trimmed the cargo. It was near the spot where their little son had died. On March 11, one of the ships in company was "supposed" to be our old acquaintance the *Lorenzo*, Capt. Robert Merriman, who had enjoyed Singapore with the Pennells. He was bound for Cape Good Hope now. This captain was to have a son, later, to put his ship's name on, one of my friends. It was good to have a Harpswell neighbor for company this far from home. It was fair enough by March 12, so John could send up the royal yards and set the royals. That day, too, he saw a double-topsail ship.

On March 14, a veteran sailor went to Kingdom Come. The old hog, a New Brunswickian, who had joined them at Buctouche two years before and had

## Captain Abby and Captain John

sailed a lot of seas with them, fell a sacrifice to a good cause. He was cut up and salted down. The Madeiras, March 16. Abby was ill. Palma Island, one of the Canaries, next. And Palm Sunday, March 20, John got into the Trades. But calms came, and left John still looking for a "decent" Trade Wind. He got a south-southwester, "something uncommon in the heart of the NE Trades Wind." It was "a strange spell of weather" to John. Off Cape Verde, John spoke a ship New Zealand-bound. Two Spanish brigs fell in with him. He observed Brother Joseph's birthday and Robert's and Job's. He lost the NE Trades just above the Line.

It was hot at the Line. John picked up the SE Trades at five degrees, South Latitude. John observed his own birthday. He was thirty-six. John observed his Brother Ben's death day. He caught a large dolphin. April 26, a heavy shower gave them a new supply of drinking water, John filled all the casks and tanks. And Abby could let herself go on a big washing. She washed three days steady. John caught a shark and a dolphin.

Gales reared their heads, and a heavy sea was on. Abby wrote: "We had to take it again." They lost the fore topsail and split the main topsail. "The heaviest squalls that I ever saw," Abby observed. She was good and discouraged. "Thought we should be torn to pieces and should not live to get anywheres," wrote she. May 23, John saw that the ocean had changed color, and he sounded with a 105-fathom line. No bottom. Very discolored, though. It must have been the mud from the Rio Plata, out here nearly 400 miles from the coast.

## Captain Abby and Captain John

Must have had heavy rains that season! More gales and still more. "Dirty weather" had set in. A large number of whales in company now. They were getting south. June 6, John swopped longitudes with the brig *Kentucky* of San Francisco, from New York, and agreed within four miles. Rains shut in again. June 10, John was "judging" himself to be forty miles from Tierra del Fuego. Sure enough, Tierra del Fuego hove into sight, and John felt his way along it.

They were nearing the Horn. Abby stopped sewing a bit, to fill her eyes with wonder. On June 10, in company with the *Kentucky*, John squared away and went into Le Mair Straits at daylight, past Cape San Diego. They made Deceit Island. Wild, twisted mountains, lonely as time, heaped themselves up here on the world's jumping-off place. And the gales were heaping up, too. Mountains of unfamiliar clouds, not the clouds of home, grim and evil and monstrous, leaned over them.

On a sudden, the cloud mountains leaned apart. There it was! A black shark's tooth of a mountain, sticking into the sky. The Horn! The last spine of the western hemisphere as it hunched up and dove down under the sea to Antarctica. Abby got her first look at that mysterious final mountain which hundreds of Yankee wives had never laid eyes on though they had rounded it often. Abby had a good chance to look it over. For she and John passed it three times! John made that sarcastic comment in his log. Around it they went, and then the gales and the mountain-high waves hurled them backward again. "The worst place in the whole world," Abby described it. She expected the

## Captain Abby and Captain John

worst. But she was agreeably surprised: "No worse weather," she wrote, "than anywheres else," as far as she could see. It was all bad, this voyage!

Still the Horn was a place she would remember all her days. There were heavy gales roaring up at them out of the new ocean ahead. Pacific gales putting their dark horns down to the Atlantic ones. Between wild days of crowding clouds, there were unbelievable days of cold, pure silver seas. Most of their time was night time, only eight hours of daylight. For this was the southern hemisphere, and it was the depth of Winter, being late June. Then silver storms of blinding snow. The decks were deep with snow often. Then between wicked clouds, the high full moon cut out sharp as a knife and lit the world and the water with unearthly splendor. It was not the moon at home, it was a strange moon, more silvery than the one at home, and it sailed at a terrible speed between Andes of rushing white clouds, too bright to look at on their upper edge. When the moon rushed out from the clouds, the bark's deck turned powdered diamonds and the whole *Book of Revelation* in place of snow. The rigging sang like ten thousand forlorn harps. Unearthly nights, lovely nights, but like something Abby might dream. Dark nights, there were strange fires clustering at the mastheads and making John's and the sailors' faces burn blue. Abby and John sailed through long nights of moonlight touched with incredible brightness on clouds and sails.

They were a month off the Horn. Abby was all turned around in her seasons. "I could not help thinking," she wrote her mother, "it was the coldest June I ever experienced." But she fought the incredible Winter as she fought Winters at home. She and John whiled away the tedious long nights, when it was "cold enough to freeze," beside a good Wood-Bishop-Bangor-Maine stove! "We kept very comfortable all the time. We managed to have a fire in our little stove that kept the cabin nice and warm. And for all we had such unpleasant weather, I really enjoyed it most of the time. For I feel so much better in cool weather than in warm, that the cold is more pleasant to me, and I feel smart, sleep well, and have a good appetite. I used to get up every morning between 4 and 5 o'clock, and make myself and John a cup of chocolate that went well in such cold weather." All the comforts of home! "And when I could stick my head out on deck, I would. But had to keep in most of the time." Abby got in a good lot of work those long nights, for all the unearthly moon and its splendor, for she was a Yankee housewife as well as a captain's spouse. "Have kept myself employed about different kinds of work, all the time, knitting by candle light, and working on worsted work when daylight. So day after day has passed."

They burst into a brand-new ocean, among unfamiliar currents and clouds and winds. But it was lovely. They had "a beautiful chance," as Abby put it, up along the west coast of their new continent of America of the South. Not too fast a speed, but coming along "well and safe." "For which," added Abby, forgetting her rather stilted mature style for a moment and relapsing into the sunnier earlier and easier idiom, "we ought to feel thankful, although we could not help

## Captain Abby and Captain John

grumbling sometimes about being so long. But we find there is other vessels that has been longer, and has heavier weather." John and Abby slanted into the coast of Chile, on July 11, made Angels' Point, next day, and down went the anchor in 32 fathoms in Valparaiso Bay, July 13, just exactly 75 years ago from the day I happen to be writing this.

"Happy I am to be permitted once more to inform you of our safe arrival at this port." So Abby began her letter home to her own mother. The years and John's schooling have changed Abby's style. And not for the better. She becomes formal and "literary" at times. It is not the sparkling naïve idiom of that sunny talk in the first diary.

The Chilean port was a white and shining one. But sadness awaited Abby in it. Sadness that had come from the other hemisphere of the world. Sorrow from Middle Bays. The little son, for all John's painstaking care in building the year-long cradle, and for all the brine, had not reached Middle Bays in a condition to be seen. The cradle had had to be closed. Abby hears the news at last, here at Valparaiso. Her heart is wrenched to read her mother's letter. No proper funeral, after all. And her mother had not seen how handsome a son she and John had had! Still, the little boy is safe in the dry earth, and not lost in the terrible shapeless sea. Abby writes of that consolation. She writes the most heart-rending paragraph I have ever read. It is like other paragraphs other Yankee sea wives had to write in the last century. But I doubt if there is one that goes so down to the depths of pity.

## Captain Abby and Captain John

"I was very sorry," she says, "to hear that our baby's body was in such a state it could not be removed. For such a thought never came into my mind but what it was pure and well preserved. But I feel thankful it arrived safe and was put into the ground. For I have felt as though I could not rest until I knew it was buried. And have always felt afraid something would happen to it, and that its little body would be swimming about the ocean. And I feel very grateful to you and father both, for taking the pains to do as you did."

Human beings can become eloquent enough, whatever rhetoric they study to cover their lives under, when they dip words up from their heart. Rhetoric falls back before a mother who writes about love.

So John's little sea-cradle lies by the pines of Bowdoin, at Brunswick, after all, and his fine carpenter work is preserved beside the bones of the hands that made that chest of love.

Abby describes Chile, the new land in her life. She is in the midst of beautiful mountains and fruit and vegetables. "I was onshore yesterday and found it to be quite a pretty place. The land is very mountainous, and the city is built at the foot of the mountains, with one long street through the city. Inhabitants are all nations, but mostly Spanish, and it looks like a Spanish port. The weather is very pleasant here now, just warm enough to be comfortable, and fruit and vegetables plentiful, and we have a good appetite for them, too!"

But Abby would swop all the Andes for Great Island, Maine! "It would be more beautiful to us if we could be with you this morning. How plain I can see you, and the pretty green fields! Oh, I long to be with you and have the privilege of walking through the fields once more! But I hope, if my life is spared, to be with you next year at this time. I suppose father is out mowing this morning. And poor little Sis going off alone to school, and you to work in the kitchen as usual. And poor Elias and I, away in foreign lands, thinking how pleasant it would be to be at home with you once more."

Through the thickness of the earth and from the midst of Winter, Abby can sense the Maine haying time. It takes a lot of years to get over that sense of the haying season. I know, for I have not got over it yet! "Tell father," Abby writes, "I feel as though I could handle a rake today as smart as ever, if I was only there. Hope you and him will not work too hard this Summer. What I see by the papers, farming is the best business there is now. How thankful you ought to be that you have so good a farm and house to live in these times, and have no one to go to war!"

Abby is despondent about that war. "It is sad to think of that. This war is going on yet. We was in hopes to hear it was over when we arrived, but hear it is going on worse than ever and that the Northerners are not gaining anything. They are smart, I think. It makes me provoked no matter if they do get whipped."

There is the usual death for Abby to bemoan. She had dreamed of home folks again. So she expected news of death when she got in. Sure enough, it was there. It is poor Aunt Bowker, this time. She had been a good sea mother. She had given all three of her sons to the sea. And now she had gone out on that greater sea her-

## Captain Abby and Captain John

self, that sea which lies waiting behind all we do, waiting for us all. "Her little family," writes Abby, "are done with this world. The last time I saw her, she told me how she longed to die. She was a good woman and lived a Christian life, and no doubt is happier than to be in this world. And how singular her three sons should all find a watery grave!" Not so singular, really, in the Maine of 1864. Many a mother outlived her husband and all her sons, and her family was made up mostly of silent ones, not seen by the rest, the girls and neighbors. The silent ones who had stolen home for good, to be with her by daylight and candle light and in her dreams, until the time came when they could take her with them for good, her lips silent like theirs, on the great sea from which no one returns twice. Abby's aunt had three tall silent ones to help her down the steps of the little Brunswick house, on my street, and out over the meadows full of strangely quiet daisies to the vast ship, so high that it made a twilight of the world, which waited her coming.

"Tell Sis to be a good girl and learn as fast as she can." For she, some day, might have tall sons to come and fetch her for that voyage Aunt Bowker had gone on this year. "I shall bring her home something pretty, and she must write me."

No. Abby has no whalebone or silk to her writing when she gets down to things that are solid and real.

At Valparaiso, John and Abby received orders to sail to Coquimbo, and they left July 14. It took them three days to cover the 180 miles because of the calms. They discharged their coal into lighters. It was slow business.

## Captain Abby and Captain John

They finished taking in ballast, August 16. They were for Callao and a worse cargo than coal. It was a cargo Abby came to hate the smell of before her sea days were over. It was guano, the leavings of millions on millions of sea birds on their bleak roosting places in the Pacific. August 25, they anchored in Callao Bay. A delegation from the Peruvian government visited them, to look them over. On the last day of the month, the surveyors "pronounced everything all right." But John had to wait for his license to take guano to come from Lima. John went up to Lima. He got the license on September 2. Next day, he pulled out for the roosting places, the Chinchas Islands.

There were gales, and then no wind at all. John lay becalmed off San Lorenzo Island, which was soon to print its name on my friend, San Lorenzo Merriman, when he would see the first light of day off there, and wail his first wail in the wide silence of the Pacific. Then John had light breezes. So light they exasperated him. "Same old weather," wrote he, September 12. Next day, he was finally there. The Peruvians took their sweet Peruvian time. John measured his hold. They fell to work. It was a long and dirty business. The evil-smelling stuff had to be brought out by small boatloads. November 25, they had finished. By John's count they had 1090 tons in. But by Mathues's, the Peruvian's, they had 1142. Mathues won out. By John's check at the voyage's end, he had been right. But that was on the other side of the world from Peru.

John pulled out on November 25. The sea was full of guano vessels. All Yankeedom was down here, among

## Captain Abby and Captain John

these God-forsaken Pacific isles, as it usually was in the Fifties and Sixties wherever an honest dollar was to be made fetching goods the world wanted. Here were the *Guiding Star*, *Witch of the Wave*, the English ship *Tudor*, and the *John O. Baker*, the Pennell ship, built the year before the *Deborah* at Middle Bays, the ship John had wished so to have the sailing of. They sailed in company. John reached Callao the 27th. On December 5, he began the long back track, for Queenstown, Ireland. Captain Miller's *John O. Baker* and Captain Todd's *Witch of the Wave* were with him. John probably felt more comfortable with those two American ships within hail, considering what was most on his mind that week. But they weren't company for long. In one day the *Witch* was out of sight, and, next day, all John could see of the other, the Pennell ship, when he looked with his four-foot spy-glass, were the topgallant-sails and royals, sitting right on the waves of the horizon, with nothing below them. She was down over the shoulder of the world.

It was December 12 that it happened. "At 4:45 AM, a little boy popped into this world. Everything passed off well, and Abby comfortable at this 12 meridian. South Pacific Ocean. Lat. obs. 19-47 South, Long. 86-00 West." John had assisted at the popping. He was all the doctor there was. Glory be! John was happy!

So to a new ocean, Abby added a new son. John was proud as a peacock, and fresh as a daisy, for all his having been up all night ushering his son into the world. The boy was a fine big boy, and it looked like him! Abby said so, too. It was a Pennell all over. John

## Captain Abby and Captain John

Pennell would never be dead while that son was walking the earth! The baby had the Pennell fists, too, big enough, John swore, to be bending a topsail already!

The other little boy, no larger than this and without a name, could play more peacefully with his small cousins up there, wherever it was, knowing his mother had someone else to think about now.

From now on, John Pennell has even more important items to set down day by day in his log than gales and calms. He records the progress of his new son. Abby is quite smart, but the little boy is only pretty well. "Handed fore topgallantsail, flying jib, gaff topsail at 7:30 ... Abby not so well today and baby sick also and very troublesome." Then the boy is quite sick. The shadow of an earlier year falls on the log's page, on December 16, and the ominous heavy dark lines appear: "Our little boy very sick and a very faint chance of his getting well again." John was fighting hard. Abby was fighting, too, but was "completely worn out." But the shadow lifts, and the black lines disappear next day: "Our little boy much better today. Also Abby is better, has set up a little today." Glory to Gideon! Abby sits up more and more. But the baby gets sick again and worries John. A heavy sea, and the bark rolls all the worse because the airs are so light there is no steerage way. John is so worried over the baby he does not take his latitudes and longitudes. He fairly shouts in writing, December 21, that the baby is better. And that day, too, he sets down his latest piece of carpentering: "Myself making a crib." John was as sure of things now as that. Maybe, though, he thought of that

## Captain Abby and Captain John

other piece of carpentering two years ago. He did a good job now. The crib was as fine a one as anybody's baby ever slept in!

There is something mighty eloquent about this picture of a Yankee sea captain sitting down and making a crib for his week-old baby, with hands made big by handling a ship, in the Pacific Ocean. I don't think you will find such an entry in the log of any British captain. I know I made the English stare when I wheeled my first-born under the towers of Oxford. Evidently no man had ever done such a thing before in all English history. He had always let his wife do it!

But the baby grew "troublesome" again. That did not mean what we mean by troublesome. A good word gone down a selfish hill! It meant the baby was fretful and uncomfortable. He was in pain most of the time, John observed. But that baby had the good sense to improve for Christmas Day, 1864, and Abby took Christmas dinner with her husband, the first day she had been up since her confinement. They felt, these two, more like a family than ever before in their married life, with a cradle with a living baby in it to rock with a foot now and then! The merriest Christmas ever in the world!

The worries kept on. John was concerned with the state of the baby's bowels. Incidentally, it had been rather rough going, to keep company with the worry over the son, and the fore topsail and jib had split. Once more the solemn lines appear enclosing the news that the boy is very sick with constipation, and Abby not so well. But next day the boy was better and Abby, too. And on

## Captain Abby and Captain John

the last day of the Year of Our Lord 1864, John weighed the baby! He went 8½ pounds. A gain of ½ pound. Not so bad for two weeks. It was the most important entry John had ever made in any log-book, and he had made thousands.

January 4, 1865, "Abby smart, also Boy." They were out of the shadows. They were getting pretty well down to the end of things, too, as the mean weather could tell you. Heavy gales were pounding them, and they were off the Horn on January 12. Next day the log is crowded. Tremendous seas are coming at them and over them. The deck is a cauldron. "Put out a 5-in. line on each quarter to cut the sea. Bark labouring and lolling greatly and shipping constant seas on deck, filling the deck full. At 8 PM weather moderating, although a heavy gale and high mountain sea prevails." Right Horn weather! And down in his snug warm crib his father had made him, Arthur Pennell was enjoying the best rocking of his life, a rocking better than his mother ever gave him. And between rolls, John weighed him again. 10 pounds, glory be! Horn weather was his meat and drink!

Weighing the baby is mixed all in with latitudes and longtitudes all the way up the Atlantic. More "high heaped" sea, and the five-inch hawser stretched out again cut them to the heart and kept the ship steady, January 16. The starboard quarter "Bull works" were stove in. "Bark rolling fearfully. Bad leak in the port side abreast main hatch, and a good deal of water among the guano, and a good deal damaged. There being so much sea on, and bark rolling so heavy, cannot find out

## Captain Abby and Captain John

the place. There is also a bad leak in the counter stern." But it moderated at last, the guano was trimmed, and the leaks mended. They flew northward. The pig breathed his last on January 24, 1865. Fresh spare ribs! Fine weather. Some calms. The crib could go out on the deck in the sun. The baby looked up at white-bellied sails with wondering eyes. The world was much taller than he had ever supposed, lying in the cabin!

Rains filled up the water casks. But February 8, they had some wind again, the *Deborah* rolled and became completely unmanageable, lying in the trough of the sea. Abby did not have to rock the cradle. "It appears to me," John wrote in the log on the 9th, "as though we were in the center of a heavy revolving storm by such a tremendous sea from all points." But that storm wore out, too. They "signalized" the English bark *Mary Woods*, from Callao. And February 12, the boy tipped the scales at 10½ pounds!

John sketched in his log the ensign of a ship overtaking them which was a new one to him. "A flag I never saw before and do not know what nation it belongs to." From John's picture, it looks like a cross between the Union Jack and the Stars and Stripes, except that the stripes are alternate red and black. It was on the bark *Everhard*. The bark was from Bremen, and John swopped longitudes with her, and agreed exactly. More vessels in company. William Renson got insolent to John and the mates, on February 20, and they put him in irons to cool off. Trinidad, the 25th. John talked with many vessels, and asked to be reported. He painted the poop deck. Then the whole ship. "Weighed our Boy,

## Captain Abby and Captain John

3 months old—11 lbs," just as they crossed the Line.

Things were going along so smoothly that Abby was able to start another diary. She has something more important than Venice to write about now. A fine baby! The first entry in Abby's new diary, begun March 13, 1865, is that the baby is rather "worrisome." Abby thinks it is the heat. She has finished his second frock and is glad they have crossed the Line. "I hope Providence will favor us with good winds to our port of destination." Abby was feeling "slim," as she finished the last frock. March 16, Abby's sister has been dead ten years. It doesn't seem half that time to Abby. "Dear sister, I trust, is better off. And I hope to be prepared to meet her. All well today." The baby sleeps well, "and is cunning as can be, talks and laughs a good deal." But the baby cuts into Abby's sewing time. She finished the skirt to his last frock.

Into the Trades at last. "These are the strongest Trade Winds that I ever experienced," wrote John. "The strongest Trade Wind I ever saw," echoed Abby. She got all her trunks out on deck and aired the mould out of them, March 27. She set down the sad news that the baby was losing all his hair but was well and "forward." Abby paints a pretty family picture, the evening of March 29: "Baby is sound asleep, and John is asleep on the sofa. So I am up all alone, but shall soon retire." Next sewing was the baby's nightdresses. April 2, the bark was "pitching bows under" and going along at a good clip. And they passed a bark! John crowed loud over passing her: "The first vessel we have seen that I could do anything with this passage." Abby cele-

## Captain Abby and Captain John

brated the event, too: "A vessel in company, cannot tell what she is, so far off, but we are coming up with her. She must be slow to let us come up with her." Abby complains of being worn out next day, the baby has been so troublesome. "I have all the care of him. Precious little help do I have from anyone." The maid Elizabeth doesn't seem to be pulling her weight in the boat. "Hope my strength will last," Abby adds. A baby is more tiring than any carnival Venice ever knew! He is a continuous one! And Abby's Sabbaths are no longer long. They are short, with a baby around. Abby had to put on heavier clothes and make some flannels for the boy. He is feeling the cold, but is growing fast, "is forward, talks and laughs a great deal, and is good. If his life is spared to us, I shall be thankful." Some days later Abby writes that the baby is good as gold and laughing all the time. Brother Job's birthday, he of the hare lip and the beautiful child, April 9, and a little way to the westward, and a long way to the north, on this side of the world, Robert E. Lee was handing his sword to Joshua L. Chamberlain, friend of Charles the Great. The long war was over. John and Abby could go home. And the boy was thinking about his first tooth and weighed 11¾ pounds, and was four months old.

Abby crowed over the baby on April 10. He "is growing cunning fast, laughs all the time, and knows me!" But two days later she is in the doldrums bad, and is afraid that 12 pounds is thin for a four-months' baby! He looks delicate to her! All fallen away to a cartload, as the Maine saying goes. Abby is aching to get home where she can give the baby some good milk. She sees

## Captain Abby and Captain John

John, too, through pessimistic eyes. She writes on his birthday, April 14, that he is thirty-seven years old and "will soon be an old man!"

Abby read a bit when she could, but the only chance she got was when the baby was asleep. They had to set the stove up again, and Abby built a fire and was comfortable once more. The baby fussed with his teeth. April 18, the guano got to smelling so Abby couldn't sleep. "It was really suffocating." And she was up and down all night with the baby. Yet next night was a great milestone, for the baby went till four o'clock in the morning without waking to feed. And then didn't he make up for it by teething and being fretful all the next day! "His gums pain him, I think," Abby wrote.

John saw a steamer, the *Emily* of Glasgow, which he suspected of being a blockade runner. He didn't know yet, of course, that the war was over. The steamer was going home. No more business in the United States, whole again, though savagely scarred. Abby was suspicious of the boat, too: "I never saw a steamer rigged like her before. We thought her to be a privateer, but think she was a blockade runner." They got her longitude, to check with theirs. Abby was up to her eyes in work on April 21 and completed a scarlet flannel cloak for the baby. She was preparing for the rigors of an English Summer. A head wind held them up day after day. Abby was impatient. She got a sty on her eye, April 26, Lat. 48-20, Long. 20-55. Her milk was all gone, the oatmeal had given out, and she had to feed the baby on arrowroot flour. He sang on it. "Baby well and good, is lying on the bed and singing out." On his

## Captain Abby and Captain John

twentieth birthday—that is measured by weeks, as all new mothers measure their first-born—the baby "is growing to be a little rogue, all the time upon the jump and spring and laughing, takes all my time to take care of him." Fastnet light at last, May 2nd, and high time, for the baby had had a spell of colic, thanks to his teeth, and, May 3, their old friend, the pilot boat *Petrel*, came out to meet them. It brought the most astonishing news, a whole chapter of history they had missed while at sea the 148 days since Callao. The war at home was done! The South had surrendered! Abby and John could go home! Abby had added a new ocean and a new son to the family history, and now she could add peace. She was bubbling over with joy. John felt like a man standing at the top of the world. He rode into town on the tug and left the *Deborah* to the pilot.

Abby stayed home and wrote down in her personal log the saddest event in American history. For the dark news followed swift on the heels of the bright. "The sad news from the States today, the murder of President Lincoln, the most wicked murder that ever took place in the world. And Secretary Seward stabbed at the same time while sick in bed. The President was shot at a theatre, by Southerners, I suppose. What a sad thing! Baby is asleep. And I feel sleepy and tired out, too, and lonely. Hope John will be back tomorrow." The Great Emancipator had lain down tired out, and had fallen asleep forever.

But John did not come back next day. He fell in with Capt. Miller of the *John O. Baker*, in a day ahead of the *Deborah*, and got his orders to proceed to Leith,

## Captain Abby and Captain John

Scotland, to unload his unpleasant cargo. Then when he started back towards the *Deborah*, it came in thick as pea soup, and John had to spend the whole night cramped up in a chair on the pilot boat, getting in the winks of sleep a captain can get in anywhere.

Abby spent the day taking care of the baby. When she got him to sleep, she started her first letter to her mother for nearly a year. She filled it with Lincoln and the baby, the two things most on her mind: "We got a paper yesterday from the pilot boat, that had the account of the dreadful murder of President Lincoln. And of Mr. Seward being stabbed. It is the most awful thing to think of. It must cause a great deal of excitement. The English papers are full of it. Not many months ago their papers were full of slander against him. And always have made all manner of fun of him. But now it seems as though they cannot praise him enough. It has changed their feelings towards the South greatly. He must be missed now." Abby is so stirred up she thinks the world is coming to an end. "What is the world coming to? I sometimes think it is not going to last long."

But the news Abby has to send is bigger news, to her point of view, than the cataclysm that has shaken the United States. The daughter springs her surprise on her mother. She leads up to it almost carelessly, though: "I expect you will laugh when I tell you that we have the second little son."—As if any woman would laugh merely over the acquisition of her first grandson!—"He will be 5 months old the 12th of this month. Was born the 12th of December, one week out from Callao. I got along nicely and have been very well. He is as bright

## Captain Abby and Captain John

as anybody's baby, I don't care whose it is. And as playful as a kitten. But is quite troublesome now. Is cutting teeth. And was very troublesome until he was two months old. But has been very good since." Too bad, though, he looks like the Pennells instead of the Reeds! "He has blue eyes and brown hair and a very white skin. Looks like the Pennell children, I think. Not so much Reed look to him as was in the other one. If nothing happens to him, you will soon see him. Is called Arthur Reed. John likes the name. And of course I had rather call him that than any other name." It was Abby's father's. And Abby winds up: "We think too much of him, I am afraid." A sin which Abby and John enjoy in company with all young parents on earth.

Abby writes that the slow-poke *Deborah* is enough to sicken anybody of a life on the ocean. "The Bark never sailed so slow. Some weeks more like a log than any thing else, drifting along." Abby is all on ache to get home and show off the baby.

John finally got back on board May 5, with the orders to Leith and letters. Abby breathed easier again, after she had run through hers. There was always the chance that even the nearest and dearest ones had died. All was well at home. She had missed the shadow this time. But the shadow did not miss poor Elizabeth, the English girl who had been helping her a year. She got the news of her mother's death. A year is a long time and can be very hard on mothers. Abby instructed her mother to send her letters hereafter care of Messrs. David Thom and Company, Leith. They headed for Leith.

## Captain Abby and Captain John

A gale gave them some excitement off the Scilly Isles and split them a topsail or two and some staysails. And the baby got his first tooth through. But Abby set down the elegiac fact that he was "growing old fast." As they went up the Channel in Spring-like weather, with a fair wind from the west, they had fifty-five vessels in company. It was a sight the world will never see again!—The Channel crowded with things like giant swans, alive in every inch of their whiteness. Abby rejoiced in the lovely sight. John mended sail.

At Beachy Head and five months, the baby weighed 13 pounds! And the English pilot had given him a nickname. He would shout out to him, "How's old Cape Horn today?" Up around England, they went. Many steamers now as well as sail. Steamers were on their way to crowd sailing ships right off the world's edge into limbo, with the dodo and mastodon. Whitby light. St. Abb's Head. And then Leith, on May 18. More letters. The shore looked very pretty to Abby. She longed to be there. She got milk for the baby at last. "Hope he will flesh up some now." [If he does, they may have to have a ship instead of a bark to get him home!]

Abby could write letters only when the baby was asleep. On May 22nd, they came into the dock and began discharging the guano. They had callers from the ship alongside them and elsewhere: Capt. Doone, Capt. Oliver, and Mr. Clarke of Glasgow. Mr. Clarke stayed to dinner. Next day, Mr. Clarke again, and Mr. and Mrs. Black. The next, Mr. Clarke for tea. Abby was dying to get on land. "Should like to take a walk onshore, but am bound hand and foot, have no time

## Captain Abby and Captain John

to go anywheres. Have the headache tonight." Abby must have said something to John, for on May 26 he hired a girl, Mary Davidson. She and the baby got on well at once. The baby, Abby wrote, was "as lively as a cricket." More callers and Mr. Clarke for dinner. And John bought the baby his first rattle! A date important enough to put down in any sea captain's log. The day following, the baby was fretful, but he had learned "how to use his little rattle pretty well." Elizabeth went shopping. But poor Abby was still on board. More callers. Capt. Cook and Capt. Thomas, and the cook, left for home. Abby set down the good news that Jeff Davis had been caught, May 27.—I spent some months in his lovely prison yard, Fortress Monroe, before I went off to war, learning calculus.—More callers. Abby took a day off, with the coming of the new steward, and sewed. The guano scented up that whole section of Scotland. But on the last day of May, Abby Pennell got her feet on the earth at long last. Praise be the Lord!

John and his wife went to Edinburgh "and found it to be a very pretty place, streets clean and broad, and pretty shops. But goods much higher than in England." That was the Scottish coming out! And relieved a few hours from the baby, Abby missed him terribly. "Left my darling baby all the afternoon. And he was as good as could be. I bought him a little hat and ribbon for the shoulders. His hat fits him nicely and is very becoming, and looks a great boy in it." Middle Bays should not find her baby unstylish or innocent of the fashions of the great world of *bon ton*. No, Sir! "I am not so tired tonight as I expected to be. So ends the last day of Spring."

There was shopping next day, and Abby got Elizabeth a black silk dress and brooch. Scottish weather set in, and Abby ushered Summer in with a cold in the nose. She had one wish only unfulfilled now: to get home. Abby and John took a momentous step on Sunday, June 4. They took the baby for a ride and introduced him to the world: "John and I took baby for a ride this afternoon. The first time I have taken him out. He was quite frightened at first." He had supposed a ship's cabin and a few sails on the sky all the world there was. "But got along with him very well. He looked so cunning with his hat on. We rode through, and saw some delightful places. The streets are broad and clean. Have not seen so pretty a place for a long time. After tea, we took a walk down on the quay, where we had a good view of the coast."

The day following, they had five callers, three of them ladies. The baby was under the weather, next day. The new steward came on board with his wife. Abby hoped they would turn out well. Elizabeth left for home. Abby and Mary and the baby saw her off at the depot. They all felt bad to part. Abby did some shopping, but came home and was homesick for the lost Elizabeth. Much as she disliked to go shopping "dreadfully," Abby went again, June 8, and bought three dresses. The baby got along all right without her again. Shopping again the next day, but the baby was ill, and they had to have the doctor. The day after, Abby was aw-

## Captain Abby and Captain John

fully worried and pleased together. "I can see he is growing thin. Darling child, I hope and pray he will be better tomorrow. John bought me a very pretty French poplin, a bright purple, am very pleased with it." The baby did get better and was "lively and playful." Mary took him for a walk. Then he was worse, and Abby had the doctor to him again. "Is 6 months old today, is getting to be a great baby. And cunning as anybody's baby." The following day the doctor assured them the baby was doing fine. Some ladies called. The next day the doctor said the baby was all well. June 15, Abby and John were in Edinburgh again, shopped, and got their chinchilla skins dressed. That evening John went out to see the soldiers drill. Another day of callers. The doctor ordered the baby out, and Abby took him for a walk. Sunday, June 18, Abby "fainted entirely away and was senseless for some minutes, but soon recovered again, and was quite smart at night. Do not know what could make me have such an ill turn." The doctor kept right on coming and telling them the baby was all right. I had an English doctor like that once, to *my* first baby. I suppose a Scottish one is still more regular!

John's wife went to Edinburgh shopping all by herself. She was discouraged at not having time to do more sewing. Shopping and the baby took all her time. The doctor came again. But Abby had a cold, so he had something to lean on. On June 14, John and Abby went to see an artillery review, but it came on a Scottish mist, and Abby got soaked. "Did not see much either." She was laid up with a cold, but the baby went on being the lively cricket that he was all along. Then the baby came

## Captain Abby and Captain John

down with Abby's cold. Of course, the doctor came as usual, to assure Abby it was not dangerous. The doctor next day declared the baby was all right. Callers. Doctor. Baby. Sewing. The days went by.

The *Deborah* was dry-docked. John and his wife went to Glasgow, July 1. But the baby was upset. "Think he knows he is in a strange place," wrote Abby. Don't babies always know it! John went to church. And Capt. Winchell of Brunswick greeted them. Mr. and Mrs. Merrow, at whose grand house they were visiting, were very kindly people. Abby got worried over the baby and had the Merrows' doctor come and tell her that it was only teeth and not a dangerous disease. The doctor cut little Arthur's gums for him and left powders. John departed without Abby for Leith. On the Fourth of July Mr. Merrow flew the Stars and Stripes on the top of his house in honor of his guest. Abby was finding it righteous hard work to hold the baby in her arms all the time. The powders were no good. The baby was frightened of the servants. Abby could not go out at all. She sat home and held the baby. The worst thing, of course, she could do. She got a letter from John each day, and wrote him one back. She was glad to leave the elegant house and elegant hosts and fly back to John by train the first chance she got.

Abby packed next day. She had a letter from James Henry, under the clouds now and exiled. Abby went into an orgy of dressmaking. She shopped, too, at Leith and Edinburgh. July 14 was a red letter day. John and Abby went to Holyrood Palace, "and went up into the top of Sir Walter Scott's Monument, where we had a fine view of Edinburgh and Leith." And in the evening, "a gentleman and his wife and three young gentlemen from Pennsylvania" came to look over the bark. The mate, Mr. Dunning, went to see his brother, Minot, like him marked for drowning at sea, at Newport. The only fly in the ointment was the baby's being under the weather. Abby visited with Mrs. Black, her Scottish friend, at her pretty home, next day. But the baby's teeth worried her all the time. She held the teething baby all day long on July 17, never let him out of her arms once. It was a wonder Abby was able to live with him at all ever after! Then the baby improved, and Abby made a bee-line for Edinburgh and dresses. She cut out a scarlet merino dress for the baby. She went to Edinburgh again. Mr. Dunning came back loaded with news of Middle Bays. They moved down to the ballast dock, July 21, and the new steward and his wife "had a spat." Abby wondered how it would end. She called on Mrs. Anderson of the bark *Maggie Hammond*, one of their old Chinchas Islands friends, and didn't she have a baby, and wasn't Abby jealous of it! It had been born in the Pacific, same month as John's and Abby's, and here it was, "as large as three of him!"

After all, the shadow did come from home, before the Pennells left Scotland. On their last day at Leith, a letter came full of the shadow. John's brother, Master Builder James Pennell, brains behind all the Pennell ships, designer of them all, the real head of the family and firm since old Deborah's death five years before, Yankee prince of the kindly twinkling eyes, dimmed now with thoughts of his oldest son's escapade, had

## Captain Abby and Captain John

stepped on a loose plank and fallen from the mast of the *Istria* to the keel inside. "Mr. James Pennell had fell," Abby set down, "and nearly killed himself. I hope to hear favorable news next mail." Bad news travelled fast, even in 1865. Master James had fallen on July 8, and Abby's entry is July 23. And there would be no favorable news. Master James had killed himself. For in two weeks' time, he would breathe his last, still unconscious. And the shadow would lie over all Brunswick, and over the Pennell yards for good. There would be only two more ships go out from there.

Their last day in Leith, Abby and John had a host of callers. Mrs. Anderson of the *Maggie* was among them, probably carrying her 39-pound Hercules—he'd have had to weigh that to be three times the size of Abby's Arthur—and gloating! Next day, it was goodbye to Scotland. Abby was miserable all day and could scarcely hold her head up. But the baby had two teeth through!

They put in at Shields, the 25th, and John was gone all day there and at Newcastle. Abby found Shields "the most out of the way place" she ever had been in. She had to walk a long ways to get to the cars in order to go shopping in Newcastle. But she went. She went again next day, in "dust thick enough to put anyone's eyes out." And she took her time. "I have to look round"—she is speaking for all women shoppers in all time—"to see where I can do the best." July 29, Abby had the baby's photograph taken. She bought carpets. Abby got so she shopped every day and all the time, coming home only for meals. She was worn to the bone.

## Captain Abby and Captain John

How she hated it! "Tired of shopping—having so much to do for other folks is much worse than doing my own. So ends another month." She had John with her August 1st, and they bought "knives and silver forks and a very pretty caster." Abby admired and walked across the splendid iron bridge over the Tyne. She finished up her shopping August 2nd, by buying herself chinaware. "And this afternoon started with bag and baggage for the ship and got on board about 6 o'clock. Found everything dirty enough, and the cabin filled with a little of everything." She took off her bonnet and sailed in. They finished loading the ship. It was coals, naturally, seeing that this was the old town of the proverb, Newcastle. Abby got a present a merchant had sent her: cologne, a toothbrush and a nailbrush, and a lot of soap. She and John sat up till one o'clock writing letters.

They left Tyne Dock August 4. "So adieu to England." And adieu to all ports till they got home. Home! —over three and a half years away! "Happy to think we are homeward bound. God grant that we may have a speedy passage and safely return to our friends at home. I feel miserable tonight. Pleasant and calm." Abby and the baby had both come down with colds. But Abby sorted her things over just the same. Another tooth came through. "Black and squally tonight. Vessels all around us, as thick as can be." Then the wind gave out. "Not a breath of air. Do not like this weather when we are bound home. All quite well today. Baby nicely and very good. I cut him out some short sack dresses today and am making him some shirts." The

## Captain Abby and Captain John

baby was still keeping Abby from doing a stitch of sewing except for him.

Across the Atlantic, in Middle Bays, the light in John's brother flickered out and left the Pennell Brothers in gloom that would never completely lift.

Calms, calms, calms. John had to anchor at times. A large host of vessels around them would do the same. The steamers went past them. Here was a reason, for all their power at times, and for all their loveliness, sailing ships were doomed. When the wind came at last, it was a head wind, and John had to beat. Beachy Head, August 12. Then a fair wind at last, and the pilot left them, taking along their letters. "Baby well and hearty." But the wind was southwest and the bark "very crank" off the Isle of Wight, and Abby looked for the worst. Next day, off Portland Head, she was miserable and had no appetite. Southwest wind. Southwest wind. Vessels in all directions and "going all directions." The lighthouse on the Start. Next night Abby saw the same lighthouse on the Start. "This is hard luck to have such luck when on our way home." But Abby had finished "Artie's second sack dress. So he is in short clothes now."—The baby had been swaddled like a mummy in dresses maybe six feet long, as the ancient Chaldean babies were, up till eight months! —"It really makes him look older." Many vessels in company. Eddystone light.

On August 18, off Falmouth, the Pennells met the *Great Eastern* steaming up the Channel, "come back with the Atlantic cable, which has proved a failure. . . . Baby very well." Probably Abby felt like crowing over

## Captain Abby and Captain John

this latest new gadget that was so unworkable. She and John little dreamed how soon the cable would be mended and their own voices running under the seas, or how fast the world would be moving around them in another ten years. This great leviathan coming home a failure and others like it would crowd them and their sails back into the times and fleets of the Phoenicians.

Next day they had still not got anywhere, as usual. Abby was cutting out a print dress when John called to her to come out and see another unusual sight. It was a ship made of iron! You couldn't believe it, but there it was! Going along and floating just like wood. People over home had fought naval battles in such things already, queer monsters out of another planet, out of the future. "She was a singular looking thing," wrote Abby. Over in Middle Bays and up the whole length of the Maine coast, the white oaks must have shuddered in all their fibres. For they would never go to sea any more.

Abby and John saw the lights on the Lizard. They dropped the Scillys behind them in the sea. "Farewell to English land for awhile." The next land would be America! The baby, proud of his new teeth, let Abby do some sewing. "Is growing to be cunning fast, and is very lively, and seems well and hearty." A proper sailor's son now. Abby celebrated her thirtieth birthday. "It don't seem possible," she wrote, "I am so old. But I suppose I am. Last year, we were on our way to Callao from Coquimbo, and thought then I should be at home this year. But we can appoint, and God disappoint." A glorious right wind at last, and Abby prayed it would last them "clear across the ocean." Abby finished her first dress late that night. It didn't last, that wind. Next night was almost calm. And next, it was the old familiar head wind. "Our fine fair wind was short. All the same as usual today." Discouraging! And Abby with a new baby to show off on Great Island! He would probably be a young man and have a moustache by the time they got him home!

Then they got a heavy sea that pitched them about so Abby could hardly keep her feet. "Not half way home yet. Oh, dear! how discouraging!" For ten days on end Abby reported herself as miserable or very miserable. But that baby was like the proverbial cricket. Abby cut him out another sack dress from the midst of misery. A gale came out of the southeast on September 1, to stir them up. "I never," said Abby, "saw the bark pitch into it so as she has today. Considerable water come into the cabin aft and wet our trunks. And that was never done before. John and I both sick today." Jessie, the new maid, caved in during the gale, and Abby had all the work to do. She was on her feet, did the baby's washing, and everything. The bark rolled so Abby was really worried. Abby observed a sad anniversary on September 5: "I no better. It is hard telling when I shall be. 3 years ago today my first baby was born. What a boy he would have been! But he is my darling little treasure in heaven." Younger even than Arthur now. Strange that such a thing could be. It was odd the way things turned out. Abby reported the baby as sitting up a good deal. Another flannel shirt for the baby, with silk embroidery! The bark rolled and turned everything topsyturvy. "It is really tiresome to be knocked about so! I managed to do a little washing for baby, but it was very hard." Waves were "running mountains high." September 10, they were on the Banks. The following day, past them. They got on through misery and head winds. Abby got a pain in her side. And the diary came to an end.

They reached Middle Bays before the month was gone. And Abby had a dozen new cities, a new continent, a new ocean, and her brand-new son to show for having been away from Maine over three and a half years. Young Arthur was the admiration of everybody on Great Island with his fine hat. The Pennells, broken terribly in their ranks here and there now, and with the light gone in the master builder's house, threw open their arms and took John and Abby and their baby to their heart.

# 15

## Sunshine on Abby and John

THE TWO CAPTAINS, back from the wide world, found something different about Middle Bays. They went the round of calls and dinners and suppers among brothers and sisters. There were some children's faces missing, as well as old people's. But there were many new young members of the family standing up and having their heights measured on the kitchen wall year by year. Yet there was something more than people missing. It wasn't merely the master builder, though it was something that had very much to do with him. Abby and John both noticed it. And they spoke of it when alone together at such times as those when husbands and wives speak their naked thoughts to each other.

Something was closed up. It was as though the great white oaks the Pennells had cut on the Plains, in the day when the carrier pigeons darkened the sky with their millions, as though the first-growth pines that once had held the sky up on their tops had all come back from under the sea and from dust and had closed in on Middle Bays where they had stood a century before. It was as though their shadows had fallen across the eight white mansions, on the lawns and elms, on the

## Captain Abby and Captain John

shipyard, and had put out their brightness. The shadow lay deepest at Master James's. Young Captain James Henry had gone from that house for good, and with him that white seraph of Pennell ships, the *Anglo Saxon*. Only two young boys were there, five and ten, Carroll and Will. Augusta had married and gone to California. James Henry had become a British citizen and a bitter exile from the country that punished blockade running. His escapade had lost the Pennells their chance of recovering some of the *Alabama* claims money for the ships the Confederate privateers had sunk during the war. There was a great emptiness, of course, in the old house on the hill. Deborah's passing had been like the passing of Sarah or Rebecca from among the Hebrews of old. She had left a hole in a nation. Ben was gone, and the second Pennell mansion had no master. Alien masters would soon be coming in.

Charles the Great was still there. And Charles was a whole town in himself. The ship's doctor was still flourishing like Jonah's gourd, albeit under the false crown of a wig. The one Capt. John's small son surprised him without! But Charles's house had become a whole new city in itself. Famous faces were seen there, and faces famous-to-be: General Chamberlain, hero of Little Round Top at Gettysburg, who had held great Lee's sword at Appomattox the moment before Grant returned it; "Bert" Peary, of Bowdoin, would be there soon, the man who was going to discover the North Pole and who would be courting one of Charles's daughters for a time; the McKeens and Gilmans of Brunswick, the Sewalls of Bath; and senators and college professors

## Captain Abby and Captain John

galore. The poet Harriet was filling the house with the literary lights of the neighborhood and all Maine. Charles's house was an open house. Open to the world. Prominent people from Boston and New York and Philadelphia were often there. But the Pennells themselves felt abashed there. They felt as if they were visiting in Boston and New York. Yes, Charles had become a citizen of the vast world outside the clan. He had overflowed his house. He had to have a house in town and a house in Boston. He rented ones in New York and Philadelphia. Charles had escaped the shadow.

But the shadow was on the rest of Pennellville, as people were now beginning to nickname Middle Bays. It was deepest in the shipyard. Alders and the wild cherry were beginning to grow up there. There had fallen a strange hush on Middle Bays after the *Oakland*, the last ship Master James's fine mind had designed, had cut open the water in 1866. The Skolfield yard, across the way in the next bay to the east, was still booming. The Skolfields were at their whitest heat, a half dozen of them. But something had gone out of the Pennell family. It was large still, but the young men were turning their faces towards the land, towards the cities. John's own baby, once he had got on his feet. There was the best Pennell captain of them all, John, still at sea. And Sam Pennell, from my house, was abroad on all the oceans. Yet there was something gone from the Pennells. Pith. It can go out of a family, when nobody is noticing. Things happen like that. The Pennells had been flourishing long before the Skolfields had come up. Maybe a family has just so much in it. Of one kind of

## Captain Abby and Captain John

strength. Maybe the Pennells' strength had been used up. The sea was running out of their veins. Carroll would grow up to be a gentleman farmer. George, at my house, would, too. The sea strain was petering out. And the world outside was changing its strengths into new forms. The shadow of family change and of changes outside families was deep upon the Pennells. The world over, sails were growing fewer on the oceans. Longer and longer stretches of days and months in the South Pacific and the South Atlantic without any sails sweeping along. Times change. Families change.

But John Pennell was flourishing still on the sea. He was riding with all sails set, light and heavy, and all filled with the winds of prosperity. Abby was with him, all but one voyage in 1877, sewing and seeing new splendors, turning out mince and apple pies, and keeping her son in good health and in dresses and combed curls till he got long enough to go into trousers, curls and all. Arthur grew. And Abby grew. John grew a better and better sailor. Abby's roll of cities lengthened out. She added new capitals of culture, new cities she always loved for being clean and having broad streets, new places of wealth, new citadels of history and romance, to her long list. Boston, Havana, Falmouth, Venice, Trieste, Gibraltar, New York, New Orleans, Havre, Cardiff, Liverpool, Queenstown, Dublin, London, Singapore, Philadelphia, Akyab, Jamestown on St. Helena, Leith, Edinburgh, Newcastle, Valparaiso, Callao, Lima; and now Anger, Yokohama, Baltimore, Astoria in Oregon, Rio de Janeiro.

Abby did miles of embroidery and cut out acres of

## Captain Abby and Captain John

fine silk dresses. She mended companies and regiments of John's pants. She cooked legions of biscuits and pies. Though she constantly wrote of the hardness of her life, with its gales and its longings for home and quiet, she kept right on going to sea, every time her husband's ship was loaded. She constantly wrote and talked of settling down to the peaceful green life in hayfields and farmhouses. But every time John packed his valise, she packed hers and the baby's and got right on the cars with him. She lived for those sudden departures and exhilarations of accelerated gaiety as voyages loomed nigh and for the long peaceful days and months where even her best friends could not reach her. Her best friends disappeared, really, as the years went by. She had none but her husband and the boy. She lived for the hours when she kept house—oh, a snug, small house!—for her small family. The hours when the world of friends and relations contracted and disappeared and left her at utter peace, save for fear of bad news when the lost world would build itself up again and come to her by letters, by faces. It was an odd, small, but very comforting life she lived, lonely yet strangely alive. Very real. She never dreamed she might be putting all her eggs in one basket. Her life was a small life in the smallest of neat houses, just a few inches, just the thickness of a plank from that vast watery universe so full of chance and sudden change, the watery universe bordered by great ports and hundreds of new coasts now and then, and the great hubbub of loading and unloading cotton, lumber, sugar, guano, ballast, pig iron, tea. Men came suddenly into being, and then vanished, and she had her comfortable wooden world again, and baby clothes to cut out. If her house tipped up and slid off every so often, it was warmer, snugger, and more of her own than any other woman's house in the world. And she had a better chance to learn to know her husband in it and to love her child. They did not go far away from it ever. They were always there at night.

And to her list of achievements, Abby Pennell added another son, Freddie, on August 1st, 1870. So now she had her heart and hands full!

Seven times around Cape Horn. Four times around Good Hope. Round the world completely. The Lord only could recall how many times across the Atlantic! Abby put a fine embroidery, like featherstitch, considering the tacking her ship had to do, along the coasts of all the continents with her goings and comings. A hundred vast storms in her itinerary. A hundred doldrums. Ten thousand tacks this way and that. A myriad of shifted sails.

Abby even added Philinque, in Lower California, to her list of places seen. She sailed with John from Philadelphia, September 2, 1868, and got there in 156 days, by way of the Horn. On the way, the pig littered; seven were added to the bark's crew. The runt, John noted, died. John also noted the "Presidential Election" Day back home, November 3. Charlotte, the stewardess, was flat on her back most of the time. John raced and beat a newfangled British iron bark. He rounded the Horn the beginning of December. He had trouble with the crew and put "Bill" and Collins in irons. He lay in the

## Captain Abby and Captain John

doldrums two days, with "Bill" and his friend still there. They promised good behavior, and John let them out. It was "awful teigeous getting up the Gulf of Lower California," John wrote, "shall be thankful when we get in and get out of this place." It was like trying to tack in a bottle, stoppered, with no air coming into it. John got to the Bay of Pichalinqui, February 6, 1869. It took 23 days to discharge his 1074 tons of coal. What they wanted of coal in a place like the inside of the fiery furnace anyway, is more than I can make out.

Callao and guano were better than this. So John went for them. The carpenter sprained his ankle on the way down, as carpenters do when you need them most. There was a gale. And John killed one of the pigs. It took 59 days to Callao. And the Peruvians took their sweet time loading the guano. John was not on his way till October 11. Callao again, October 24. John's orders were to go to Hampton Roads. He left November 1. Round the Horn, with no trouble, December 13. Gales after, though. John butchered a pig that dressed off 235 pounds. More gales, and a topsail yard arm went. Another gale on January 2, 1870, "a violent Pampero," out of the pampas grass of the Argentine, and it kicked up a sea that started the boats on the forward house, took the topmast studding sail, stove in the poop bulwarks, and sent the whole hen coop and all the Rhode Island Red biddies to Kingdom Come! The bark started several leaks, the guano was awash. But John came through it all and repaired the damage done to all but the poor hens. Abby repaired John's pants.

## Captain Abby and Captain John

John filled in the time between gales by carving a name board for the *Deborah Pennell*, thinking of his mother's death eight years before. He tarred the mizzen rigging. "Commenced to paint aft myself and carpenter." The perils of an omitted comma!—John means a routine bit of ship's business. He does not mean here that he was reverting to the woad-tinting of their backsides practiced by his British ancestors! Doldrums for some days at the Line. John drew a diagram of the *Deborah's* cabins. The last pig went to the happy rooting grounds, March 12, 1870. John holystoned the dining cabin floor. He kept busy all the time. Gales once more, and water in the guano, off Hatteras. The fat was often in the fire on ships off thereabouts. John anchored in Hampton Roads, March 26. He sailed up the Chesapeake to Baltimore, and delivered his guano. From Baltimore he chartered to take coal to Portland, Maine, "at $2.00 per ton for gas company, they discharging the coal at their expense." He got 1090 tons and sailed April 21. May 3rd, he made Cape Elizabeth light and anchored in Portland harbor.

And Abby hurried home to Great Island with the news of her expecting an addition to the family. She and John stayed on land for a few months. And J. Frederick Pennell saw the light of day, August 1, in Pennellville.

But Abby was back on the *Deborah* just as soon as she could get on her feet and get some dresses cut out.

So it went.

One prop to Abby's and John's prosperity was their first mate. John had made his man, as we have seen, and

## Captain Abby and Captain John

he kept him for use now on the *Deborah*. Elias Reed sailed as their first mate, and he kept things shipshape and Bristol fashion as John had taught him to do. He was a broth of a man, built big into his trousers, and a character like blue steel just out of the foundry.

That was all to the good for Captain John Pennell. For one melancholy sign of change in the American logbooks after 1855 is the growing frequency of trouble among the crews. The character of the men who worked the sails was changing fast. In the old days, a Maine sea captain had sailed with a whole crew made up of incipient Maine captains of his own background and kind and blood. All hands had usually got on well together. But with the crowding of competition, more and more the captains had to pick up their crews where they could find them. There weren't apprentice sea captains enough to go around. The captains picked up crews in ports along their way. Ships were being filled up with drifters and loafers and fly-by-night men. Many of them were scoundrels of the first water. And captains had to use strong-arm methods to secure even these.

So the third mate came into being. A child—and usually a tough one—of necessity. It was the third mate's chief duty to collect men and make them toe the line once they were aboard. That gentleman would ferret them out in ports and pay the debts they had contracted. Sailors, both the good ones and the bad ones, owed money to everybody. Then the mate would liquor them up and bring them aboard. Having usually been one of his quarry, he generally knew the ropes of the game. Sometimes the men were brought aboard by port

## Captain Abby and Captain John

bullies and toughs who rounded them up, shanghaied them, and then collected for them from the grateful captain at so much a head, delivered. When the men sobered off, they would find themselves far at sea with a job on their hands. The third mate might have to use his fists on them to make them go aloft. He was generally a good man with his fists, and had a big pair. He had to have, to live. Sometimes, too, it was a case of the biters being bit. For often when the new crew came to, they turned out an utter set of wild-cats, hyenas, and scalawags of the first magnitude and made the captain's and the third mate's lives a misery and a burden.

With such crews aboard, mutiny began to be a frequent occurrence. Of course, captains themselves were often enough the cause as well as the men. A weak or an unfair captain was headed for trouble sure as he had a parting in his pants for the wind to go between his legs. Sooner or later, trouble came.

Captain John D. Pennell was an A-1 captain. He was straight-grained as they came. He was a quiet man, but he had his way with people. He was thoroughly fair and even ready to love his men as his ancestors had loved them before him. The new men weren't the lovable kind. But he got on with them. He was level-headed. He was gentle. But he was a stickler for decorum, that quality without which a ship ought never be given her papers to go to sea. Witness the ships of our merchant marine in this Year of Grace and Harry Bridges, 1939! John even made his crews observe the Sabbath. And such a man was bound to be respected by even the

## Captain Abby and Captain John

dyed-in-wool scamps. So John steered clear of mutiny for years.

But even John Pennell had one on his hands at last. It was at Port Key Francis, 100 miles from Havana, in April, 1869, and he was loading sugar. It was ungodly hot weather. And that may have had something to do with it. Mutinies often had roots in the weather. Anyway, the men got out of hand over the question of hours of labor. John tried to "gentle" them and reason them back to work. But they weren't the gentle kind. One of them up and knocked John unconscious. But the tough had forgotten all about the first mate. It was an unlucky day for him that Elias Reed was on board. Elias came running. He sailed in without the usual preliminaries and pleasantries. He straightened things out with his bare hands in about two minutes on his pants' clock. The ringleader saw Mars and Mercury in conjunction. For Elias was good with both left and right. When Elias was through, all three ringleaders were in the land of Nod. And the rest of the men were like a lot of sucking doves, cooing around their mate. Elias was built like a Great Island ox. He had a temper like a July thunderhead. He was resourceful and quick where John was calm and quiet. Elias was jovial and a good mixer with the men, where John was the aloof and gentleman-scholar type. They made an ideal sailing pair. Elias's nature was the one thing needed this hot day among the sugar barrels. It saved the day.

Elias Reed had been in hotter water than this mutiny. He had lived through one on an earlier ship as first

## Captain Abby and Captain John

mate. There had been a great fracas between the officers and a crew of blacks. The second mate killed one of the mutineers. All three mates decided it was best for them to leave the ship before awkward questions were asked. So they took the long-boat and lit out. They scuttled the boat on the coast of Uruguay. They traversed a jungle in the night and heard the rhythmic tapping of poisonous snakes as they waded the swamps. They were pursued by bloodhounds and escaped them by wading up to their necks in water. They separated. Elias got to Montevideo, he secured a first-mate's berth on a Yankee ship, and he came home rejoicing. A mate like Elias Reed could not be kept down!

Most crews respected the man John Pennell had built. Especially after that two minutes' affair among the sugar barrels in 1869.

The years rolled on, and the bark *Deborah* rolled on over all the waters of the world. John succeeded in port and out. He became a high-up Mason. He became interested in church movements such as Sunday Schools. But his way remained on the ocean. Abby sewed and rocked her new baby and kept a weather eye on Artie. He was growing handsomer every day he lived. But one thing about the older boy was plain: Pennell looks or not, he was never going to be a sailor. He was all landsman, for all he was spending his boy's best years on the water. But the children's father and mother had the sea deep in them now. They could call it a day and rest home for good almost any time now. But they could no more do that than they could fly. They went on sailing.

And another fact is clear from the log-books of John

## Captain Abby and Captain John

Pennell. American ships are thinning out on the ocean in the 70's. Fewer and fewer sail are in company as the days and months and years go by. There are a greater proportion of Britishers than John used to report. Britannia's use of the Civil War to get back her place as mistress of the seas had had results. The privateers had thinned the Yankee ships out. But English sails are fewer, too, all sails. There are more and more steamers. A hand is writing on the wall of the high skies over the sea.

Like all American ships that sailed the seas continuously and took great chances, the bark *Deborah Pennell* had a number set on her days. It was the fog that got her at the end, no gales. On December 20, 1873, she went ashore in the murk on the Dutch coast near the entrance to Rotterdam. But Captain John Pennell wasn't there handling the wheel. It was his man, Elias Reed. But even John Pennell couldn't have saved his old ship that wild night. The waves came in low and long under the blinding mist. They were like sledges against the Maine oak. The North Sea waves picked the bones bred in Maine. Maybe old Deborah stirred a little in her grave under the pines in Middle Bays that bitter night, where she had lain quiet for twelve years. And if the dead have tears, maybe her eyes were moist at the passing of her ship. And maybe, too, the unnamed Pennell boy in heaven, whose cradle the *Deborah* had been for more than a year, stopped his play a moment, and was sad.

Abby Pennell wept when she heard. But ships were bound to have an end. As people.

## Captain Abby and Captain John

John Pennell's prosperity might go on. But it would be for only a little time, a matter of a few years now, under sail. He had grown fairly well off with his carrying business. But a man has only so many good years ahead of him. So it is best for him to drink in the sunshine while he can.

## 16

## Last Page Out of Homer

IT WAS THE BRIGHTEST and the bluest day of the blue-and-golden October of 1874, October 27. The sun was as clear as a ball of solid gold in a sky without a cloud. The last terrific yellow flames of Fall were burning among the birches, and the maples were still burning red in the swamps.

The old Twelve-Rod Road out of Brunswick towards Maquoit was afire. Smoke went up from it from the town's end and down to where it forked to the left and went on to Middle Bays. It smoked along the high elms with the Pennell Brothers' houses behind them. It smoked right down to the dark blue bay at the shipyard.

It wasn't a common fire, though. It was the Fall dust being churned up in the sunlight by hundreds of carriages. Everybody in town who owned or could borrow a buggy, a buckboard, a carryall, or even a gig, was there. And lots who couldn't on foot. Everybody who was anybody was on the road. And some who weren't. There were horses that looked as if they had staggered out of the ark and buggies built before the Flood. There were horses that were all nervousness and breeding so exquisite that it hurt them like horseflies and they

## Captain Abby and Captain John

couldn't keep still. There were new buckboards which put people's eyes out with their blazing on their bright new black-and-gold, black-and-red wheels in the sun. There were old ladies with snowy hair and bonnets no bigger than a teacup with strings that tied under the chin, ladies so delicate that the breeze might break them into shining splinters any minute. There were huge fathers of families, huge as only the men in our fathers' day could grow, wide in the beam, with moustaches that swept like a mass of golden wire away back to their ears, half buried in spite of their bigness under a baker's dozen of children in striped stockings, velvet dresses, or pants with bursting seams and pearl buttons at the knee. There were big bugs and little bugs, and all the bugs in between. There were girls like bouquets of flowers tied up with flying ribbons. Boys as dangerous as dynamite, sitting in farmers' express wagons and jolting along with their legs hanging down over the tailboard. They had innocent eyes of angels, but they might go off any minute and strew destruction over the earth. There were farmers' wives who had put all the nice things they had in the house on their backs. The livery stables of Brunswick and Topsham stood empty as last year's crows' nests. Every horse was hired for the day. People had come by the steam cars from Portland and Bath. They had even come from Boston.

A page in the history of Brunswick was about to be turned, and all the town was going down to Middle Bays to see it go over.

At the end of the road, the carriages were turning

## Captain Abby and Captain John

into the field which swept up to the headland. Charles Pennell's yard was crowded, and Ben's. The shore was alive with people.

Up in the house of Charles the Great, tables were spread and waiting. Tables were spread out on the lawns, too, and in under the apple trees. The white linen cloths were held down by round pebbles to keep them from ruffling in the wind. Glass pitchers were there, green with lemonade and red with raspberry shrub. Platters of cold tongue and beef and chicken breasts. Caraway cookies and cinnamon cookies and pumpkin pies big as the Fall sun, apple pies, mince. Turkey meat and cranberry sauce around it. Tarts heaped with red jelly. Swarms of late bees burned in the sun over dishes of strawberry jam. The feast was ready.

And over the heads of stout fathers sitting on the dry grass and being careful of the seats of their pants and boys and girls careless of theirs, in the midst of them all, the largest ship ever built in the town of Brunswick lay quiet above the billows of Queen Anne's lace. Twenty-four feet high, 218 feet of curved beauty, 1433 tons of solid and honest Maine oak. The ship *Benjamin Sewall*, built by the Pennell Brothers, waiting the word to go out on the Atlantic and around the world! She was the last word in loveliness and strength, "the finest ship ever launched," all finished in her cabins with solid mahogany. She was alive with pennons from her noble stem under Charles the Great's parlor windows to her stern over the thatch and dead sea lavender of Middle

## Captain Abby and Captain John

Bay. It was the peak in the history of the Pennells and of Middle Bays. It was a peak in the life story of Brunswick.

It was close to twelve o'clock. It was tip-top high-water mark of the highest-run neap tide of the year. And even so, the bay had been dredged out for the ship's coming. The air ran with excitement. A thousand voices were murmuring under the hill. All eyes were on the ship. It was the moment of a lifetime.

There was a knot of people high overhead on the ship's topgallant forecastle, under a cloud of flags. Benjamin Sewall himself was there, the business man from Boston for whom the ship was named. He was eighty years old, but his eyes were like those of a boy who has skipped school, or is at least running away to sea. The President of Bowdoin College was there, General Joshua L. Chamberlain, who kept the Stars and Bars off Little Round Top and so off the Capitol at Washington, that bloody Second Day at Gettysburg. Reverend Professor John S. Sewall of Bowdoin was there. The Honorable Charles J. Gilman, head of the Republican party and civic righteousness at Brunswick.

And three other people stood on top of the ship. On top of their world. On top of the highest moment in their life together, Captain John D. Pennell, Abby, and the boy, Arthur, born in the Pacific, up to his father's shoulder now. And maybe another boy, two years taller by measure of earthly years, whom nobody but Abby could see, with the face of an angel, the boy who had been cradled at a mainmast and who had sailed there around half the globe and back. Abby and John were

## Captain Abby and Captain John

standing on their ship, the ship John had designed, the ship they had dreamed of all their life together.

But the third boy in the family was down in the crowd under the lofty prow, among the common run of cousins and uncles, and he was crying as if his heart would break. Freddie could see his mother and father and brother up there on the sky, and he thought they were going to go away and leave him for good with the thousand strangers around him. He sobbed and sobbed. He was only four years old. His cheeks were rivers of tears. And up in Charles the Great's apple tree, the young daughter of Charles the Great, Helen Pennell, was crying bitterly behind the bandage over her eyes that was going to keep her from seeing what would have made her weep to see anyway. Helen had sore eyes, and she had to be in darkness this greatest day in the life of the Pennell family!

Helen and Freddie, as Sancho to her blindness, had raided the bathtub up in Helen's house filled with sickel pears put there against the coming feast. They had filled their blouses with the fruit. Helen had eaten many of them, but her clothes were still bulged out with pears here and there. But the raid and that feast had been half an hour ago. Her heart was breaking now, she knew. No one had noticed her and Freddie in their raid, because everybody was all excitement over the preparations. The raid had been too easy a one. Helen's heart was a long ways from it now. She was weeping internally, she felt, though her eyes were scalding under the bandage. Helen leaned on the tree trunk for comfort. She felt a pear give way. It was miserable.

## Captain Abby and Captain John

All the Pennell brothers who were left were there under the ship's nose, with their wives and children. Widow Pennell with Master James's son, Carroll, thirteen years old and gorgeous in a new blue sailor suit with a real sailor cap and tie. James Henry was missing. But perhaps his father was there for one moment, on the spot where he had fallen to his death nine years before. Old Jacob was there. And Robert and Joseph. But Job of the unhandsome hare lip and the handsome child and Ben and old Deborah were all up under their marble stones a mile away, and could not come.

General Chamberlain was saying something high up on the sky. Too high to hear. And people were talking. The General's long white hair and moustache flowed out back from his face in the light breeze and burned with ineffable brightness in the sun. Then Professor Sewall raised his two hands against the blue, and bowed his head. A hush came over the crowd. The thousand heads there bowed, too. The prayer floated out half-heard and was lost in the wind and sunlight. Something about God's holding the ocean and ships in the hollow of his hand. In the hush people could hear the seagulls calling out over the bay clearer than the words of the prayer.

The preacher's head went back. The mauls and hammers began. The hard, seasoned supporting beams rang like bells in their fibres. The whoa-haish! and gee-haw! of the bearded men goading their oxen and dragging away the fallen beams. Cries of sweaty men. The sound swept up like a sudden gale. The people drew back in their best clothes from the dust and the sounds. Higher

THE SHIP *BENJAMIN SEWALL* ON THE WAYS

## Captain Abby and Captain John

and faster the sounds crowded, quickening and quickening up to a terrific crescendo. And then they stopped as if they had been cut off by scissors in the air. All the blows on metal and wood stopped at once. The sudden silence hurt the ears. An instant of utter stillness. Every man drew in his breath. It was like something at the very core of the process of being a man and creating man's kind. Then there was a last small and inadequate-seeming blow. Like a great bowstring, maybe, snapping somewhere out beyond the headland to the south.

"There she goes!"

No one believed it for a moment. The ship seemed as still and dead as ever. But there was something different. And then the ship came slowly to life, as a planet might come to life, gathered her strength upon her, gathered speed, went on her way, lonely, independent, went on her way from out of the people's midst. Down the ways and into the high water. Two long and lovely ripples curled up each side, turning to green gold in the sunlight. John and Abby and their son rode backward into the bay, a handsome family, their faces to their brothers and the people on the shore, their faces turned up and full of sun.

But their other boy, the four-year-old, broke from his aunts and ran after them, ran after the ship that was taking his parents away. He held up his hands and sobbed deep as they went, as a man might, wounded deep. He cried to them to stop, to wait for him. But the ship went away. He saw it glide half the width of the world away on the water. He fell on his face in the grass. No one heard his sobs any more. And the little

## Captain Abby and Captain John

girl up in the apple tree felt the tears hot on her bandage. The *Benjamin Sewall* stood up suddenly tall and comely on the bay, even and straight, as she would stand up till the day she got her death.

It was finished.

The crowd gave three cheers. Everybody threw up his hat. Young Master Carroll Pennell seized his sailor hat to throw it into the air with the rest, with the hundreds of others there. But he had forgotten the elastic under his chin. The hat snapped back upon him and covered his face and eyes. He swore the first oath of his life. "God damn the thing!" His mother did not hear him. Nobody heard him. Nobody heard young Freddie Pennell crying on his face where the ship had been. Everybody was cheering, cheering. The only sound was joy.

Nobody could hear the sound of waves rolling in upon rocky Formosa where this ship would break her heart and leave her ribs to bleach among the wicked rocks in the sun. It was too far to hear those waves, for the thickness of the world was between them and the people. Nobody heard an even lower sound, something like a whisper about her captain's lying cold and still in far-away Rio de Janeiro. And not one there heard the whisper, as low as the faint Fall wind that day, that this, the loveliest Pennell ship and the greatest, was the last. The line had stretched out for a century. But this was the last ship of them all.

The page of history had turned over. The people of Brunswick had seen a sight that would be like a page out of Homer in a handful of years.

# 17

## Happy Family at Sea

A TUG TOOK THE NEW MEMBER of Captain John Pennell's family to Portland, Maine, for her masts would be put in her and she would be rigged out there. Helen Pennell had her chance to sail on her, after all, for she went along with Freddie the twenty-odd miles, and the bandage was off her eyes. Freddie had gotten over the pears, too. It was a lovely trip.

The year 1875 saw the maiden voyage of the *Benjamin Sewall*, in which John Pennell held five of the sixteen shares. It was a grand sail. It was one and a half times around the globe. And the whole family were together most of the way.

They did not start together. John took the ship over with a cargo to Liverpool all by himself, to spare his wife and children the Winter crossing by sail. It was a sign of the times that he coddled his family so and had them go over by steam.

Abby herded the boys and trunks to Boston and embarked on the Cunard steamer *Atlas*. They had a taste of the wintry Atlantic, but on the kind of boat that did not pay any attention to the weather or the winds but plugged right along in spite of everything. Arthur was

## Captain Abby and Captain John

on his back for five or six days. He had no sailor in him. But small Freddie was up and about and looking for mischief after one day's seasickness. The *Atlas* was not so fast as a sailing ship. She contented herself with eight sure knots an hour. But she got the Pennell family there in March all right.

Abby and the boys joined Capt. John at Liverpool. And from there they headed for the sunrise side of the world, March 22, 1875, around the Cape of Good Hope, with a cargo of Welsh coal for the Empire of the Rising Sun. Freddie was wearing his first pants, and was very chunky in them. His light hair was parted on the right, his shoes were high, buttoned ones, and he had a sailor blouse on in honor of his father's profession. That's how he was rigged in the photograph that inevitably accompanied the family's start on such an extended holiday. Artie was in long trousers, eleven, and on his way to being a complete man. Abby wore the white ruching that she always wore at her neck, made by her own hands, and she creaked in wide silks. John was brilliant in his blue frock coat and high silk hat, the costume in which he always celebrated the ceremony, if there was not a gale, of taking the sun. The whole family took the sun all right. They were a family good to look upon!

The *Sewall's* family counted twenty-three souls. There were three mates, sixteen sailors, besides the captain and his family. The sailors were dressed out of the ship's chest: stout overalls, dark blue flannel blouses, oilskins, and rubber boots. Captain John's first law was cleanliness. The men radiated it. The captain and fam-

## Captain Abby and Captain John

ily and the mates ate at first table, the men after. The staple food and foundation for all meals was pilot bread, in three-inch squares, grayish, and tougher than canvas. It came in barrels. After that, there was pork and beef and molasses. And after these, if Abby's hand was in—and it generally was—mince and apple pies, to restore a man's soul. All through her years at sea, no matter what silks or satins she wore, Abby Pennell was a housewife before she was anything else. The ship's first lady always did some cooking, just as she always sewed and washed and ironed. Lord only knows how many mutinies that woman staved off with her pumpkin pies!

The *Benjamin Sewall* gleamed with fine mahogany. She was lighted by kerosene lamps and candles. The ship's port and starboard lights were oil. In uncharted waters, where ships were infrequently met, they were not lighted, in order to save oil. Abby had a bath tub, as well as a whole chicken-farm establishment. She often notes proudly in her diaries that she has taken her bath. But her son Fred recalls that he and Arthur took their Saturday evening baths in a half hogshead, on the deck. Grinning sailors doused them from two sides from big canvas buckets, under the evening star. There is something very human and very American about these two small boys being bathed out there in the infinity of the ocean in the Saturday religion of the Yankee race, two small white bodies glimmering against darkening blue eternity! Somehow, that seems as eloquent to me as any Greek frieze of youths carrying sacrifices to Demeter and Athena. Fred says it was lovely when the buckets

## Captain Abby and Captain John

the sailors threw on them were dipped up from the Gulf Stream, but the Pacific buckets made their eyeteeth rattle! The last bucket was always cold as the ocean is three miles down. The boys often stood up together under the deluge. But sometimes not. For a boy of five and one of eleven are as dangerous a combination as trinitrotoluol, and might upset the hogshead, demolish it, the sailors, maybe, and maybe themselves. What one boy does not think of the other will. Abby kept everything else, as well as her boys, shining like a looking-glass. She was neat as a pin and busy as an ant. No floor of her house on the *B. Sewall* was without its rugs, braided by Abby's hands out of her dresses and John's pants. She had pictures to her walls, as well as a sewing machine, and canary cages to her curtained windows. She made a ship a New England house and a complete home.

The vast new ship was like a dream come true. The beauty and comfort and speed of her were a constant wonder and joy to Abby and John. After all the years of seeing barks and brigs go past them, they now were on a vessel that left everything behind. Liverpool to Yokohama in 128 days! And that after five days lost off England becalmed. The *Sewall* passed even the clippers on her route. Handsome as a holiday, she took the old gales that used to damage the *Deborah* on the nose and cut through them like a mackerel hawk, and was out in fair weather before they got used to the foul. She minded the wheel like a pilot sloop, John said. She handled easy for all her great length and tonnage. She

## Captain Abby and Captain John

made a man proud. She was a fine thing to have worked for and lived for, these many years.

The Pennells were a happy family in the Spring of that year 1875, going down the Atlantic along Africa. John had two boys that he said were handsome as the morning and the smartest wife that ever kept house for a captain, he was sure. His life was at high tide. The other Pennell families might be on the ebb, he and Abby were on the crest of their life coasting to comfort and a long and happy age, with children to be proud of. John was forty-seven, at the top of his strength. No man could ask more. John could not look around the corner of time and see what lay ahead. After 1878, the steamers, used until then chiefly for passengers, would quicken up, and size up, too, and they would take over freight. And all that intricate science of making winds from whatever quarter move a great mass along, even against their own strength and will, would begin to fade out into archaeology and join the lost sciences of the Egyptians. John could not see ahead. And so he was happy at the peak of his powers and pride.

John and Abby never saw land once, after England, till Java Head, high beauty burned into every sailor's brain in the past century, rose up like the staircase to Paradise out of the sea, green with leaves by day and lighted by fireflies like wandering stars at night.

"Passed several vessels." "Distance run these 24 hours 253 miles." "Robert's birthday, 49 years." "Twenty-two days from Liverpool to the Line." So the new log runs. It is like sailing the waters bordering heaven. "Barometer falling." A gale to try her out on! Two, three, four weeks of gales. The Atlantic was going to harden this family for their round-the-world picnic right at the beginning. "Terrific squalls . . . tremendous sea." But the *B. Sewall* waded right through it all with only a few sheets of copper, "Muntzes metal," put on at Liverpool, started on her starboard side. A bark in company, "we passed her about night." Another gale, "a heavy sea boarded, staving off port bulworks, stove starboard boat and forward house doors." But the seas did not slow her up much.

"We have had some fearful gales," Abby wrote home. "It seemed as though the ship must go to pieces. I found I did not feel any more safe in a large ship than I did in a small one. She rolls and tumbles about fearfully, and the sea washes right over her all the time in heavy weather. She may be called a wet ship, I think. But the best of all is she is tight and a good sailer. We don't make any vessels astern, and pass everything we see. She has made some splendid runs, and her strength has been tried pretty well this passage." Abby wished she might race her brother Elias, who is now graduated to captain of the fine Pennell ship *Oakland*. "Tell Elias, when you see him, I would like to fall in with the *Oakland* and have all the wind we could carry all sail to! She works well, and steers like a pilot boat, John says."

Five-year-old Freddie watched the green serpents of ocean water coming in under the cabin door. He was always locked in the cabin in a storm. He sat on his berth, the top one. The whole room was going it. It was better than any rocking-horse his father could have bought

## Captain Abby and Captain John

him in Boston. He crowed with delight seeing the water come in and all his mother's braid rugs awash. Freddie took off his shoes, and jumped down and went paddling. He rigged up one shoe as the *B. Sewall*, and let her sail around. Overhead, the oil lamps were swinging like the pendulum on Uncle Robert's clock back in Middle Bays. It was great fun, a gale.

It wasn't for the boys' mother. Abby wrote later to her mother from Yokohama: "I have suffered more with fright this voyage than I ever did before in my life. I never want to go another long voyage." She never meant a single word of this, though. "Gale after gale ... I never saw anything like it. They expected to see her masts go every minute. But she come out of it with but little damage, after all. . . . The wind struck her very sudden, before they could get all sail in, and there was such a noise! Fred began to cry and say, 'I wish the wind not blow so.' But they soon got used to it. For we had no more moderate weather after that till we got into the Trade Winds in the Indian Ocean. We had a month of the worst weather I ever experienced. The ship rolled fearfully and was so heavy the seas would wash right over her. She never was dry for more than a month."

When they were having only a common gale, Freddie and Arthur had high old times at games of slide on their mother's polished floor below the brass steps of the companionway. Each boy got an oval braid rug and sat on it. The roll of the ship carried them back and forth like sixty. They played they were ships. Artie made Freddie be the *Oakland*, and he was the *B. Sewall*, and of course beat Freddie all hollow. They often collided, and the *Oakland* always had to be the ship that went down. Sometimes the real sea water came in. Then it was more like real ships. The boys might get their trousers as wet as their father did his.

The boys liked gales. They did not have school hours then, when gales were on. Fair days, except Sundays of course, mother made them work at reading and writing and doing sums. She kept their noses to the grindstone. She kept regular school hours, too. She could sew and teach at the same time. She put in her bill to the town of Brunswick and drew a teacher's pay, when she got home, for the schooling she gave her children.

A ship was about as good a place as a boy could ever be in. And sea captains probably made the best fathers under the light of the sun. Capt. John often played with his boys. It was an important part of his ritual of the day, in fair weather. He thought it important enough to set it down in the log. "Played with Freddie on the after house."

Freddie liked to get on the end of a rope and make believe he was helping the sailors hoist sail. He and Arthur would rig up a canvas bucket full of dunnage and play it was a sail. They pulled it up and let it fall back by the hour. Freddie had inherited his father's voice. He would sing a song he had picked up from the crew as he and Arthur pulled on their sail:

>   Haul on the bowline,
>   The fore and main top bowline,
>   Haul on the bowline,
>     The bowlin' haul!

## Captain Abby and Captain John

>Haul on the bowline,
>The ship is a-rolling,
>Haul on the bowline,
>  The bowlin' haul!

>Haul on the bowline,
>The main topgallant bowline,
>Haul on the bowline,
>  The bowlin' haul!

And so on for endless stanzas till all the lines on their imaginary ship were tended to.

Fred knew the halyard song, too, *Whisky for My Johnnie:*

>Oh, whisky makes me pawn my clothes,
>  Whisky, Johnnie,
>Whisky gave me a broken nose,
>  Whisky for my Johnnie.

Freddie didn't sing that one when his father was around. For Captain John was a temperance man. Freddie had another song he had picked up from the men at the capstan. He didn't sing this one, either, when Daddy was present:

>In Amsterdam there lives a maid,
>Mark you well what I say,
>In Amsterdam there lives a maid,
>And she is a mistress of her trade.
>I'll go no more a-roving with you, fair maid.

## Captain Abby and Captain John

They hit the bottom of their wide curve around Africa, June 4, but they were well past the bulk of the continent then. The winds were against them. But that meant little to the *Benjamin Sewall*. Great gales came at them, "fearful sea running." But all the harm was a few more strips of copper loosened on the starboard bow. And of course the decks were under water most of the time. Capt. John broached an iron water tank and found salt water had got in and made it brackish. The men showed signs of scurvy. So John began dosing them all with lime juice every day. And he stopped giving the men salt beef and pork for a time. John Jury complained of a bad leg. They saw diving fowls. John saw a whale and let the boys up out of their caulked cabin to have a look at him. He was a sixty-footer. He sailed along with them companionable as could be. Freddie could count the eye-winkers, he said, by his little dark eyes. He went alongside for miles, matching his speed with the *B. Sewall*. Then suddenly he said goodbye, blew and filled the deck with a rainstorm of spray, and nearly blinded Freddie. There was a sound like a thousand choked foghorns. And John Henry Whale was gone to the bottom of the sea for supper. Freddie saw that whale in his sleep a long time after that day.

Freddie's father saw patches of kelp, June 13. Another gale hit them, and a sea boarded their port quarter, loosened the rail, and stove in the forecastle doors. The seamen had a free bath. They made 200 miles in the gale's heart. Mr. Raling, the third mate, "got hurt bad by a sea," and was laid up. So was a sailor. The carpenter sprained his knee. But on June 22, at last,

## Captain Abby and Captain John

John had driven through to good weather. "Opened all shutters and companionway doors, all being caulked in for one month, to keep water out of the cabin." The boys could come out at last and play on the deck.

July 2, Java Head lifted up and smiled upon them.

The tropical night came down like a velvet curtain. But there were mysterious figures in the curtain. It was starred by great fireflies. They felt their way along the velvet through the night. Strange sounds came off the land like unearthly music. And dawn came like a great explosion and showed them they were coasting along by a rainbow. Mountains ran up, incredible layers of green and gold shading off into blue. Iridescent showers trailed islands like pieces of mother of pearl. The sea ran silver and the color of wine. Feathery islands looked like big butterflies resting on azure tablecloths of smooth sea. The ship sailed through a continuous rainbow. The ripples ran out from the bows in long mounds of jewels. Twenty or so ships were in company, each with those ripples of crushed diamonds going out from them. The sun went suddenly down in a world of powdered gold. It was red, and it was gone. Blue evening turned the mountains dark, and then it was black night. They could fairly hear the black curtain rustle down. At nine o'clock, they let go with the steam anchor off Anger Point.

Day exploded again, and John hove anchor and let the ship drift with the current through Sunda Straits. They were close inshore now, and Freddie could see plainly they were in the place where his fairy stories came from. Feather dusters for trees, and somebody had spilled a whole box of jewels down the hill. Only it was little houses of a village. "It done our eyes good," Abby wrote her mother, "to see the green trees. . . . If you had been with us, Sis, you would have a chance to do some drawing and oil painting! The scenery in Java is lovely!"

They drifted to Anger. And Abby added another city to her collection. It was a city that no other Yankee housewife could add to her set, in a few years more, for it would be erased forever by an earthquake and tidal wave as though it had never been thought of. John let his anchor go.

And in a second the water was alive with little boats bearing down on them from every side. A hundred dugouts crowded with naked men standing and singing like sirens. A whole floating city of boats! Men right out of fairyland came alongside in boats down to the water's edge with golden nuggets and wisps of the rainbow. Fruit for the first time in three months! Melons as big as their heads, grapes the size of plums at home, yams and sweet potatoes, coconuts and bananas. Bananas!— Fred will remember the taste of those bananas to his last hour. For he ate them till he foundered! Everybody ate them. But nobody so many as Freddie. He made a business of it. The ship's family cut into coconuts and drank the cool milk from the hairy bottles. And there was good water at last, after the stringy and brackish water in the casks. They filled up all their tanks. John bought three hundred bunches of green bananas and hung them on the yard arms to ripen, high enough to be out of the boys' way.

## Captain Abby and Captain John

While they ate bananas in Sunda Straits, Abby wrote her mother about the boys: "Artie and Fred have both got along nicely and have been well. But both have been homesick at times, and will set up and talk about home and what they had that was good to eat at Grampa's, and what Yarney and Ella done. Artie never will make a sailor. Fred is fat as a little pig, and the greatest little rogue you ever saw. They are both favorites with all hands. They are well. Was not seasick but one day. Fred is hearty, but Artie is about the same as at home."

No mutinies, this voyage. They are all one happy family. "We have a good peaceable crew and good officers. Mr. Sewall, the mate, we like very much. So we have been favored in many things."

In the midst of islands like the Islands of the Hesperides, and with the rainbow's end in her lap, Abby's thoughts are in the humble places of home, at the Bowdoin Commencement and in the hayfields of Great Island! "I would like to know how you all are at home, and what doing. My thoughts have been with you in Brunswick the last thing at night and the first in the morning. Who is living in the house we left? Is all living and well, of our neighbors? Give my love to them all when you see them. Next week will be Commencement Week! Is Elias at home? How beautiful it is at home now, almost haying time! And all sweating to it, I suppose."

The anchor came up, and they were on their way next morning with the big sun. Fred still recalls how those golden bunches of bananas looked swinging back and forth, back and forth, at the yard arms as the ship

## Captain Abby and Captain John

rolled. Fred's eyes were on them big as saucers. He could not get them out of his mind. He could not reach them, all right. But he had his friends who could, and they wouldn't let a small boy suffer for the lack of a banana or two. The crew were taller and used to living in the rigging night and day. And they also liked bananas. So the bunches of fruit grew smaller night by night. The bananas disappeared at a great rate. Soon some of the bunches were only stems. Freddie's friends obliged him in the daytime, not to mention obliging themselves at night. So it was natural that Capt. John should have a sad note to set down in his log: "Several of the crew and 2 mates attacked by cholera morbus. Also Freddie." The red-handed were all revealed. The Old Boy's chickens had come home to roost! The thinned bunches of bananas swung unmolested after that, keeping time with the waves. The patients all recovered.

It was tricky sailing now. The sea was sown with islands as thick as caraway seeds in a cooky. There were shoals and reefs like teeth in a shark. But it was fair weather, and John threaded his way through the hazards of Malay waters and out into the wicked currents of the China Sea as though he had sailed these waters all his life. It grew very hot, and the tar boiled in the seams of the deck. Freddie blistered his bare feet. "Thermometer in the coolest place 88," noted John. They sailed up the Formosa Channel. Was there no whisper from the rocks there where twenty-eight years later the *Benjamin Sewall* would go to her grave? They met several barks, two junks, and a steamer. In they went between Aknisi and Suwa Sima and burst out into

## Captain Abby and Captain John

the North Pacific. It was squally off the coast of Japan, July 27. They took pilot and came to anchor in Yokohama Roads, July 29.

They commenced discharging their coal, August 2, and finished, August 30—1972 tons of it. The Japanese coolies made the Welsh dust fly. "We are discharging quite fast," Abby wrote her mother. "It is very warm, and we are all black with coal dust. Fred is black as a little negro. He is fat and hearty, and Artie is, too. They have been homesick at times. Artie has wished himself at home many times. We have all been well. John is very thin, and I am myself. It was a great change for me to stop working or stop doing housework. I have to wash all the time for the children. They keep me busy."

The boys' mother wrote that business was very dull at Yokohama. They did not know what they would carry next or where they would go. Again, on the edge of a new wonderland, Abby's mind was on Great Island: "I suppose you are hard to work haying. Artie said the other day, he wished he could be down to Grampa's and help him hay."

The long silence of half a year from home had been broken at last, as usual, with news of death. Abby had the passing of two friends to bewail. One lament was for Arabella, wife of John's Brother Joseph. Abby had often felt very much at home at her house. "Poor Arabella! I cannot realize she is gone from our sight forever. I should have thought of everyone else before her. What a loss to Joseph and Josie! He must feel very lonely, poor man. But they have a good home now. It is

## Captain Abby and Captain John

not like his own, though. We miss their letters. They always wrote us long letters. We received two long letters from Arabella before we sailed from Liverpool. I trust she is happier. She was a good woman. It must be some consolation to Joseph to have her die so happy. Who is to go next? I hope not any more while we are gone." And Abby is bitter against their Skolfield friends and rivals across the bay over the loss of her friend Capt. Jordan. One pair of Skolfield ears must have burned, August 9, 1875: "Capt. Jordan, I suppose, is lost. It seems very sad to see a man throw away his life by going in old leaky vessels. He knew what she was, and told John he did not want to go in her. And John told him not to go in her to please anyone. But he went, and is lost. I pity his wife. If Capt. Clem Skolfield has any conscience, I should think he would feel bad."

Brother Elias is married now, to a Harpswell girl, as a Harpswell man ought to be, a Purinton of Cundy's Harbor, and he evidently has started right in on his family. "Hope we shall get letters from Elias and Min," Abby writes. "Am sorry to hear they are going a long voyage again. It will be some time before we shall see each other again. Am glad to hear Min is so well. Wish we might meet somewhere. I pity Min," Abby writes out of the midst of her coal dust, "to have to be on board of a ship discharging coal in a hot climate with children. It is dreadful. Give our love to them."

John wrote his "Father and Mother and Sister Reed" from Japan that same mail, too. And he put his letter

## Captain Abby and Captain John

with Abby's in an envelope marked "Via San Francisco and overland," so their letter would not go blundering off down around the Horn. There was a railroad right across America now. Distances were lessening. John crowed over the new ship and the records he had broken: "123 days from the Smaller Irish Channel. A good passage for a ship as deep as we was, 22 feet. The best passage from England here for a deep loaded ship. Beat some of the tea clippers. Had some very bad weather, especially in the South Atlantic and Southern Indian Ocean. We had very heavy weather. Could hardly tell the ship from the ocean, at times, but for the masts and rigging. And now we are here well, the children safe, which will lighten your hearts, I know, to overflowing pleasure." John wrote that he had telegraphed his safe arrival to Sewall, Day and Company, Boston, so the folks at home must have heard, long before this letter reached them, that John had arrived safe. Distances were dwindling to nothing. John was keeping step with the new world and its modern improvements. He wrote that he was having a hard time finding something to carry home: "I cannot get an offer of any kind. Ship too large for Tea. Small vessels better. But even dull for them. I expect I shall go to Manila seeking. San Francisco dull, no prospect there at present."

John also expressed his disappointment that the new house he had acquired in Brunswick, on Union Street, the Hospital today, had not been rented yet. The weather was sultry. He expected every minute to get a typhoon. "They blow with violent force here and cause immense amount of damage. Sept. is the worst month, and when I shall be leaving."

He mentioned his brother's bereavement: "How very sudden! How sad and lonely for him! I pity him and poor Josie." And John wound up with thoughts, like Abby's, that ran on the haying going on under his feet at the other side of the world in the fifty-foot hayfields of my Great Island: "Suppose you are now about through haying. Hope you have got along well and get a good crop. It is too bad for you to always be alone on your Farm. The Best thing you can do"—here is a man's typical and universal solution for everything— "is to get some smart young man to come and take Mary [Sis] for a wife and make him do your work and carry on the Farm, so you can have an easier time. Hoping this will find you all well, with love to you all and also Friends, I remain yours ever, J. D. Pennell."

John didn't go to Manila to seek a cargo. He loaded a general cargo of whatever he could lay hands on: tea, fireworks, toys, and Japanese knick-knacks, and headed for the United States, for Oregon, the wheat center of the world at that time. But before he left, he had taken the boys for a ride in a rickshaw and bought them some colored paper lanterns. And Abby had let herself go on enough silks to cover all her friends at home and half of Great Island besides! They sailed from Yokohama on September 10, 1875.

They dropped the Jap pilot, with the wind "flying all around the compass," probably in preparation for that typhoon of John's, off Cape Sagamia. September

## Captain Abby and Captain John

12, 243 miles. September 13, 255 miles. They bowled right along in the new waters of the North Pacific. 227 miles. A gale, for variety's sake, September 20, and all the ritual of handling their vast new sails, more than enough in total spread to cover Abby's father's hayfields!—397 yards of cotton in a single sail, the foresail, made by Emmons and Houghton, Liverpool—in the teeth of the wind and in six shakes of a Spring lamb's tail! An exquisite litany of hard work that reads like Choctaw to us who have allowed one of the finest sciences to go into limbo: "At 3 PM reefed Topsl. and stowed Mizen Topsl. 4 PM reefed and stowed Mainsail. Reefed foresail and stowed upper fore and main topsls. 7:30 stowed foresail, fore and mizen topsls. Hove to on starboard tack. Blowing heavy from ESE. Middle hours heavy gale ESE. 10 AM change wind from SW. Set fore and Mizen Topsls. Course East. Ends fresh gales SW. Heavy sea." September 21, 251 miles. Next day, 257. The next, 272. The typhoon would have to travel to catch them now! They were flying. 245, 244, 146—another gale cut them to this. But as chipper as ever the 28th, and 256 miles. The days went by all alike. Sunlight, and Abby sewing with rainbows of Japanese silks on her lap as she rocked in her rocking-chair, two fine boys playing on the deck and the roof of their house. No ship in company. A really big ocean and plenty sailing room this time! One gale more, taken in stride. And John made Cape Cook, October 9, and Vancouver's Island the following day. The Pacific Ocean in a pretty leap of one month! The *Deborah* had taken six weeks from Trieste to Gibraltar! This was

## Captain Abby and Captain John

riding on the back of an angel of light, and no fooling! Only a fast steamer could keep up with the *B. Sewall* today.

It took almost as long to get into port as it had to cross the Pacific! John struck a thick fog and felt his way down the West Coast. "No telling when we shall get the sun again. Judged the ship to be off Columbia River." He heard breakers on October 16, judged that he was off Shoalwater Bay, and lit out of there on a tack to the southwest in the fog. The fog lifted next day, he went in near land, peering. Made out a can buoy striped black and white. More breakers, flew out again. "Unable to see any pilot or be sure of position. Off to sea again, tacked back and forth." "No signs of any pilot." More tacking. "No prospects of any pilot." He might as well be sailing in the land of the dead. The day following, the same groping all over again. This time John saw a lighthouse, "supposed to be Tokey light." Still no sun to tell John where he was at. Next day, after more feeling in the fog, he felt a pilot, and the steam tug *Astoria* towed him in over the bar to Astoria, Oregon. John subtracted a day from his life and made his October 19 into October 18, "being the difference of time in sailing from East Longitude of 180 degrees into West Longitude or Sailing around the World. And so," John added in his log, "we have 2 Mondays." I hope to goodness Abby did not wash twice! Being a New Englander, she probably did!

John swopped his knick-knacks and tea for good, solid and honest American wheat, 2000 tons of it, hove anchor on November 24, and away for Liverpool,

## Captain Abby and Captain John

around his old friend, the Horn. He noted his eighteenth wedding anniversary. Fine weather, and flying along fast. Spoke the ship *Itaska* of Bath, Maine, near the Line. Oiled the poop deck. Near the Line the *B. Sewall* struck what helped spell the end for sail: doldrums. The doldrums mean all life ends here, on sailing vessels. The sails droop, and she sticks fast to the ocean. The *B. Sewall* stood still eight days. While waiting for the wind, John amused himself by putting out a bottle with his latitude and longitude in it. "This is the hardest time I ever had in Doldrum, if so it is. Hope every hour and minute for a fairer and better breeze." One can understand the grim force in the Maine phrase, used on the land now, of somebody's being in the doldrums. It means being no more use to himself or anyone else than a last year's crow's nest. And that's pretty useless.

A breeze came at last, and John gave the crew a holiday because it was Christmas and because they were crossing the Line, too, killing two occasions with one stone! The day after New Year's, Mr. Raling, the second mate, nearly finished them. John came up on his watch just as a squall hit them from the east and "caught him with all light sail set. Came near capsizing the Ship. Striking Ship hard alee got off light Sails and got Ship off and wore round to South." A close shave! John told Mr. Raling things he would never forget. Then he went back to work on the wheel house. John started keeping a diary of his own on January 4. He caught water in barrels that day. There was a ring around the moon, January 6. John oiled the main deck. Freddie had a fine time skating on it. Far, far south,

## Captain Abby and Captain John

but it was Summer down here and fine weather. Albatrosses began to appear. On January 26, they swept around the Horn. Freddie saw Horn Mountain clear as a crystal. Not many Maine boys ever saw it, for all they cut their teeth and learned to creep while teetering round it on a ship. "I saw it," Captain John wrote in his diary.

They turned north and flew faster. "The girls have got us by the tow rope," the sailors told Freddie. That was why they were going faster now. Sailors always said, on the homeward trip around the Horn, that their sweethearts were pulling them home.

She has dipped her yards under, hove to off the Horn,
   In the fog and the floes she has drifted forlorn,
Becalmed in the Doldrums a week long she lay,
   But the girls have got hold of the tow rope today.

Freddie couldn't understand it all, being only five and a half. But he was glad they were going faster. They went so fast they almost collided with a bark on the starboard tack, January 29.

And Freddie saw his first albatrosses close to that same day. He had seen the birds sailing along overhead, sailing for hours without flexing their narrow wings. But now ten of the most graceful of all flying things settled right on the deck at Freddie's feet. They let him come up to them pretty close, rolling their innocent blue eyes at him. They were much bigger than a five-year-old boy. They weren't afraid. Fred went up to stroke one, but it lifted its beak and snapped a pair of

## Captain Abby and Captain John

sea shears that were strong enough to take off a boy's hand at a single clip. The crew all roared. Freddie ran howling for mother's skirts. After that, he kept his distance. He sat on the deck with the strange and lovely visitors all around him. The sailors ran and got pork chunks and hard-bread and fed the albatrosses. The birds swallowed down huge pieces of the salt pork and winked their eyes for more. They walked about ungainly and shouldered up nearer to the source of supply. The men talked to them and fooled with them for hours. They became good friends. It was a mighty pretty sight seeing the men and the birds and the little boy visiting. But the men said it was time for good albatrosses to be going on home at last. And they began to help them go one by one. They did that by shoving them to the rail and boosting them over. These vast birds could not fly off the deck. It wasn't long enough for them to get a start. They had to take off from the sea. They struck the ocean with loud thumps, shook themselves to see if they were all there, and then struck out with their wide wings and webbed feet. Once they were clear of the wash of the ship, they began to rise, one by one. They lifted themselves with their enormous wings beating the air and the water. They beat harder and harder and kicked back with their feet. Four long lines of splashes showed where their wings and feet hit the waves. They went for fifty yards before they were off the water, then they slanted up low into the wind, got altitude, and wheeled off on their way to live in the air for another week or two, till the next queer birds, bigger even than they were and with longer wings,

## Captain Abby and Captain John

should come along, and they could ride on their backs and take strange tasty food from little creatures, crawling on the big birds' backs, that were neither bird nor seal nor good red herring. They went off full of peace and salt pork of New England and strange stories to tell their grandchildren as they floated along by the Southern Cross on a cold Winter evening in June!

Fred would always remember those lovely things, so alive and so wild and yet friendly, wheeling sure as a planet wheels in astounding majesty through the air. He would always remember them along with the dark saw-tooth of a mountain that his father had told him was the end of the world, with the shape and loneliness of Horn Mountain.

But some of the albatrosses that day did not go home to the water. The men had picked out the biggest ones, the grandpappies of the lot, and herded them into one corner of the deck. Now they sent them home in a different way, to a home strange even to one of these vast birds so used to loneliness and strangeness. The men got great clubs, and they sailed in and knocked the gentle things on the head, right before the surprised little boy's eyes. They knocked them on the head and skinned them and took their wide wings to put up in the forecastle for decorations. The deck ran with blood. One bird had a wing spread of ten feet. They stripped the wonderful feathers off, hide and all. Stray feathers floated like little ships on the red pools of blood. Freddie thought it was a shame. He felt like crying, but he didn't cry, for he was fascinated by seeing what was going on. He had seen his father kill a rat. But this

## Captain Abby and Captain John

wasn't the same thing at all. He had never seen death come so close and look, some way, so good to look at. One of the men gave him one of the ten-footer's wings. It was still warm. Freddie ran and put it up over his berth. And he felt odd and like a man doing it.

A gale with all the fixings of lightning-fast work on the yards, on February 6. Then good weather again. "Freddie and I was playing on top of the house today," Captain John noted in the diary. John saw "plenty of whale feed," the 9th, and set the observation down in the log. He described it more at length in the diary: "Last night we passed through large quantities of whale feed, which was of a reddish color, somewhat like blood but not so deep." John noted also that the days were growing shorter. A shark came around. John got a hook and some salt pork. He sent off a fine dinner to the shark. The pirate took it, and he took the hook and all and came back smiling up at John for more. They overtook a bark and a ship. "On deck most of the day playing with Freddie," the diary runs. One bark kept up with them several days, but they shook her at last. They passed barks, ships, brigs, and brigantines. They spoke the ship *Lydia Skolfield* from home, bound for Falmouth from Callao with a load of guano. And didn't John's own brother-in-law, Captain Dunning, come over and make them a call and borrow some flour and bread! And probably some of Abby's mince pies. No getting away from a Dunning, even down here in the southern hemisphere! They had a lovely call and heard all the news of Middle Bays and Great Island. Next day John lost sight of the *Lydia Skolfield*, astern. No

## Captain Abby and Captain John

keeping up with a Pennell these days! Ships were all around them thicker than thieves. There was hardly elbow room in the South Atlantic. Not so many Yankees, though, as in the old days before the war. John began painting the ship, to while away the time and to keep the crew out of mischief.

"Some bonitas around," reads John's diary.

John and his boys went a-fishing. No round-the-world family picnic would have been complete without that. They ran into a school of bonitas one sunny morning. The sailors got out the fish lines. The best man got the best line, took it in one hand and a bag in the other, straddled the jib-boom, and worked along on his bottom with his legs as handy as hands. When the sailor got out where the jib-boom clears the prow, he settled down there with his feet supported by the brackets, lit his pipe and settled back to home comfort with his line trailing in the sea below. He was as comfortable as in a rocking-chair. In no time at all, his line whistled taut. The man sat up and took notice. This way and that, the line sawed the water. Finally the sailor braced back his shoulders, and hove up his catch. A great fish, blue as the sea, twinkled in a lovely arc in the sunlight, the man flapped at him with his free hand, and he fell smack into the mouth of the dangling bag. All the crew and the boys cheered. Another fish leapt his arc into the sailor's pouch.

Other people clamored to try it. And Artie loudest of all. John let his older son go out. A big sailor went with him and established him right on his smaller back cush-

## Captain Abby and Captain John

ions, and came back and left Artie alone in his glory. Arthur got his bite in a minute's time. He held on like a good fellow, and let the bonita have his tear. Then everybody yelled, "Land him!" Artie took a big brace, leaned back and brought up his fish. He didn't have any bag. The bonita sparkled through the air and landed right smack in Artie's lap. The surprised boy stared at him. He wasn't able to do a thing about it. He just sat. Sat there with an uncomfortable feeling in his lap that made him think of babyhood, with the yard-long fish lying across his knees. The bonita was as surprised as Arthur was. The sailors roared. One of them started shinnying out at last. But the bonita got tired of his perch, slapped the boy a big slap, dove into the sea, and broke off the hook and away.

Freddie howled and danced for a chance to try his luck, too. But his father wouldn't let him go. They retrieved Artie. And then the sailors filled the deck with flopping fresh suppers. Capt. John let Freddie hold one fish he had hooked on his line, and the child's arms were strained at their sockets as the fish sawed the line back and forth. He was glad to let his father land the catch. But that fish was his fish. He even tried to pick it up when it got quiet in the sun. Abby cooked it, and Freddie ate himself nearly out of his jacket that night.

Another day they caught bonitas by trailing a line with a hook baited with a piece of John's red flannels. The line was looped over a slender stick fastened upright to the rail. When the stick snapped suddenly and fell down, John was sure Mr. Benjamin Bonita was there on the flannel, waiting to come to tea. John had to look lively before the fish got a purchase on the line and parted it and got away.

They crossed the Line, for the fourth time this picnic, on March 8, 1876, and saw among the fleet around them a skysail-yard ship, "crowded with studinsails, water and ring-tail sails." It was a regular circus of a ship! They got into the North East Trades. John gave the deck two coats of white lead. It took 150 pounds. They tethered the boys that day in the cabin!

One fine day, when there was a following breeze and his father was taking the sun with his sextant, tall hat and all, Freddie looked over the rail and saw six dolphins below him. Six rainbows shedding green and gold beads by the million in the sun. It looked exactly as if somebody had broken a bag of beads open and was spilling them all over the waves. The fish came out of the water together, alive down to the last point of a fin, curved together, and went into a wave's side, came out through together on the other side, flashed abreast in the sun, and into the green again as fast and final as arrows. It made the boy catch his breath, it was so pretty! Freddie shouted to his father to come see. John went over and took a look. He ran for his harpoon. He threw it, and missed. Threw it, and missed again. Mr. Raling, who had nearly upset them that day, threw over a line with a rag on the hook. A dolphin went for it, took it, and away in a shower of bubbles like sparks. And Mr. Raling nearly lost both arms. They cracked at their sockets. He held on and braced his feet in the scuppers. He held the green sea stallion for maybe half

## Captain Abby and Captain John

a minute, leaving his heel marks in Middle Bays oak. If the line hadn't snapped at last, no knowing but that dolphin might have dragged them the length of the Equator!

John and the men often did harpoon dolphins, though. And ate them. They made excellent eating. John harpooned porpoises, too, their northern cousins, but they were nowhere near so tasty or tender.

"Two or three schools of flying fish," wrote John in the diary.

Freddie saw flying fish almost every day. You looked for them most at the bow, right where the bone in her mouth sent up tiny rainbows. And other times the dolphins would come chasing them and going into the air right after them, and snap them up a yard above the sea. Sometimes the flying fish flew right on to the deck and fluttered about with azure wings at Freddie's toes like watery butterflies. They often ate these butterflies of the sea. It seemed sort of a pity, they were so bright-eyed and smart. But they tasted fine. Much like the smelts of Middle Bay. Abby baked them the same way, with pork scraps crisscrossed on them and binding them together in the pan.

The days ran on, and every one of them was a picnic. They burst into the Sargasso Sea, graveyard of ships and cradle of all Atlantic's infants, from eels to sea serpents. "I see," John wrote in the diary, "some seaweed called Sargasso weed. We caught a piece tonight and there was some tiny little crabs in it, with a kind of yellow berries." At times, the weed was so thick it was like sliding through the meadows of Great Island.

## Captain Abby and Captain John

"Long windrows which the ship went through." Green as home. The sailors rigged up hooks of heavy wire and let them down and brought up whole forests of seaweed for the boys. There were those crabs by the hundred in those forests. And Freddie hunted them out and let them run over his hands. His father fixed him up an aquarium on the deck. Freddie kept a lot of them in there. He and Arthur matched them up and had fights.

One day Mr. Raling had hauled up a big clump of seaweed and forgot about it. He was walking around, big as Billy-Be-Damned, and he stepped right on the clump. His feet shot out from under, and he sat down hard. It rattled the whole ship. Mr. Raling was a heavy man, and his sizable bottom made a big impact when he sat down that far. Freddie yelled for joy. The mate was hopping, hopping mad. But Capt. John laughed, too, till the tears ran down.

Another day they fell in with a whole host of some kind of jellyfish with sails on them going along over the water. They stood out of water six inches. Their sails were like the wings of the fairies in Freddie's fairytale books. The sailors had a name for them, men-of-war. Fred wished he had one for his aquarium. But they never caught one.

In all these lovely days of whitecaps and sun, and all through this holiday that girdled the globe, the Pennell boys came very close to the sea. They dipped their hands in it. They knew it close to. They sat down and wet their seats in it in rough weather. They heard the winds and saw them at work in the white sails they could almost touch. No boys in the world now, no mat-

## Captain Abby and Captain John

ter how often they cross the ocean, will ever be so close to such a dangerous and exciting and beautiful a playmate as Fred and Arthur had every hour of the day. Civilization and steam have taken us a long and high way above such danger and loveliness. We have let steamers erase the wind, as our automobiles have erased our hills. No boy knows now the ecstasy I knew, as a boy in a buggy, of feeling the land go uphill and down. No boys today can know the sea as these boys knew it, so near they could reach out and touch it with their hands. And few boys, even in 1876, had such a father to play with them and their dangerous shining playmate as John Pennell when he played with his two sons. Such fun comes only once or twice a century.

The Pennells passed ship after ship. John overtook a large iron one with skysail yards, and passed her easily. Wood would beat iron any day! forever! They lost the Trades, March 16. They met an English ship showing a "Rendezvous Telegraph," whatever that was. And John added in the diary that she had a windmill between mainmast and mizzen. They "signalized" the famous clipper ship *The Three Brothers*, 93 days out of San Francisco for Liverpool, Lat. 32-44 N, Long. 39-01 W. Gales hit them in the middle Forties. But on April 11, John wore the ship to the northwest, and there on their lee were the mountains of North Wales. Holyhead light blinked at them at nine o'clock that night, and the Pennells, still warm with their holiday in a stolen, double Summer, took their pilot in a storm of snow. John tried to dock that night "but was sent to the river." The tide was too low in the Mersey. He docked

## Captain Abby and Captain John

next day at East Waterloo Dock, ready to discharge his 2000 tons of wheat for its consignees, Barflow, Williams and Company, 19 James Street, Liverpool.

John walked around the docks a while, waiting to unload. He saw a wire-rigged ship. They all went out to Sefton Park and saw a lake, "and there was ducks and geese in it, and there was boys in it sailing boats, yachts, and schooners." I bet there was! If there ever were water without boys and boats in it, I don't know the kind. John's boys were scornful of these British ones, having the *B. Sewall* for their plaything. John carefully noted the weather each day, though in dock. On Sunday, May 30, the whole Pennell family went to a Sunday School in Liverpool.

The long holiday was not done even yet. There was one more ocean to cross. They got 2000 tons of coal and headed for Philadelphia, May 18, 1876. John had a surprise ending for his family. They picked up two new mates, Mr. J. H. Caton of New Orleans and Mr. William H. Clark of New York—to strike a proper balance between the North and the South—and Mr. Raling could go and look elsewhere for more ships to capsize. The Pennells flew through a wilderness of vessels, passed a "large gun boat ram," met six ships, four barks, and two brigs—all bound for Europe; met six more barks another day, were among the Grand Banks fishermen before you could say Jack Robinson, picked up pilot and hove anchor twelve miles below Philadelphia, June 17, just 29 days from Liverpool. The Atlantic was a fish pond to this new queen ship of Middle Bays!

And to cap the climax of the year-and-a-half holi-

THE SHIP *BENJAMIN SEWALL*

## Captain Abby and Captain John

day, Capt. John Pennell took his whole family to the big doings in the City of Brotherly Love, the first American world's fair, the Philadelphia Centennial Exposition! John had planned the whole thing a long time ahead as a surprise. It went off like clockwork. This made three world's fairs for Abby and John, for they had done the Crystal Palace and the London Exposition before. Abby was in ecstasies over the elegant assemblage of Victorian beauty and utility at Philadelphia. John was pleased, too. Freddie saw a steam engine running a "walking beam," and was scared almost out of his wits by a steam whistle. It nearly took the tops of people's heads off. It was one of the most eloquent prophecies of the loudness of the mechanized, brave new world of the future!

Abby has left her fine touch on this long holiday. She decorated the inside covers of her husband's logbook of 1875–76 with some of her best spatter work. In case you are ignorant of this fine art work of our grandmothers, it is done with a fine brush full of black paint drawn across the teeth of a comb. You put down the floral or whatever design you want on your paper, you draw the brush across the comb a few times, lift up your pressed flower, and there it lies argent in a field dotted sable. It is delicate work and looks like our dainty Victorian grandmothers themselves. Abby did a piece of Sargasso seaweed for John, what looks like a banana leaf, and a graceful spray of some other plant surmounted by the Cross. It was like her, lacework and piety together! She got all the designs on upside down. She didn't look inside to see how the text lay. Maybe

## Captain Abby and Captain John

the French trade mark misled her. It is upside down, too. Or maybe John is the one to blame, for Abby may have put the design on before he put a single mark in the log. Anyway, Abby's designs are beautiful, right side up or down! So the masculine chronicle here has its sweet feminine frame.

# 18

## Earthquake, Loup-Cervier, and Reunion

A MONTH AT HOME resting up from the wonders of the future world, and helping with the Great Island haying, and John was ready for the sea again.

This time, he left his family home. It was the first and last and only time he ever did so. But he felt they needed a rest after their long holiday on the ocean. He established them in a great sea captain's house on Park Row, one house from School Street, and a Skolfield for good company, overlooking the dubious trickle of Mall Brook, and he was off for 'Frisco. Abby felt awfully being left behind. So did the boys, especially Freddie. John cut two tresses of Abby's hair, coiled them up in a folded paper, and put them next to his heart. Two rings of life to keep him safe on the oceans! "August 3, 1876, parted with dear wife and children."

John left Queen Street, Philadelphia, August 8, and sailed down past Cape Henlopen, near where he had piled the *Deborah* high and dry on the shore years ago. Faint and baffling airs kept him within 150 miles of the Delaware Capes after five days. Then a real breeze. "A lonesome Sunday," with no Abby there. But Monday brought a gale to take up John's mind. "Three weeks ago this morning I left home and wife and children. O, what a lonesome three weeks it has been for me!" This note runs like a refrain through all the latitudes and longitudes of the log. "O how I would like to see dear ones at Home!" A near collision with a gigantic bark. But Abby's hair was coiled over John's heart, and he escaped. John saw a "very bright star" right overhead at noonday, the last day of August. A meteor, or Abby's spirit? Who can say! An eclipse of the moon, September 4. "Suppose Arthur and Freddie commence going to school today."

They did. And didn't they go to the Brunswick Grammar School where I myself would sit, homesick for Lost Paradise Farm, woebegone and wretched, twenty-seven years later! They hated it. So did I. So would any boy who had known the freedom of five seas or of my Great Island universe! It was like putting dragon-flies in a bottle!

John spotted a case of peaches broken into in the half-deck and nineteen cans taken, just this side of the Equator. He was 38 days to the Line. Good winds at last. "O if I could only see loved ones at home today, what would I give! To me it is a lonesome day."

Freddie was tying a girl's pigtails to his ink-well cover. He was getting acclimated to town.

John bent his Cape Horn sails. He had sails especially made for that place. He hit a stiff "Pampero" on October 5. He set down the observation, October 22, that this was the "hardest chance" he had ever had to get to the tip of South America.

Freddie was home from Topsham Fair, with a whole

## Captain Abby and Captain John

houseful of McGinty's babies. And he had just been down on his grandfather's farm on Great Island picking the ancestors of the cranberries I would pick on my father's marsh-meadow under Misery Hill.

John made out the peaks of lonesome Tierra del Fuego, October 25. It was 74 days he had taken to the Horn, and he was disgusted. There was no seeing that elusive peak this time. It had drawn its gales about its shoulders and howled unseen. Around went John, October 27, and headed up. He unbent his Horn sails and bent the old ones, November 7. It was Election Day at home, he noted. Three days of doldrums. 104 days out. "A hard chance," wrote John. "Where are the SE Trades?" He got them at last, but very faint. Over the Equator, December 6. After one day of good wind, John wrote sarcastically, "Sailing distance down to the old mark again. That is *Small*." Three days of calms. "This is hard." It wasn't the ship's fault. It was the wind's. San Francisco at last, 152 days out, January 8, 1877. A hard "norther" swept down on the harbor. It damaged a great many vessels, but not John. He had Abby's hair over his heart. John commenced discharging on January 12.

Freddie was snowballing on the other edge of the United States. And Abby was cutting out a new dress.

John hauled out of San Francisco for his old port of Callao on February 13. It was guano again. Too bad, for such a fine lady as the *B. Sewall* was! But business was business. John passed the ship *Elwell* after a race of two days. That warmed his heart a little. "Lonesome Sunday," five days out. The steward was laid up. Almost at the Line, and the doldrums came, two livid weeks of them! John got over the Line, March 6. He opened a case of salmon. "Very bad. Tins blown, and those that appeared good salmon, bad." The fish came from Hanley and Snow, San Francisco. Something to take up when John got back to that overblown town! On March 7, John "broke a wish Bone with the mate, got the longest piece." Anybody in the wide world could guess what John's wish would be. Sure enough: "Wished to meet Abby in Callao." If wishes had been horses that Spring day, Abby Pennell would have got the biggest jarring of her life! The steward got laid up again. John turned the cook out of the galley into the forecastle and put the steward in his place. Maybe the steward could cook. But no, the steward got under the weather again, and the cook had to be put back. John swopped them around again twelve days later! April 17, John made Callao and went into quarantine till the doctor gave him his bill of health.

John began a new log. He ran for the Haunillios guano bed, and made "a very good passage" of sixteen days. Wednesday, May 9, 1877, John got out his ballast and took the first launch load of fertilizer aboard. Maybe the fine lady *B. Sewall* had a secret understanding with the clean rocks and elemental fires deep under that remote spot in the far Pacific. Maybe she was insulted with this malodorous cargo. Maybe it was merely blind chance. Anyway, at about half past eight that quiet evening a good part of the mountains on Haunillios Island disappeared all at once into the sea. The mountains disappeared with a roll of thunder like the

## Captain Abby and Captain John

cracking of earth's foundations on the Judgment Day. The drums of doom began to beat a steady and mighty tattoo. Flames ran down the mountains that were left. The sea rose up in a new range of mountains and came hurtling in on the shore. The twenty-eight vessels in the harbor ran uphill and crashed together. They slipped dizzily downhill and buried themselves to their lower yards in crazed waves. The screams of dying men and women could be heard even above the rushing together of mountains and sea. There was a sickening sense of all steady things being spun in, somehow, on their centers. Hell opened suddenly in the Pacific.

The *B. Sewall* snapped her anchor cable like twine, spun in a great arc. John Pennell went prone on his face. Stupendous and unendurable sound rang in his brain. John Pennell all his life had been very susceptible to earthquakes. Something inside his head could sense even the slight ones far below the sea. And they made him deadly sick. This moment his head was a furnace of molten brass. His lovely ship, the peak of his life, with her wheel spinning wildly above him, went up an evil sudden hill and locked yards with another vessel, splintered and cracked, then she went down the hill, buried herself in water, spinning giddily. But she came up again, shook tons of doom off her shoulders, and rocked hurt but saved. John felt the cold sea run off his shoulders, and he rose up, too. For John Pennell had two strong loops of life on his heart, and they had saved him from destruction.

John wrote the earthquake, with the heat still burning terribly in his head, into his log: "About 8:20 PM,

## Captain Abby and Captain John

the ship began to tremble by the shock of an earth quake, and immediately came on terribly, the ship shaking terribly, and with a fearful noise in the air and on shore from the rocks rolling down the mountain. The ship began to swing around rapidly, and by a tidal wave that came on. Ship rushing back and forth, swinging around and around, taking her anchors at a speed, I should judge, of 10 to 15 knots. The Norwegian bark *Atlantic* cut across and fouled on my starboard bow and fore rigging, fouling anchors and chains. We continued together all night, surging together, carrying away cat-head channels, chains, damaging ship's sides very badly, carrying away jib-boom and gear, fore topgalnmast, etc., etc, damaging ship very much. Swinging around and around all night. The shocks following every few minutes in a lighter form, and continuing on in the same way in the morning of Thursday, the 10th. Got out stern anchor with about 540 fathom line. Slipped the starboard anchor with 75 fathom chain. And got clear from the Norwegian bark and clear from the fleet, and let go the port anchor with 50 fathom chain. The sight and the noise of the ships crushing together, the falling of spars, and the hollering of people was most terrible. Words cannot describe it. And the scene next morning was a sad one. The whole fleet lying damaged, more or less in hull and spars. And total losses and loss of life was mournful. The tidal wave swept away nearly the whole settlement on shore, the landing mole, the Governor Buildings, etc., etc. The noise sounded like broken quick crashes of thunder, only of one continuation, for some time, I don't know

## Captain Abby and Captain John

how long. The tumbling of the rocks down the mountain and the flashes of fire flying from them was most terrible. No description can make it realized to any one. What a terrible night it was! It seemed that the whole mountain was going to tumble and bury ships and all for ever."

A ship from Bath, Maine, the *Geneva*, rode right up into the town and wedged between houses, and her Captain McLoon escaped over the roof tops before she went to pieces. John Pennell listed the vessels that were a total loss: besides the American *Geneva*, the *Conference, Conway Castle, Avenmore*—all English; the "Store" ship. Those that were damaged were: Americans, the *Benjamin Sewall*, the *Resolute*, the *Theobald;* and English, the *Jeremiah*, the *Thompson*, the *William Levitt*, the *King Celtic*, the *Sir John Lawrence*, the *Governor Tilley*, the *Ugland*, the *Atlantic*, the *Eliza Campbell*, the *Samuel*, the *Conqueror*, the *Duke of Rothsey*. Only four of twenty-eight vessels escaped damage. Captain Corfield, his wife, three children, servant, and steward of the *Avenmore* were drowned; Captain Trick of the *Arctic;* Mrs. Garvin of the "Store" ship; and others on the shore.

It was lucky it was night. "Had this happened in the daytime," John wrote in his log, "there would of been a great loss of life among the launches, at the chutes, and from various other ways. But at that time every one was on board their own ships."

John sailed to Callao for repairs. Capt. McLoon, Mr. Trott, his mate, and eight of his crew, went with John. They felt shocks of earthquakes on their way un-

## Captain Abby and Captain John

der the sea. It was a five-day run for them. They arrived May 15. While the *B. Sewall* was dry-docked, other cripples came limping in. John's ship had to be recaulked and sea-metalled. The quake had started her seams. While they were recoppering her, the third mate ran away, as third mates were known to do. The job on the ship cost John five hundred dollars.

John was bound to get his guano, earthquakes or not. There were some guano islands left in the Pacific. He sailed to Pabelon de Pica for it, a passage of sixteen days, arriving July 13. He had kept the Fourth as a holiday on board. "Myself thinking of home, sweet and dear ones at home." He had met another earthquake and had felt the ship shake. Evidently Mother Nature was doing a lot of furniture moving under the ocean that Summer. John had passed what was left of Haunillios. At Pabelon de Pica, he had hard work getting through the surf to the shore to hire launches, he had to climb "Jacob's Ladder" getting there. They loaded. John observed each Sabbath and Freddie's birthday. There was another earthquake, but the new island was still there in the morning. Capt. Otis and family, of Brunswick, paid John a visit. Abby's birthday. The Pennell ship *Oakland*, Capt. Purington now, came in. John was sick for three days. It was his head. Something the earthquake had done to it. But he finished loading his 2000 tons of guano, September 21. A lot of friends came on board to bid him goodbye—one never knew for how many years or for eternity—as he sailed the 24th for England. John clipped a salvage notice from a newspaper just as he left. On the back of it is

## Captain Abby and Captain John

the item that Horace Greeley, who advised young men to go west, had gone east and been arrested in Paris, June 20!

There was no comedy, though, on the other side of this clipping. It was tragedy, and a family one. The great Pennell ship *Ellen Hood* had gone ashore at Key West with a load of $150,000 worth of cotton. The ship's value was given as $45,000. This made a huge hole in the Pennells' fortunes.

John rounded the Horn, October 25. It was getting to be an old story. How many more times would he make it? Northeastward, in squalls of snow.

Above John, at the top side of the world, his son Freddie was all excited over a wild animal he had seen on grandpa's farm, big as an ox. It was the loup-cervier. "Lucy-Vee," the Great Islanders pronounced it. They also called it "Isaiah Jordan's lion," because it had clawed the old fellow most to death one moonlight night. Brother Arthur had seen it before young Fred. He took his brother up back of the barn and showed him its tracks, big as saucers in the October mire. Freddie dreamt of the creature that night. And next day, when his grandfather and another man were shingling the roof of the farmhouse, they yelled to Freddie to come out and see the loup-cervier. It had just jumped the pasture stonewall. It had come up from Quahaug Bay and was headed towards Misery Hill. Fred looked off towards Misery, and he felt his blood run cold. There it was, sure enough, jumping off the ground in big leaps high as a man. It was tawny color and big as a barn door. It was headed towards the hill where I

## Captain Abby and Captain John

would often be driving our horse up from Lost Paradise Farm, once I had got myself properly born, the hill where my heart always stood still as I listened for the sound of the heavy padded feet on that great cat out of the earlier, heroic days, the cat that had set his mark on Isaiah Jordan's face and back. Freddie did not go for beechnuts under Misery any more that Fall.

Gales hurried John up towards his children. He was sick off and on. But he began painting ship. Did not a cold wind off the stars blow upon him at Latitude 20 South? Rio lay over there in its beauty. From the Horn to the Line in 27 days, "a fine run." But it was dull without Abby along and no Freddie to play with on the house aft. A topsail schooner, November 25. Wedding anniversary again. "Bent our best suit of sails," December 8. John came to anchor in Falmouth Roads, just 90 days from Pabelon de Pica, the day before Christmas. Letters. All well at home. John drew a deep breath. The best Christmas a man could have: wife and children well. Christmas Day, John was ordered to Brest. And there he docked, December 28, and began unloading.

John received 14 Brunswick *Telegraphs* from Abby. On February 8, he telegraphed to Abby to start over with the boys. He could not bear being separated from them any longer. No discharging on the 11th, "lumpers all *drunk*." The last of the guano went off Washington's Birthday. John was ready for a tug, March 2. And across the Atlantic, Abby was washing and ironing at her mother's and getting ready for the start next day. Elias drove Abby and the boys to the village.

## Captain Abby and Captain John

Abby was riding to Boston as John was pulling out of Brest for Cardiff. She put up at Capt. Sewall's in Boston. Fall River Line to New York. Abby and company left New York on the Cunard steamer *Batavia* as her husband anchored at Cardiff. Abby was seasick. It took time to get sea legs back! There were only four "ladies" besides herself on board, two Sisters, an elegant French woman, and Mrs. Wickham, from Pennsylvania, with her husband. John started loading his coal. Abby got her sea legs back and enjoyed herself with her friends. "We have a jolly set aboard." At Queenstown, Abby had a despatch from John. John took the train to Liverpool. Artie and Freddie were on pins and needles and could not sit still with excitement. And on Sunday, March 17, the Pennell family met in a tender in Liverpool harbor. Fred remembers to this day how his handsome father could not wait but leaped from the tender's deck over a wide rift of water and took his mother in his arms. The Britishers must have blushed British red to see such an American husband's embrace in public! The two boys danced and cheered, waiting their turn. Their turn came. Freddie got tossed high, too, and smacked on his breeches. "Feel happy once more," Abby wrote in her fourth diary, which she had started on leaving America this Spring. "Boys delighted." Life was too short for her and John to be apart. They would never be so again. John said so right there in the tender. The British blushed.

They sailed from Cardiff, April 4. They had the Spring at their bow and a good lifetime before them. They headed towards Rio de Janeiro, Brazil. The great

## Captain Abby and Captain John

new dry-dock in the harbor down there needed a vast supply of coal to work its steam pumps. And John was going to supply it. Rio was a coming center for ships of all the world. They would be often there. "At home now and happy," wrote Abby. "Have a good cook and steward. Cabin looks prettier than ever." John's ship was home. Forever now. Home was nowhere else. Abby could ask no more of life than she had. "Done some washing myself and ironing. Found my same old iron. John had taken care of it." The patent iron John had bought her so long ago! Life was good! It was made up of flatirons and homely little parts. All in place. Always there. Where a husband had saved them for his wife. They stopped and "got some nice mackerel of a fisherman off the Scillys." The old happiness of housekeeping had begun again. Small housekeeping on a mighty backdrop of the infinite ocean and sky. Things back in their grooves. And Abby would coddle the boys no more: "Boys commenced studies today," Monday, April 8. Porpoises by the rail! Harpoon away! It was like old times. It was a holiday that would last, now, for good. John had a sick headache, April 14, a rather new and uncomfortable kind, but he soon got over it. Abby pounced on some flannel and began to cut them all out some shirts. Plenty of men's backs to cut out shirts for now! Abby cleaned and put away Winter clothing and worked away "regulating trunks." She finished her new bonnet and wore it on deck. "Feel smart today, done a considerable little cooking."

The Sargasso Sea and new crabs for the old aquarium. Freddie and Arthur were up to their elbows in

## Captain Abby and Captain John

glory. And there was a great glory the night of May 3. John described it in the log: "Water full of phosphorus. Looked all afire" And Abby in her diary: "Saw a beautiful sight last night. The ocean was glittering like silver." The husband and wife stood side by side and looked down at the fire in the flood the Ancient Mariner saw. Where the ripple ran out and broke was a sheer cloth of flame. They were sailing together through a milky way hazed with ten million stars. These two who knew each other so well knew they would always know each other so and never be lost among stars here or hereafter.

Next day Abby took sick and had to go to bed. John was up with her all night for three nights running. He kept track of her recovery in the log. "Abby still mending." It was the old times, the two of them worrying about each other and doctoring. Abby was up just as they crossed the Equator. Abby and John saw Brazil lifting up in the west. A new land for them. Abby cut Freddie out some shirt waists. She washed and ironed. They had gales, May 20. But fair weather followed. "I done a large washing. So everything is clean now." A calico nightdress next for Freddie. Another vast gale slowed them up. But they beat into Rio harbor the last day of May, and hove anchor off Fort Villegagnon.

# 19

## Where Rio's Mountains Preach Eternity

"LOOKS BEAUTIFUL ALL AROUND US."

That is the way a Yankee housewife would describe the harbor of Rio de Janeiro, Brazil. Out of a bay so deep it shades from sapphire into indigo, mountains sweep up and hold clouds on their sides. A white city curves along below. Islands like pieces broken off Paradise shine on the dark water with unbelievable green and golden splendor. Whales can come in there, for it is the deepest harbor in the world. Nothing is low or drab. All things shine and sweep up. Everything shouts out its beauty full throat. Even the winds run bright and leave wakes of crushed diamonds where they go. At night, lights wind up like trails to fairyland along the high shores. But the hills shine as bright by day. Mountains break off sheer and go down under the sea. One of them stands immense and lonely by itself tipped up from mystery and deep water. Mountains wall all the sparkling bay. Mountains that will never be moved stand up above time and preach patience and eternity.

At the mountains' feet a brave and happy little American family were resting now from the great winds of the world. They did not ask much of life. Security and love were all they wanted. A few rooms as neat as

## Captain Abby and Captain John

those back in New England, a sewing machine, a patent flatiron, two sons growing up good as their father. A husband and wife nineteen years together, with never a single quarrel, looking forward to a few decades more and peaceful gray hair and the satisfaction of seeing their sons turn into men. Another son who was forever a baby, in a place they believed in as they believed in the oak in their ship. They were good people. The sailing vessels, that meant their life and security, floating all around them. Children of the winds and dressed all in white. These things were strong and must surely last. They had not seen a single steamer on this whole voyage down to Brazil. But above this family and the ships they lived by were the mountains. Measured against them, these white fleets were mayflies, and the small cabin and the four happy people in it were less than a rib in a mayfly's brief wing.

Freddie watched the natives carrying the baskets of coal on their shoulders. They were black as the coal. The only thing white about them were the whites of their eyes. They grinned up at Artie and him. The ship was tied up at Multnegee Island discharging. Abby was in the cabin eating fruit that was "nice and tasty" after the voyage. She had been into Rio. The dazzling city had turned out dirty and disappointing from inside, as Abby had learned that white foreign cities were apt to do. It was hot. Far to the north, they were thinking about haying on Great Island. The Pennells might yet be there for the last of it. Eight of the crew had run away. The family had been out to one of the islands. It had been lovely there, all right.

## Captain Abby and Captain John

Abby put up mosquito bar in the boys' room. The black stevedore was turning out "quite a gentleman." Abby and John took the boys to the Botanical Gardens in a new miracle among modern improvements, horse cars. The world was moving along faster and faster! What would people think up next? The Pennells saw "many pretty places," and they put up at the *Hotel de Europe*. But the beds were hard. Abby bought some feather plumes, with a hat in the offing. But the plumes were expensive. They went to visit the Emperor's Palace, but the ride there was through very dirty streets. They were glad to go home to the neat ship. The men had a rumpus with the cook over the hardness of his flapjacks. John had to put two of the men in irons. The family and the crew observed Sunday. Abby washed Monday. Then they made calls on the Americans in port. Artie took sick. They all went up a mountain, first part by horse cars, then by carriage, then by foot. The three levels of civilization! The mountain had a hotel on the top, *White's*. Civilization had got that far. The Pennells dined there and stayed on overnight, to see the famous view in the morning. But they could see nothing next morning, it rained so. "Glad to get back," wrote Abby. It was their last picnic, in Rio. Capt. Strickland in the *Invincible* of Bath, for Hong Kong, came in dismasted. Abby baked custards. John wrote the last day of June, 1878, into his log: "Sabbath observed." He was tired. He did not write any more. He and Abby sat a long time on the deck together, very quiet and very happy in the evening under the mountains, and watched dark come on.

## Captain Abby and Captain John

July 2, John came back from Rio with a headache. The headache that bothered him lately. Abby gave him oil and soaked his feet in mustard water. It was a New England stand-by, good for almost everything that ailed anybody. But John was still under the weather next day, and was hot and feverish. Abby had the doctor to him on the Fourth. It didn't seem like a holiday. "Suffers with his head," she wrote. The doctor thought it was a bilious attack. But July 5, John was much worse, and the doctor said he must go to the hospital. Captain Drinkwater of Yarmouth, Maine, happened to be on hand, and he took John and Abby over to the hospital. Captain Drinkwater also took the two boys on his vessel. Abby stayed with her husband. It was hot in the little room and very quiet. The quiet mountains outside everywhere seemed to have come very near. Their quietness seemed to have got into the room. They grew dim with the sudden twilight, but they were still there in the room around Abby and John. John was very quiet. But after a great while, he drew a deep breath and murmured something. Abby could not make it out. She put her head down close to John. She heard what John said. He wanted to go after frogs and not sit in school. It was too good a day, he said. Poor John, his fever was so bad his mind was wandering on nothing. He kept speaking low every so often. It was hard to hear, and most of it did not make sense. It grew even quieter. Abby heard a clock somewhere strike nine. Then John spoke up suddenly clear as a bell. "Get me the rock salt, and I will put it in his cradle." Abby put her handkerchief to her mouth and bent over him quickly, with her eyes

*337*

## Captain Abby and Captain John

gone wide. A terrible look came into her face as she looked at her husband close. . . . "Then I saw he was to die with me alone in a strange land. With strangers around me. No one to speak to. Only two in the house that could speak English."

John Pennell died a half hour after midnight. The logs were finished, the voyages done. When Abby took her hand from his heart she found a packet of paper. She unrolled it and found two locks of her hair.

One great felicity John Pennell had. He died early enough so he did not see sails driven by steam from all the oceans. He died before his life's business died. It is a good thing to die when a man is in the flower of his strength and work.

The rest was a fever and a dream. Abby's diary ceases to be a diary. Days merge and time stands still, time leaps dizzily ahead. But never back. Captain Drinkwater was always there in the background helping all he could. All a man could. He told Arthur and Freddie, for one thing. That was a good thing. He heard what Abby said over and over. And so he moved all the mountains of red tape he could. He got the body embalmed. He got papers. John could go home. Captain Drinkwater's ship was Abby's home and the boys' home. Days went by. But all of them meant nothing. It was a dream. Maybe Abby would wake up.

"Oh, my God, what affliction! How can I bear it. It seems too hard to lose such a good kind husband and father as he was. God alone knows my sufferings. Am obliged to keep up and do my best for my children's sake. I have got no one to look out for me now. My

## Captain Abby and Captain John

guide, my protector, and all have been taken from me. I feel alone in the world now. Oh, my God! have mercy on me and spare me to reach home in safety."

Captain Drinkwater was kind. And she could take John home. The papers were ready and the arrangements all made. Abby went back to the *Benjamin Sewall* and "got a few things together." "I must prepare," she wrote, "to leave my ship forever, bid adieu to the sea I have travelled 20 years. My heart is nearly breaking." She found the little flatiron. John had bought it. And the canary cage. It was like hearing carnival music ghostly and far away.

A lot of people were kindness itself. They made it easier. A despatch came ordering John to Callao. They would not have gone home, after all. Callao, and the terrible heat in John's head he had told her about. The heat that had done something strange to his head! No, John was going home instead. Abby set her lips and went over and packed up the last things. When she went the last time through this cabin door, she'd be walking forever out of the great house of the sea. Well, she could do it. She got out the things, and she washed and ironed for the last time on board the *Benjamin Sewall*, July 16, put the cabin to rights, took up her goods, and walked out of the door and a part of her life that was finished for good. She closed the door firmly behind her. "Farewell to our old happy home forever." She walked bravely across the deck. Her real happiness was back behind the door she had closed.

John's body went aboard the steamer *Tycho Brahe*, for New York. Abby and her boys went aboard, too.

## Captain Abby and Captain John

As they went past the *Benjamin Sewall*, they saw her flag at half-mast. So Abby and John started out on their last voyage together. Out past the lovely islands, out past the mountains that stand up and are like patience and eternity.

The Atlantic can heal a mind. The lamentations in the diary grow calmer, as the steamer goes on through the days. The sea preaches eternity and patience, too. Freddie had a birthday. Abby mended Freddie's clothes. The old items of existence that add up to a day and a week and a year came back one by one. There would be happy days. A different kind of happy days. Not John's kind again. Not the sea's. "Voyages are over," Abby wrote calmly in the diary.

New York, August 9, and the Fall River Line boat to take her and the boys. The *Tycho Brahe* dipped her flags as Abby went past her up the East River. It was a last salute to two brave captains leaving the sea. Boston, somehow, and the vast arms of Elias, her brother. Brunswick, and John's brother, Charles the Great "with arms open to receive me. For the first time I lost control of myself, nearly fainted, but was helped into the hack." Home in time for haying, after all.

The box was opened. This time all was "in good condition." Not like that other box which came to Brunswick years ago. "His dear body was at rest in his brother's house." Abby's father and mother came. They were old now and had had many years together. Abby and John had been separated in the middle of life. Abby thought of how hard that difference was. Good friends all around her here. But her place would be elsewhere, and among strangers. This was a part of the old life, and it was melting away.

Abby fell asleep and dreamed; and in her dream she saw John's face, and she saw John and his old Mother Deborah were together, Deborah who had escorted him to school and to sea so long ago. The mother and son met face to face and smiled. Abby woke comforted. Professor Packard of the college came. His beautiful flowing hair and side-whiskers were showing the snows of the recent Winters. He was like a benediction in the house.

And next day, August 14, the Bowdoin teacher who taught longer than most teachers ever lived, a tower, too, in the town of Brunswick, and a man handsome as learning itself, the preacher who had hailed many of the tall Brunswick captains as they came home the last time from sea, preached John's funeral sermon in his brother's house. "Dr. Packard was very happy in his selection of language," the Brunswick *Telegraph* reported, "and very touching in his references to the family." The paper went on to relate an incident that happened in Rio at the time Captain Pennell died. His two sons looked out that morning and saw every flag half-mast on every vessel in the harbor. " 'Is it for poor papa?' asked one of them. When that son and mother met, the mother said, 'Oh, I hardly know what we shall do.' 'Do the best we can and trust the rest to God,' was the reply of the little fellow, thoughtful beyond his years—he is thirteen years of age. Dr. Packard fully improved the incident."

The funeral was a milestone in the town's history. One

## Captain Abby and Captain John

of the largest ever held. "The turn-out of shipmasters was very large." Captains came from Maine towns far and wide. Captain John had had many friends. The six bearers were all shipmasters. Thirty carriages drove to the grave. Abby scattered the flowers on the casket herself. She stood up to the end like the captain she was, among the others. Then she went home and made the last entry in her last diary, August 17; noting that the first of the everlasting rains that would fall on her husband's grave was falling now on the mound where he lay beside his nameless, first-born son, who had come home before his father from the sea.

In the front of that last diary of Abby Pennell's there is a little pocket. In it are some pieces of yellowed paper carefully folded. The marriage intentions of Abby and John are there, dated November 13, 1857, and signed by Nathaniel Badger, Town Clerk. And there is a very yellow newspaper clipping of four lines from the poem which Longfellow spoke in 1875 at his fiftieth anniversary at Bowdoin. The lines are the ones describing the pines John Pennell rests under:

> O ye familiar scenes, ye groves of pine,
> That once were mine and are no longer mine—
> Thou river, widening through the meadows green
> To the vast sea, so near and yet unseen.

The other papers are packets of hair. The one is that which John Pennell wore over his heart in the earthquake in the Pacific: "A piece of my dear wife's hair, for many years in procession, 1876. My dear Abby's

## Captain Abby and Captain John

hair." The brown curls still shine with the golden glints of life. In the other packet, there are four curls. One is from John's head when he was six years old, and had curls on his shoulders. It is as golden and alive as cornsilk. The next is John's hair bleached out a pale yellow after years in the sun at sea. The last is hair touched with gray, and Abby has written on that packet, "My dear John's hair taken off after he died July 6, Saturday morning, Rio Janeiro."

People now may smile at the customs and institutions of our Victorian grandparents. But there is a whole family history in those paper packets. A whole saga of happiness. That hair rankles with amazing life. Good as gold. Such love does not go out of date. It will last and go on shining, here or somewhere in the universe, long after the fire in these curls here has burned out to dust, for it is too good a thing ever to be lost. It will go on shining long after the time when there will be no more mountains at Rio looking out on the sea.

## 20

## Captain Abby Ashore

THE REST IS NO PART of this chronicle.

Abby Pennell went on being a strong captain. But she was a captain on the land, and the lines of her life ran out beyond Maine. It was a full life and a fine one, though people say she was never the same woman after John left her. Never the sparkle, never the gay sense of life and power. She did a life's work, though, and did it well. But that is another story. Her life with John is the life of this book.

Abby brought up the sons John had left in her charge. She brought them up splendidly. They had the best. Abby went to Andover, Massachusetts, with them and put them through Phillips Academy there. She took boarders to support them. And then she moved on with her sons to Yale, and took more boarders there. She brought the miracle of Great Island cooking into maybe a hundred lives and left them better lives. She saw her sons through their college education. That is usually a ticklish sort of business. So far as I know, Abby is the only mother besides the Lady Magdalen Herbert, the mother of George Herbert, the poet and mystic, who successfully went to college with her sons.

## Captain Abby and Captain John

Arthur, the boy who was never cut out to be a sailor though born a-sailing, was graduated at Yale in the class of 1887, went on into the Law School, and graduated in 1889. He became a successful lawyer. Fred, who took to the sea more, went through Sheffield and graduated from Yale in 1890. He went into a business that borders his father's, ships' supplies and kindred iron and steel products, in New York City. He has done very well indeed. He has all the integrity and Yankee love of things that work well and are in good order that his father had before him. And the same bedrock faith in hard work and in life. He is a man I am very proud to have as a friend. His mother lived to be very proud of having been a schoolteacher to this son.

Abby Pennell lived to be proud of both her boys. She brought them back on her visits to relations and friends in Brunswick. Abby is still remembered in my town. People recall her as the woman who did such exquisite embroidery and always wore white ruching at her neck. These are two good things to be remembered by. She is remembered also for her gentleness, her sweet disposition, her courtesy, and pleasant ways. Those are good qualities to be remembered by, too. They say she always seemed young. That is another thing they all recall. Never seemed old even after her hair grew gray. Maybe that was because she and John had no gray years together. People in town remember that Abby's favorite exclamation was "Sho! sho!" That was when she was surprised. And being always young, she was often surprised at life. And she always washed her face in water with cucumber peelings in it, to keep

## Captain Abby and Captain John

her skin white and fine. She became a kind of myth while she was still alive. A myth of fine manners and fine housekeeping and fine dresses. My brother-in-law, Andrew Pennell, Carroll's son, remembers her very clearly as a small boy. He says she wore silks that seemed to have water on them *and creaked*. He remembers the sound of her, and the grace of her, very well.

When Abby Pennell hove her anchor up, February 22, 1909, there were, maybe, two figures waiting at her door. One would be tall and fine as a man, and the other one small as the smallest child, but wonderfully alive because he had always been young. And the three would go off together on a voyage past the surf that flows over the August elms in a Middle Bays night from the north to the south of the sky. And maybe some equivalent of the little patent flatiron would go along with them and make Abby completely happy.

What was Abby's body was brought home to Brunswick and joined John's under the pines. Abby had been buried there before, though. Twice. Once when her first baby went into the ground there. And the very best part of her when John went into his grave.

But Abby's best ship, the *Benjamin Sewall* had a grave on the other side of the globe. In October, 1903, the queen and last of all the Pennell ships, the best of all Brunswick ones, went ashore in a wild typhoon on the coast of Formosa. She broke her stout Maine heart in pieces on the wicked rocks there. The men took to the boats. But when they approached the land, the savage cannibals of Botel Tobago fell upon them like

## Captain Abby and Captain John

wild animals and drowned and cut many of them to pieces. And some, it was said, had a worse fate in the evil green glooms of the high mountain ravines above, where nature is so lovely that she becomes a fiend.

The incident became a famous one in the annals of international affairs. The United States, through Secretary of State John Hay, asked the Japanese to punish the treacherous natives of Formosa. A punitive expedition was sent out, and some huts were burned and some savages taken. But the red-handed ones could not be identified. All Formosans, like all Japanese to us, looked alike to the Japanese. And what could these famous lovers of law and order, the Japanese, do? They would like to know. They asked, through diplomatic channels, John Hay. They had been having their hands full of these Formosans for a decade. They had lost a lot of their own heads. They had finally built a fence all around the hateful race of people and charged it with electricity. But the natives felled trees on it and got over and collected Japanese heads just the same. The Formosans were a hard lot. The way of the Japanese peacemakers was not easy.

The ribs of Brunswick oak on the black reefs whitened out in the fierce China Sea sun. And on the beaches books filled with the fine lace of the handwriting of Captain John D. Pennell bleached into oblivion. The log-books had still been aboard the *Benjamin Sewall*. Fred had seen them when he visited his father's old ship in New York harbor in 1897. John had brought home only his personal first drafts. Now the ship's logs perished with the last Pennell ship. It was like a swan song of all the clean and trim vessels the Yankees of New England had built to be their monuments.

But John Pennell had his monument in other places, safe from the ruin of suns and winds. He had it in his sons. He had it in this blue sea-chest full of his papers from which I have tried to make him and Abby stand up alive.

# 21

## The Roll Call on the Headland

AND NOW, here in the cabin I have built on the headland beside the spot where the Pennell ships were launched, I bid the blue chest and Abby and John goodbye, with the bay a cloth of silver in the moonlight at my elbow as I write. But before I do, I should like to tell them what has happened to the place they loved so well and where their ships were built.

Suppose I let my handsome daughter, Mary-Alice, do it for me. For she wrote a fine graduation part about Pennellville last month at Brunswick High School: "The wharves and ways of Pennellville stood empty. The mudflats crept in over the channel. Year by year, the rotting piles sank deeper. Grass grew over the forgotten ways and cradles. The sheds fell into ruin. Time and change scattered the Pennell family, and the little schoolhouse stood empty. Fishermen and farmers tread the paths where once the Pennell captains strode with rolling gait. Today, the only landmarks of the booming shipbuilding days are the houses built by the ships' carpenters. These lasting memorials of a seafaring race are still as upright and beautiful as ever. For many years to come they will remain, with their windows looking out to sea, standing by the narrow rutted road that ends abruptly at the open ocean."

John Pennell never had a house there. That is partly why I have tried to build him this one made of pages in a book.

Before I finish, too, there is one more rite I should like to do. The full moon is with me, and Middle Bay shines with beauty borrowed from the moon. It is midnight. Who knows but midnight and the full moon might help me? I should like, if I could get the virtue and power from this night and the moon, to go out of my cabin and stand on this headland and call the roll of the Pennell sea captains and builders. Now, sixty-five years after the last Pennell ship slid into this bay, I might see them come up, from the grave and the sea, at the sound of their names being called.

Those shadowy old three Thomases, faded out by a hundred years and more. Dim as figures from the *Book of Genesis*. That William, who built my old house and planted my elms for me, with sea spray shining in the moon on his lips. And great patriarch Jacob would come from under the broken gravestone at the white pine's root in his own field, rejoicing like his namesake in the *Bible* at having founded a family like a nation. Deborah would rise from her crumbled marble stone, too, and march down here with a ghostly white birch switch in her hand.

I have tried to give these people life. Maybe they might answer the roll if I called it.

Jacob the Younger, who rebuilt my house and robbed the front hall to add to the lovely long west room, who

## Captain Abby and Captain John

plastered even the shed and dated the plaster in 1859. And his son, Captain Sam, who sat in his old days in his armchair in the room where my Peggy sits now, and looked out under the loveliest elm of all Pennellville on Middle Bay, silvery in the moon, azure in the sun, through days and nights and days, till they found him with his eyes closed for good. Job would stand up, his disfigured lip not seen in the moonlight, with his handsome boy with him. Ben, sorrowful without sons, would come, rejoicing in the sons of the others. And Master James with the moonlight showing the twinkles at the corners of his eyes and the great hurt of him from his last·fall on him no more. He would bring a dozen ship models in his wide hands, as mediaeval builders bring their cathedrals, and he would bring the gold watch and chain his sea captain son had given him.

Charles the Great would step out from his south porch—it is only a step from me here—where he used to pay off the yard hands on Saturday evenings, he would step down and come over the meadow with his tall hat on top of his wig and his gold-headed cane in his fine long fingers. His poet daughter would come, too, with her pen in one hand and her scrubbing brush in the other. Eliza and Paulina. And Paulina would have a mind no longer touched by the moon and her great sadness at losing sons to the sea, she would come without the moon in her mind here under the moon. Joseph and his wife, with their lost little son by the hand. Robert and his wife. James's wife with her sisters from the Bunganuc hill. Susan Chase would come. Maybe the poet Longfellow, too, if Susan would add her voice to

## Captain Abby and Captain John

mine in the roll call. The Harpswell preacher, who drove his yoke of oxen every year to the Bowdoin Commencements and wrote books for a million boys, Elijah Kellogg, would come. For Charles had saved him from drowning in this very bay. And the author of *Uncle Tom's Cabin* would come to me through this moonlight tonight since she built a whole book out of Pennells and Orrs. Maybe even the great Son of Destiny himself, Napoleon. For Abby's sake, because she picked a flower from his grave on St. Helena. And who knows how strong the chains of sentiment are, especially with a soldier!

And the ships themselves would rise from the oceans' bottoms, if I had my will, and come home, too. They might hear me and come. That *Guadalupe* that sank on her maiden voyage out of Portland. The *Jacob Pennell* would rise from under Ireland and bring the hundreds of Irish babies and men and women back to the light of life with her as she rose. The *Deborah Pennell* would come up from her grave in the North Sea, and old Deborah's eyes would shine to see her namesake. The *James Pennell* would break from the ice floes of Antarctica, at the call of me and this moon, and head north and come up here fast as thought to this family reunion. The *Istria* from deep down in the South Pacific, with the dark star gone from her masthead and the dark stain of Master James's fall gone from her hold. The *Anglo Saxon* with her sins washed away and white as her sides used to look in the sun. James Henry, her master, would come with her, young again, and his sins washed away, too, and his hurts forgiven and forgot-

## Captain Abby and Captain John

ten. And the great *Benjamin Sewall* herself would come up from under the reefs in the China Sea, and come hither home. All the vessels would come home, young and healed, to their people.

Gussie might come from far California. And Aunt Nell with the sweet frostflower-blue eyes, and no pail of molasses to carry, and no fear of great Deborah upon her! The little nameless Pennell would come surely from playing with Frankie in heaven. And Frankie, too. And all the little Pennell boys who never grew up or old.

And all the men who ever handled Pennell ships till they sank in the sea would come up and climb this headland to join me. Davey Lewis with his madness gone from him. And the old master and maker of captains, William Woodside, vomiting no more blood, healed and hale, with the gold watch he was so proud of, gripped in his big hand. The little cabin boy, Johnnie Ottagan, would come up from his dark watery place in the Atlantic north of St. Helena. All of them would come here, down to the unnamed men who slipped from the yard arms in the storms of snow. All the men down to the last Smiths and Peter Angulias, who froze their hands and feet in the rigging.

They should all come home tonight if I had my way. Come home to this shipyard of the Pennells and answer to their names under the moon. And these silent and empty shores would ring tonight with their voices. And over three-score ships would ride here under my window with a thousand sails full of this moon's silver light. There would be a greater fleet than Tyre or Sidon ever knew at one time here in this bay tonight, and a whole

## Captain Abby and Captain John

small nation of people around my cabin on this shore.

And, last of all, John and Abby would come, I hope. John walking between his two fine sons, the named and the unnamed, and Abby with her face turned up to his. Rio would be a name forgotten. I should have a chance to thank this man and this woman for the goodness of becoming their friend. And this shipyard and this bay would shine with a light much purer and much brighter than the moon or the sun. It would shine with a great family affection and great goodness, as well as with the light of family glory. For wherever John and Abby stood, there would be the best light men have to live by, the light men call love.

**THE END**

# Appendix 1

## THE ROLL OF PENNELL VESSELS

| | |
|---|---|
| By 1807 | Schooner *Farmer* |
| Around 1807 | Schooner *Independent* |
| | Sloop *Eliza* |
| | Brig *Favorite* |
| | Schooner *Harmony* |
| During War of 1812 | Privateer *Dash* (Sailed from Brunswick, never heard from again) |
| | Ship *Charles* (Never launched, rotted at wharf) |
| 1815 | *Fair American* |
| Before 1825 | Topsail schooner *Exchange* |
| ?) In 1830's | Ship *Union* |
| 1834 | Brig *Charles,* 160 tons |
| 1834 | Schooner *Harriet,* 128 tons |
| 1836 | Ship *Jacob Pennell,* 233 tons (Lost off Ireland, 400 passengers and crew drowned) |
| 1838 | Ship *Eliza* |
| ?) Around 1838 | Brig *Cyrus* |
| 1840 | Bark *Tennesseé* |
| 1840 | Brig *Mary Pennell,* 233 tons |

# Captain Abby and Captain John

| | |
|---:|:---|
| 1844 | Brig *Guadalupe,* 188 tons (Sailed on first voyage from Portland, Maine, December 14, 1844, Capt. Berry, lost in great gale) |
| 1845 | Bark *Oregon,* 347 tons |
| Middle 40's | Ship *Majestic,* 714 tons |
| 1848 | Ship *James Pennell,* 570 tons (Abandoned off the Horn) |
| 1848 | Ship *Cornelia* |
| Before 1849 | Brig *Robert Pennell* |
| November 1, 1849 | Ship *Tempest,* 861 tons |
| October 5, 1850 | Ship *Governor Dunlap* |
| By 1851 | Bark *Tadesco* (Lost on beach near Lynn, Mass.) |
| 1851 | Ship *Calcutta* |
| 1853 | Ship *Redwood,* 1165 tons |
| 1854 | Bark *William Woodside,* 462 tons (Sunk by Confederate privateers, 1862) |
| 1855 | Ship *Charles S. Pennell,* 968 tons |
| 1855 | Ship *Ellen Hood,* 1046 tons (Wrecked at Key West, 1877. Loss: $187,891) |
| 1855 | Ship *United States,* 1082 tons |
| 1859 | Ship *John O. Baker,* 797 tons (Named for a business man in Portland, Maine, lost in the North Sea, 1878) |
| December 1, 1860 | Bark *Deborah Pennell,* 599 tons (Lost in the North Sea, near Rotterdam, December 10, 1873) |
| 1862 | Bark *Anglo Saxon,* 543 tons (Lost in blockade running) |
| 1864 | Brig *George W. Chase* |
| 1864 | Ship *Mary Emma,* 1067 tons |

## Captain Abby and Captain John

|  |  |
|---|---|
| 1865 | Bark *Istria,* 811 tons (Lost in the South Pacific) |
| 1866 | Ship *Oakland,* 1237 tons |
| October 27, 1874 | Ship *Benjamin Sewall,* 1433 tons, 202 feet on deck, 218 feet overall, 39 feet wide, 24 feet deep (Lost in the China Sea on the coast of Formosa, October 5, 1903) |

# Appendix 2

## BRUNSWICK SHIPMASTERS

Names of Brunswick, Maine, shipmasters from the third decade of the nineteenth century down to about 1899, as set down by Charles Pennell, 1899:

Amos Tappen
John Peterson
Daniel Stone
Harry Minot
Daniel Giveen
John Lane
James Otis
Jesse Snow
William Curtis
John Skolfield
Peter Jordan
Ephraim Harding
William Thomas
William Stanwood
Daniel Chase
William Woodside
Henchman Sylvester
Thomas Snow
William Simpson
Thomas Merriman
John H. Marshall
Joseph Alexander
John O'Brien
Joseph McLellan
Robert Giveen
Anthony Chase
Robert Giveen, 2nd
John F. Hall
John Dunlap
Henry Merritt
Hiram Henry
Joseph Skolfield
James Cowan
Robert Harding
Charles Thomas
Benjamin Woodside
James Lunt
Anthony Morse
Robert Simpson
Jesse Snow
Samuel Blake
Richard Merryman
Isaiah Hacker
Thomas Alexander
Charles Skolfield
Isaac Woodward
Bartlett Adams
John Woodward

## Captain Abby and Captain John

Cowan Jordan
William S. Giveen
Abel Goodrich
Lewis Giveen
Jacob P. Dunning
John Giveen
John D. Pennell
James H. Pennell
Robert Stevens
Joseph Melcher
Benjamin Melcher
Abner Melcher
Robert Chase
Israel Rodix
Henry Orr
Thomas Skolfield
Samuel Berry
Caleb Adams
James Ross
Joseph Badger
Charles Badger
Richard McManus
Asa McManus
Nehemiah Larrabee
Robert Foster
Joseph Alexander, 2nd
Isaac Linscott
Charles Snow
Jordan Woodward
Jabez Lewis
John Rogers
Randell Doyle
Robert Giveen
Minot Dunning
Robert Giveen, 3rd
Isaac Pennell
Robert Simpson, 2nd

John Card
George Melcher
Thomas Giveen
——— Littlefield
Robert Chase, Jr.
——— Bisbee
Joseph Brown
James Skolfield
Osborn Dunlap
Frank Jordan
Isaiah Elder
Nathaniel Badger
Benjamin Dunning
Robert McManus
George McManus
Peleg Curtis
William Murray
Francis Jordan
Leonard Merrill
Robert Bowker
Thomas Skolfield
William Decker
Clement Martin
Matthew Martin
Charles Boutelle
Joshua Boutelle
Horace Patten
Alfred Merryman
Albert Otis
Robert Stanwood
James Causland
Alfred Skolfield
Edwin Forsaith
Thomas Minot
Israel Gross
Samuel Skolfield
Benjamin Pennell

# Captain Abby and Captain John

William Mountford
Robert J. McManus
Elisha Connely
James M. Winchell
Samuel Harding
Charles H. Chase
John Thompson
Dana Simpson
Harmon Orr
——— Street
David Coombs
Amherst Whitmore
George F. Mustard
Thomas Martin
Clement Martin, Jr.
William Boutelle
Arthur Woodside
Curtis Merryman
Charles Bates
Henry Otis
Adam Woodside
Nathaniel Lincoln
Lincoln Skolfield
James Otis, 2nd
Jacob Merriman
William Grows
Robert Skolfield
Lewis S. Pennell
Henry Merritt, Jr.
William Merryman
Robert Ross
Joseph Dunning
Robert Harding, 2nd
William Hinckley
Wildes Thompson
James Drummond
Alcot Stover

William S. Skolfield
Horace Coombs
Charles Sylvester
Josiah Melcher
Norman Perkins
Thomas Moulton
Albert Minot
William Potter
Isaac Sylvester
Israel Clark
——— Bagley
William Otis
John Bishop
Edward Thompson
Bradbury Minot
Jeremiah Merryman
Lincoln Patten
Edward Otis
Sylvester Dunning
Dana Humphreys
Stephen Morrison
Horatio Hall
James Sylvester
Samuel Skolfield
Lemuel Stover
Samuel C. Pennell
Harrison Snow
Ephraim Wilcox
George Curtis
George Skolfield
Albert Otis, 2nd
Charles Dunning
Bell Hall
Robert Sylvester
Charles A. Boutelle
Charles Humphreys

# Index

Abaco, 105
Abbe, Mr., 90
Abenakis, 78
*Acacia*, 107
Academy, Venice, 146
accordion, 173
Adams, Bartlett, 358
Adams, Caleb, 359
Adams, Parson, 181
*Aerial*, schooner, 122
Africa, 122, 125, 126, 218, 291, 296
Aknisi, 300
Akyab, 215, 216, 221, 268
*Alabama* claims, 266
*Alabama*, ram, 62, 218, 221, 222, 266
albatrosses, 211, 308-311
Alexander, Joseph, 358
Alexander, Joseph II, 359
Alexander, Thomas, 358
Almería Bay, 159
American Consul, Venice, 131, 138
Anderson, Alice, 30
Anderson, Mrs., 258, 259
Andover, 344
Androscoggin River, 13
Angels' Point, 237
Anger, 268, 298
*Anglo Norman*, steamer, 90
*Anglo Saxon*, bark, 61, 216, 266, 352, 356
*Anglo Saxon*, steamer, 98
Angulia, Peter, 99, 353
Antarctica, 58, 234, 352
Antwerp, 194

Arctic, 327
Argentine, 20, 271
Ascension Island, 223
Astoria, 268, 306
Atlantic, 9, 13, 75, 76, 88-100, 102-122, 167-172, 190, 196-200, 203-205, 207-211, 218-226, 231-235, 245-252, 262-264, 270, 271, 287, 288, 290-292, 311-318, 321-323, 329-340
*Atlantic*, bark, 326, 327
Atlantic cable, 261, 262
*Atlantic Monthly*, 188
*Atlantic*, ship, 197
*Atlas*, steamer, 287
Augusta, 158
Austria, 158
Austria, Point, 156
Austria, Prince of, 134, 152
Austrian Empress, 136
*Avenmore*, 327

Bachelder, Capt., 107, 108
Badger, Charles, 359
Badger, Joseph, 359
Badger, Nathaniel, 342, 359
Bagley, Capt., 360
Bahama Banks, 105
Bahama Keys, 96
*Baker, John O.*, ship, 48, 59, 145, 155, 242, 250, 356
Baltimore, 110, 268, 272
bananas, 298-300
Bangor, 199
Bangorani, 156
Banks, the, 116, 198, 264, 318

*361*

# Index

Barcelona, 88, 89
Barflow, Williams and Co., 318
Barnabas Church, 146
Barnegat light, 172
Barnum's Museum, 183, 201
*Batavia,* steamer, 331
Bates, Charles, 360
Bath, 48, 190, 198, 205, 266, 280, 307, 327, 336
bathing, 289, 290
Battery Wharf, 100
Baxter, Helen, vii, 283, 286, 287
Beachy Head, 253, 261
Belfast Loch, 93
Benani Keys, 96
*Ben Bolt,* 109
Bengal, Bay of, 220
Benton Academy, 189
Benton, Maine, 187, 189
Bermuda, 171
Berry, Samuel, 359
*Bible,* 75, 170, 213
Birch Island, 66
Bisbee, Capt., 359
Biscay, Bay of, 121, 232
Bishop, John, 360
Bishop, John, 195, 360
Black, Mr. and Mrs., 253, 258
black-fish, 82, 83
Black Head, 93
Blake, Samuel, 358
Blanchard, J. P., 75, 76
blockade, cotton, 62
Bolongo Island, 216
Bon, Cape, 156
bonitas, 312-314
Booker, Emery, vii
Boston, 16, 31, 50, 52, 76, 90, 91, 98, 100, 102, 103, 127, 140, 177, 182, 267, 268, 280, 282, 287, 303, 331
Boston Bay, 91, 100
*Boston Budget,* 51
Botel Tobago, 346, 347
Bougarina, Cape, 125

Boutelle, Charles, 27, 359
Boutelle, Charles A., 27, 360
Boutelle, Joshua, 27, 359
Boutelle, William, 27, 360
Bowdoin College, 23, 36, 37, 40, 50, 64, 72, 121, 238, 266, 282, 299, 342, 352
Bowker, Aunt, 239, 240
Bowker family, 180
Bowker, Robert, 359
bowline song, 294, 295
Brazil, 333-341
Bremen, 170, 194, 246
Brest, 330
Bridges, Harry, 274
Bristol Channel, 208
British, 13, 33, 34, 90, 94, 96, 118, 122, 163, 206, 218, 223, 251, 253, 277, 331
Broadway, 171, 173, 178
Brown, Joseph, 359
Brown, Minister, 30
Brunswick, vii, viii, 13-73, 75-78, 97, 101, 102, 177-182, 185-187, 190, 201, 205, 227-229, 238, 240, 257, 259, 261, 264-268, 272, 279-286, 303, 322, 328, 340-342, 345, 346, 349-354
Brunswick Grammar School, 322
Brunswick High School, 349
Brussels, 20
Buctouche, 197, 232
Buenos Aires, 118
*Building of the Ship, The,* 36, 37
Bull Run, 197
Bunganuc, 15, 37, 38, 40-42, 45, 48, 126, 133, 351
Burma, 215, 216
Byron, Lord, 80

cabin boy, loss of, 223-226
Cadiz, 11,
Calcutta, 11, 87
*Calcutta,* ship, 58, 356
California, 189, 266, 353

*362*

# Index

California, Lower, 270, 271
Callao, 241, 242, 246, 250, 251, 262, 268, 271, 311, 323, 324, 327, 328, 339
Campbell, Daniel, 38
*Campbell, Eliza,* vessel, 327
canaries, 146, 170, 171, 203
Canary Islands, 233
Cape Breton, 197
Cape Cod, 90, 98, 103
Cape Florida, 90
Cape Horn sails, 322, 323
capstan song, 295
Card, John, 93-97, 359
Cardiff, 62, 198, 214, 224, 226, 268, 331
Carmer, Carl, 85
Carroll, Mr., 150
Casco Bay, 13, 84
Causland, James, 88-91, 95, 109, 359
Chamberlain, Joshua L., 248, 266, 282, 284
Channel, English, 231, 253, 261
Channel Islands, 28
*Channing,* ship, 218
*Charles,* brig, 54, 355
*Charles,* ship, 34, 355
Charleston, 196
Charlotte, stewardess, 270
Chase, Anthony, 359
Chase, Charles, 360
Chase, Daniel, 43, 358
*Chase, George W.,* brig, 63, 356
Chase, Hannah, 48, 56
Chase house, 37, 38, 48
Chase, Julia, 49
Chase, Robert, Jr., 359
Chase, Susan, 37, 39-45, 49, 103, 120, 126, 133, 134, 138, 140, 143, 144, 181, 351
Chesapeake, 272
Chile, 237, 238, 240
China, 60
China Sea, 26, 300, 347

Chinchas Islands, 241, 258
chinchilla skins, 256
Chinese junk, 214
cholera morbus, 300
*Christian Register,* 51
Civil War, 62, 185, 195, 196-251, 254, 277, 282
*Clara Anna,* ship, 113
Clark, Israel, 360
Clarke, Mr., 253, 254
clippers, 290, 303, 317
*Cloud,* ship, 90
Cloutman, Thomas, 31
coal, 93, 94, 96, 198, 207, 214, 232, 240, 260, 271, 288, 301, 302, 331, 335
Coffin, Margaret, vii, 351
Coffin, Mary-Alice, 349, 350
Coffin, Robert P. Tristram, 47, 48, 53, 54, 78-81, 82, 83, 84, 85, 111, 112, 117, 118, 139, 140, 142, 145, 178, 196, 198, 231, 232, 239, 241, 244, 256, 323, 330, 349-354
Coffin, Robert P. T., Jr., vii
Colcord, Lincoln, 84
Cole, Capt., 108
Collins, 270
Columbia River, 306
Commencement, Bowdoin, 121, 299, 352
Confederates, 62, 196, 204, 217, 218, 221, 222, 248, 250
Confederate privateers, 197, 204, 217, 218, 221, 222, 266
Confederate States of America, 196, 248
*Conference,* 327
Congregational Church, First Parish, Brunswick, 30, 49, 52, 60, 64, 70, 181
Connely, Elisha, 360
*Conqueror,* 327
*Conqueror,* steamer, 90
*Conway Castle,* 327

# Index

Cook, Cape, 305
Cook, Capt., 254
cook of the *William Woodside*, 120, 210
Coombs, David, 360
Coombs, Horace, 360
Coquimbo, 240
Corfield, Capt., 327
Cork, 92
*Cornelia*, ship, 58, 356
Cornwall, 118, 119
cotton, 75, 76, 185, 194, 329
Cowan, James, 358
crew, 288, 289
crews, deterioration of, 273-276
crews, methods of collecting, 273, 274
*Cruickshank, James*, bark, 124
Crystal Palace, 206, 207
Cuba, 81, 90, 91, 92, 96, 97, 106-115
Cunard Line, 287, 288, 331
Cundy's Harbor, 302
Curjola, 158
Curtis, Angus, 109, 110, 111, 112, 119
Curtis family, 180
Curtis, George, 360
Curtis Library, Brunswick, vii, 32, 35
Curtis, Peleg, 359
Curtis, William, 358
Cushing, Elder, 73
*Cyrus*, brig, 54, 355

*Dash*, privateer, 33, 355
Davidson, Mary, 254, 256
David Thom and Co., 252
Davis, Jefferson, 196, 254
Deceit Island, 234
Decker, William, 359
*Defiance*, tug, 93
Delaware Capes, 203, 321
De Soto, Cape, 124
Devil's Back, 80

diphtheria, 203
"Dixie," 146, 203, 204, 218
Dog Banks, 106
Dog Keys, 91
doldrums, 240, 272, 307, 323, 324
dolphins, 171
Doone, Capt., 253
Double-Headed Shot Keys, 91, 96, 106
Doughty, Angelina, 181, 182
Doughty, Henry, 112, 113, 181
Doyle, Randell, 359
drafting, Civil War, 229
dried apples, 121
Drinkwater, Capt., 337, 338, 339
Drummond, James, 360
Dublin, 202, 204, 205, 207, 268
*Duke of Rothsey*, 327
*Dunlap, Governor*, ship, 58, 69, 356
Dunlap, John, 358
Dunlap, Osborn, 359
Dunning, Andrew, 226, 227
Dunning, Benjamin, 26, 46, 359
Dunning, Charles, 26, 360
Dunning family, 45, 46, 73, 78, 87, 102, 180
Dunning, Gil, 78
Dunning, Jacob, 53, 219, 223, 226, 227, 228, 258, 311, 359
Dunning, James, Lord Ashburton, 46
Dunning, Joseph, 26, 46, 360
Dunning, Minot, 26, 53, 96, 103, 258, 359
Dunning, Reed, 226, 227, 228
Dunning, Rufus, 141
Dunning, Sylvester, 26, 360
Dunning, Thomas, 53
Durham, 14
Dutch, 213

earthquake, 324-328
East River, 200, 340
East Waterloo Dock, 318

# Index

Eddington light, 261
Edinburgh, 254, 256, 257, 258, 268
Elder, Isaiah, 359
*Eliza,* sloop, 32, 355
*Elois,* bark, 127
*Elwell,* ship, 323
Embargo Act, 33
Emerson, Capt., 109
*Emily,* steamer, 249
Emmons and Houghton, 305
Emperor's Palace, Rio, 336
England, 9, 17, 46, 118, 119, 194, 205-208, 216, 218, 226, 229-232, 253, 259-262, 287, 288, 290, 328, 330, 331
*Ensign,* brig, 118
Equator, 211, 213, 217, 223, 233, 247, 272, 291, 307, 314, 322, 323, 330, 333
Erskine, Capt., 112, 119
Etna, 127, 156, 158
*Everhard,* bark, 246
*Exchange,* topsail schooner, 26, 34, 35, 255

*Fair American,* 34, 255
Fall River Line, 331, 340
Falmouth, England, 113, 115, 118, 119, 131, 216, 226, 231, 268, 311, 330
Falmouth, Maine, 29
*Farley, E. Wilder,* ship, 115
*Farmer,* schooner, 30, 31, 355
Fastnet light, 204, 250
*Favorite,* brig, 32, 355
Fire Island light, 199
Fisk, Capt., 119
flatiron, 151, 332, 339, 346
Florida, 90, 98
flour, 88, 89
flying fish, 315
Flying Point, 15
Forest Church, 72, 73
Formosa, 286, 300, 346, 347
Forsaith, Edwin, 359

*Forward,* sloop of war, 90
Foster, Prof., 188
Foster, Robert, 359
Fourth of July, 117, 197, 217, 257, 328
Franklin, Dr., 32
Freeport, 30, 72, 88
French, 186
French, Capt., 112
fruit, 122, 123, 145, 298-300
Furbish, Alice, vii
*Futty Alum,* bark, 217

Gardi, Cape, 126
Garese, Mr., 163
Garvin, Mrs., 327
Geneva award, 62
*Geneva,* ship, 327
Genoa, 11, 20
George Town, 219
Gestolini, Mrs., 137
Gettysburg, 217, 218, 282
Gibraltar, 89, 123, 155, 156, 157, 160-166, 268
Gibraltar, Rock of, 123, 160, 161, 162, 174
Gilman, Charles J., 282
Gilman family, 266
Gilman, Mary, vii
Girard College, 202
Giveen, Alvah, 167
Giveen, Daniel, 26, 358
Giveen, Elizabeth, 143, 144
Giveen family, 23, 26
Giveen, John, 26, 50, 359
Giveen, Lewis, 26, 359
Giveen, Mary, 48
Giveen, Robert, 26, 358
Giveen, Robert II, 26, 358
Giveen, Robert III, 26, 359
Giveen, Robert IV, 26, 359
Giveen, Thomas, 26, 359
Giveen, William, 26, 359
Glasgow, 194, 249, 253, 257
Gloucester, 29

# Index

Golita, 156
gondolas, 134, 136, 144, 146
Good Hope, Cape of, 212, 218, 220, 221, 222, 232, 270, 288
Goodrich, Abel, 359
*Governor Tilley,* 327
Grant, General, 266
*Great Eastern,* steamer, 141, 142, 261, 262
Great Island, 77-80, 84-87, 102, 112, 113, 114, 141, 142, 178-181, 191, 229, 238, 239, 272, 275, 299, 301, 304, 311, 321, 322, 323, 330, 335
Great Stirrup Key, 105
Greeley, Horace, 329
Greenock, 93
Griffin, E. D., 43, 44
Gross, Israel, 359
Grows, William, 360
*Guadalupe,* brig, 57, 352, 356
guano, 241, 245, 249, 253, 254, 271, 272, 311, 324, 328, 330
*Guiding Star,* 262
Gulf of Mexico, 97, 98
Gulf Stream, 90, 96, 98, 105, 171, 290
Gun Key, 106
Gurnet, 72, 78, 79, 85, 180
Gurnet Bridge, 78, 180

Hacker, Isaiah, 358
Haiti, 76
Hall, Bell, 360
Hall, Horatio, 360
Hall, John, 358
halyard song, 295
Hamburg, 194
*Hammond, Maggie,* bark, 258, 259
Hampton Roads, 272
Hanley and Snow, 324
Harding, Ephraim, 358
Harding, Robert, 358
Harding, Robert II, 360
Harding, Samuel, 360

Hare, Capt., 107
*Harmony,* schooner, 32, 355
Harpswell, 8, 27, 36, 37, 50, 52, 64, 72, 73, 77-87, 102, 109, 110, 111, 112, 113, 114, 141, 142, 158, 178-181, 195, 214, 229, 232, 238, 239, 299, 301, 304, 321, 322, 323, 330
*Harriet,* schooner, 54, 355
Harriman, Capt., 106
*Harrisburg,* ship, 115
Hatteras, Cape, 62, 171, 175, 272
"Haul on the bowline," 294
Haunillios Island, 324-327, 328
Havana, 31, 91, 93, 96, 97, 103, 106-115, 131, 158, 207, 268, 275
Havre, Le, 75, 194, 196, 268
Hay, Capt., 107
Hay, John, 347
Hayden and French, 200
haying, 142, 239, 299, 301, 304
Henlopen, Cape, 321
Henry, Hiram, 358
hens, 94, 115, 116, 124, 217, 271, 289
High Head, 158
Highland light, 100
Hills, Capt., 31
Hinckley, William, 360
Hinds, Amos, 169, 187, 188, 195
Hinds, Lettice, 141, 169, 182, 183, 184, 187-190, 194, 195, 202, 203, 204-207
Hinds, Lucy, vii
Holland, 199
Holyhead, 62, 317
Holyrood Palace, 257
Hong Kong, 336
*Hood, Ellen,* ship, 59, 329, 356
hoopskirts, 132, 137, 147
Horn, Cape, 2, 11, 26, 48, 57, 232, 234, 235, 245, 253, 270, 271, 308, 310, 323, 329
horse cars, 336
Hospital, Brunswick, 303

*366*

# Index

*Hotel de Europe,* Rio, 336
Hoyt, Capt., 111, 112, 113
Humphreys, Charles, 360
Humphreys, Dana, 360
Hyde Park, 206

ice, 103
ice cream, 147
"In Amsterdam there lives a maid," 295
*Independent, The,* 188, 190
*Independent,* schooner, 31, 355
Indian Ocean, 9, 212-214, 216-218, 293
Ireland, 55, 81, 93, 194, 204, 205, 207, 231
Irish, 204, 205
iron ships, 262, 270, 317
*Istria,* bark, 63, 259, 352, 357
Italians, 131, 136, 137
Italy, 127-148, 156, 158
*Itaska,* ship, 307

Jacobs, Elizabeth, 82
Jacob's Ladder, 328
Jamestown, 220, 268
Japan, 268, 288, 290, 293, 301-304, 347
Java, 11, 297-299
Java Head, 291
Jefferson, President, 33
Jersey, Isle of, 28
Jessie, maid, 263
Jesuartz Church, 146
Jordan, Capt., 302
Jordan, Cowan, 27, 359
Jordan family, 201
Jordan, Francis, 27, 359
Jordan, Frank, 27, 359
Jordan, Isaiah, 85, 329, 330
Jordan, Peter, 27, 358
Jury, John, 296

Kamerling, Samuel, vii
Keller, Helen, 52

Kellogg, Elijah, 52, 352
Kelsey, Mr., 44
Kennebec, 182, 187
Kennebec and Portland RR, 177
*Kentucky,* brig, 234
Key Francis, 275
Key West, 329
*King Celtic,* 327
King, Mr., 151
King, Mr., mate, 182
*Kingsland, Mary,* steamer, 97
Kish lightship, 93

Lagosta, 157
Laguia, 111
Lane, John, 358
Larrabee, Nehemiah, 359
launchings, 13, 14, 15, 34, 54, 55, 58, 59, 63, 64, 75, 139, 145, 150, 155, 186, 279-286
*Lawrence, Sir John,* 327
Lee, Robert E., 248, 266
Legata, Cape, 156, 157, 158
Leghorn, 11
Leith, 250, 252, 253, 268
Le Mair Straits, 234
*Levitt, William,* 327
Lewis, David, 94-96, 353
Lewis, Jabez, 359
*Life of Napoleon,* 117
Liffey, 205
lighting of ships, 289
Lima, 241, 268
lime juice, 296
Lincoln, Abraham, 201, 250, 251
Lincoln, Nathaniel, 360
Linscott, Abram, 85
Linscott, Isaac, 359
Lisbon, Maine, 13
Little Andaman Island, 215
Little Round Top, 282
Littlefield, Capt., 359
Liverpool, 76, 112, 194, 195, 205, 207, 231, 232, 268, 287, 288, 290, 291, 302, 305, 306, 317, 318, 331

# Index

Lizard, the, 118, 226, 262
Lloyd, Mr., 132, 137
London, 115, 198, 205-207, 268
London Exhibition, 206
Longfellow, Henry W., 36, 37, 39-42, 44, 60, 103, 342, 351
Long Island, 199
Long Wharf, 76
Longwood, 219
*Lorenzo,* ship, 214, 232
Loring, Capt., 107, 214
Lost Paradise Farm, 78, 79, 80, 81, 112, 322
loup-cervier, 85, 329, 330
Lower California, Gulf of, 271
Lundy Island, 208
Lunt, James, 358
Lynn, 35

McKeen family, 266
McKeen Street, 14, 15
McLellan, Joseph, 358
McLoon, Capt., 327
McManus, Asa, 26, 359
McManus, George, 26, 359
McManus, Richard, 26, 359
McManus, Robert, 26, 359
McManus, Robert J., 26, 360
Madeiras, 167, 210, 233
Magdalena Islands, 197
Magg, Mr., 119
Main Street, 14
Maine, 2-73, 75, 77-87, 97, 101, 102, 113, 114, 141, 142, 177-182, 264, 279-286, 340-342, 349-354
Maine, District of, 29, 31
Mair Brook, 14
Mair Point, 15, 72
*Majestic,* ship, 58, 356
Malay, 20, 213-216, 300
Malays, 213, 214
Mall'Brook, 321
Mall, Brunswick, 70, 134
Manila, 303, 304

Maquoit, 14, 15, 37, 72, 279
*Marengo,* ship, 112
*Margaret,* bark, 157
Marrow Bone, 91
Marshall, John H., 358
Martin, Clement, 27, 359
Martin, Clement, Jr., 27, 360
Martin, James, 99, 353
Martin, Matthew, 27, 359
Martin, Thomas, 27, 360
*Mary Emma,* ship, 63, 356
Massachusetts, 28, 29, 35
Matanzas, 92, 96, 106, 113
Mathues, 241
May, Capt., 106, 107
Means, Capt., 107
Mediterranean Sea, 88, 89, 123-167, 175
Melcher, Abner, 26, 359
Melcher, Benjamin, 26, 359
Melcher, George, 26, 359
Melcher, Joseph, 26, 359
Melcher, Josiah, 26, 360
Meleda, 156, 157
men-of-war fish, 316
Merrill, Leonard, 359
Merritt, Henry, 358
Merritt, Henry II, 360
Merro Island, 213
Merrow, Mr. and Mrs., 257
Merriman, Jacob, 26, 360
Merriman, Robert, 214, 215, 232
Merriman, San Lorenzo, 241
Merriman, Thomas, 26, 358
Merryconeag Sound, 81, 84
Merryman, Alfred, 26, 359
Merryman, Curtis, 26, 360
Merryman, Jeremiah, 26, 360
Merryman, Richard, 26, 358
Merryman, William, 26, 360
Merrymeeting Bay, 14
Mersey, 317
meteor, 322
Middle Bay, 60, 61, 66, 350, 351

# Index

Middle Bays, vii, 2, 4-7, 15-73, 75-78, 84, 97, 101, 102, 141, 145, 167, 178-182, 185-187, 190, 201, 226-229, 237, 259, 261, 264-268, 279-286, 311, 348-354
Mill Street, 14
Miller, Capt., 250
Minorca, 89
Minot, Albert, 27, 360
Minot, Bradbury, 27, 360
Minot, George, 31
Minot, Harry, 27, 358
Minot, Thomas, 27, 359
Minot's light, 35
Misery Hill, 85, 112, 329, 330
Mississippi, 90, 97, 98
Mobile, 75
Monsoon, 213
Montevideo, 276
*Morituri Salutamus,* 41, 342
Morrison, Stephen, 360
Morro, 92, 109, 115
Morse, Anthony, 358
Moulton, Thomas, 360
Mountford, William, 360
Multnegee Island, 335
Muntzes metal, 292
Murray, William, 359
Mustard, George F., 360
mustard plaster, 160
mutinies, 273-276

Nantucket, 90, 99
Napoleon, 112, 117, 118, 146, 169, 219, 220, 222, 352
Napoleon's garden, 146
Napoleon's tomb, 219
Narrows, the, 199
New Brunswick, 197, 232
*New England House,* 182
New Meadows, 15, 72
New Orleans, 75, 76, 89, 90, 97, 111, 115, 185, 190, 194-197, 268

New Wharf, 16, 64, 66
New York, 50, 76, 109, 161, 171-177, 181, 182, 183, 185, 267, 268, 331, 340, 345
*New York Tribune,* 188
Newburyport, 97
Newcastle, 259, 260, 268
Nicholas, Capt., 106, 107, 108, 109
*Nimrod,* steamer, 93
North Pole, 266
North Sea, 48, 199, 277, 352

*Oakland,* ship, 64, 267, 292, 293, 328, 357
O'Brien, John, 358
*Odessa,* bark, 76
*Old Clock on the Stairs, The,* 40
Oliver, Capt., 253
Oman, Fred, 94
Orange Keys, 91, 106
Oregon, 268, 304, 306
*Oregon,* ship, 48
Orr, Charles, 193
Orr family, 81, 169, 201
Orr, Harmon, 192, 193, 194, 360
Orr, Harriet, 141
Orr, Henry, 359
Orr, Joseph, 81
Orr, Lettice, 81, 112, 123, 168, 169, 170, 189, 219
Orr's Island, 48, 60, 73, 80-84, 112, 159, 169, 178, 189, 192
Otis, Albert, 26, 359
Otis, Albert II, 26, 360
Otis, Capt., 328
Otis, Edward, 26, 360
Otis, Henry, 26, 360
Otis, James, 26, 358
Otis, James II, 26, 360
Otis, William, 26, 360
Otranto, 127, 156
Ottagan, Johnny, 223-226, 353

Pabelon de Pica, 328, 330

# Index

Pacific, 9, 11, 20, 63, 235-245, 258, 271, 282, 290, 301-308, 323-329, 352
Packard, Alpheus Spring, 50, 341
Palma Island, 233
Palos, Cape, 156, 157, 165
Pampero, 271, 322
Pentelleria, 127
Park Row, 321
Parliament, Houses of, 206
*Patten, George F.*, ship, 118
Patten, Horace, 359
Patten, Lincoln, 360
peaches, canned, 322
*Pearl of Orr's Island, The,* 60, 61, 78-82, 188, 189, 190
Peary, Robert, 266
Pennell, Abby J., vii, viii, 1-3, 73, 79-87, 97, 101-265, 268-272, 276-278, 282, 283, 285-321, 323, 324, 328, 330-346, 354
Pennell, Agnes, 46
Pennell, Arabella, 227, 301, 302, 304, 351
Pennell, Andrew, vii, 54, 346
Pennell, Arthur, 242-264, 268-270, 276, 282, 285, 287, 288, 289-299, 301-303, 305, 312, 313, 316-319, 321, 322, 330-336, 338-341, 344, 345
Pennell, Augusta, 140, 144, 167, 168, 266, 353
Pennell baby, 202, 208-215, 222, 223, 226, 227, 229, 230, 232, 237, 238, 243, 263, 277, 282, 335, 337, 346, 353
Pennell, Benjamin, 4, 26, 46, 48, 50, 54, 56, 70, 178, 196, 233, 266, 281, 284, 351
Pennell Brothers' firm, 6, 37, 47-65, 68, 201, 258, 261, 279, 281
Pennell, Carroll, vii, 266, 268, 284, 286
Pennell, Carroll, Mrs., vii
Pennell, Catherine, vii

Pennell, Charles, 7, 25, 46, 50-53, 54, 59, 62, 70, 103, 110, 119, 174, 177, 178, 187, 203, 248, 266, 267, 281, 283, 340, 351
*Pennell, Charles S.,* ship, 59, 356
Pennell, Clement, 28
Pennell, Deborah, 4-7, 16, 46, 47, 49, 55-57, 59, 60, 69, 70, 87, 98, 119, 174, 178, 180, 181, 182, 186, 187, 190, 266, 272, 277, 284, 350, 352, 353
*Pennell, Deborah,* bark, 59, 68, 166, 186, 187, 190-204, 207-264, 268-273, 275-277, 290, 305, 321, 352, 356
Pennell, Eliza, 46, 48, 351
Pennell family, 28-65, 69-72, 252, 265-268, 349-354
Pennell, Frankie, 226, 227, 228, 353
Pennell, George, 268
Pennell, Hannah, 56, 58, 144
Pennell, Harriet, 46, 53, 56, 102, 138, 226, 227, 291
Pennell, Harriet Giveen, 51, 267, 351
Pennell, Helen, vii, 283, 286, 287
Pennell, Henry, 155
Pennell, Isaac, 26, 359
Pennell, J. Fred, vii, 51, 52, 174, 266, 270, 276, 282-288, 289-303, 305, 307-319, 321-323, 328-336, 338-340, 344, 345
Pennell, Jacob, 6, 7, 30, 34-36, 45-47, 54, 55, 187, 350
Pennell, Jacob, Jr., 7, 46, 48, 70, 178, 180, 284, 350
*Pennell, Jacob,* ship, 55, 353, 355
Pennell, James, 7, 46, 49, 54, 56, 61, 62, 63, 70, 88, 178, 182, 216, 217, 258, 259, 261, 266, 267, 284, 351
Pennell, James Henry, 26, 49, 62, 88, 103, 116, 124, 140, 143, 144,

# Index

151, 167, 187, 195, 201, 216, 217, 221, 223, 257, 259, 266, 284, 352
*Pennell, James*, ship, 55, 57, 58, 69, 102, 352, 356
Pennell, Job, 7, 46, 49, 50, 233, 248, 284, 351
Pennell, John, 31
Pennell, John, vii, viii, 1-7, 16, 25-29, 34, 35, 45, 46, 47, 48, 53, 57, 58, 59, 60, 64, 65, 66-67, 79, 80, 83-87, 97-265, 268-278, 282, 283, 285-343, 346-348, 354
Pennell, Joseph, 7, 46, 53, 179, 182, 185, 226, 227, 233, 284, 301, 302, 304, 351
Pennell, Josie, 301
Pennell, Julia, 49, 144, 284, 351
Pennell, Lewis, 26, 360
*Pennell, Mary*, brig, 55, 355
Pennell, Mary Ellen, vii, 40, 44, 56, 88, 144, 353
Pennell, Moses, 60
Pennell, Paulina, 46, 53, 227, 351
Pennell, Robert, 7, 46, 53, 97, 101, 102, 119, 146, 152, 179, 185, 233, 284, 351
*Pennell, Robert,* brig, 57, 69, 356
Pennell, Samuel, 26, 48, 49, 56, 267, 350, 360
Pennell ships, 30-65, 85, 355-357
Pennell, Thomas, 28, 29, 350
Pennell, Thomas II, 29, 350
Pennell, Thomas III, 7, 29-31, 33, 66, 350
Pennell, Thomas IV, 30, 34
Pennell, William, 26, 30, 48, 350
Pennell, Willie, 144, 266
Pennells' Wharf, 16, 34
Pennells' Wharf Road, 7, 24, 63
Pennellville, vii, viii, 267, 272, 278-286, 349-354
Penobscot Bay, 84
Perkins, Norman, 360
Perry, Mr., 201

*Persia,* ship, 198
Peru, 241, 242, 271, 324
Peterson, John, 358
*Petrel,* pilot boat, 196, 250
pets, 125, 127
Philadelphia, 50, 202, 203, 204, 267, 268, 318, 319, 321
Philadelphia Exposition, 319
Philinque, 270
Phillips Academy, Andover, 344
phosphorus, 333
Pichalinqui, 271
pies, 116, 117, 120, 121, 122, 123, 124, 125, 150, 167, 168, 289
pig-iron, 199
pigs, 116, 170, 198, 232, 233, 270, 271, 272
pilot bread, 111, 289
*Pilot-Fish,* 111
Pinkham, Capt., 106, 107, 108, 207
Pisa, 20
Pithyusae Islands, 124, 156
Plains, Brunswick, 27, 73, 78, 265
Plata, Rio, 233
Plymouth, 231
Pola, 128
Portland, 36, 43, 54, 57, 67, 70, 82, 102, 140, 142, 150, 163, 177, 181, 214, 272, 280, 287, 352
Portland Head, 261
Portugal, 122
potatoes, 92
Potter, William, 360
Pound, Elizabeth, 219, 248, 252, 254, 255
Powell, John, 30
Presidential Election, 270, 323
*Prince,* steamer, 207
Purington, Capt., 328
Purington family, 302

Quahaug Bay, 84
Queenstown, 194, 197, 268, 331

# Index

Race, Capt., 109, 110
Raling, Mr., mate, 296, 307, 314, 316
Randell, Martha, 73
*Redwood,* ship, 58, 356
Reed, Abby, 73, 79-87
Reed, Alta, vii
Reed, Arthur, 81-87, 142, 143, 180, 191-194, 195, 229, 299, 301-304, 340
Reed, Caroline, 82, 84, 114, 158, 189
Reed, Elias, 82, 118, 135, 141, 142, 164-166, 177, 178, 180, 182, 191-194, 198, 200, 204, 207, 222, 228, 273, 275, 276, 277, 292, 299, 302, 330, 340
Reed family, 48, 79-87, 180, 229, 252
Reed, John, 112
Reed, Lettice, 141
Reed, "Sis," (Mary), 82, 113, 145, 159, 164, 165, 177, 180, 193, 222, 228, 229, 240, 298, 302, 304
Renson, William, 246
*Resolute,* 327
Revolution, 1688, 29
Reynolds, Alec, 88, 89, 90
Rialto, 12, 134, 136
rice, 216, 218, 232
Rich, David, 193
Richardson, Charlotte, 189
Richmond, 204
Riding Rocks, 96
Rio de Janeiro, 64, 268, 286, 331-341, 343
Rio harbor, 334
Rodix, Israel, 359
Rogers, John, 359
*Rose of Annandale, The,* 169
Ross, James, 359
Ross, Robert, 360
Rotterdam, 277
Routh, I. H. W., 90
Rovigno, 129

Royal Navy, 34
rugs, 290, 293

Sacratif, Cape, 124
Sagamia, Cape, 304
Sagarovich, Mr., 152, 153
Saguenay, 82
St. Abb's Head, 253
St. Helena, 219, 220-222, 268, 352, 353
St. Lawrence, Gulf of, 197
St. Mark's, 133, 134, 137
St. Petersburg, 194
St. Vincent, Cape, 122
Salem, 101
salmon, canned, 324
salvage, 328, 329
*Samuel,* 327
San Diego, Cape, 234
San Domingo, 90
Sandy Hook, 172
San Francisco, 23, 63, 234, 303, 317, 321, 323, 324
San Lorenzo Island, 241
Santa Argo, 89
Sargasso Sea, 315, 316, 319, 332
Sargasso weed, 315, 316
schoolhouse, Pennell, 4, 6, 66, 67, 73, 167
school on shipboard, 294, 332
Schuylkill River, 202
Scilly Isles, 118, 253, 262, 332
Scotland, 38, 93, 251-259
Scott, Tristram, 181
*Screamer,* ship, 73
scurvy, 296
Sebascodegan, 77
Sefton Park, 318
Seven Days' Battles, 204
Sewall, Benjamin, 282
*Sewall, Benjamin,* ship, 64, 166, 281, 284, 318, 340, 346, 347, 353, 357
Sewall, Capt., 299, 331
Sewall, Day and Co., 303

# Index

Sewall, John S., 282, 284
Sewalls, 266, 282
Seward, Secretary, 250, 251
sharks, 311
Sharpness, 197
Sheffield, 345
"She has dipped her yards under," 308
Sherine, Thomas, 89
Shields, 259
"ship's doctor," 50
Shoalwater Bay, 306
Sicily, 127, 156, 158
Sierras, Spain, 160
Simpson, Dana, 360
Simpson family, 64, 66
Simpson, Robert, 358
Simpson, Robert II, 359
Simpson, William, 358
Simpson's Point, 15
Singapore, 207, 214, 216, 232, 268
Sinnett, Capt., 118
Sinnett, Mrs. 176
Sir Walter Scott's Monument, 257
Skolfield, Alfred, 26, 359
Skolfield, Charles, 26, 358
Skolfield, Clement, 302
Skolfield family, 64, 73, 87, 180, 201, 267, 302
Skolfield, George, 26, 360
Skolfield, James, 26, 359
Skolfield, John, 26, 358
Skolfield, Joseph, 26, 358
Skolfield, Lincoln, 26, 360
*Skolfield, Lydia,* ship, 311
Skolfield, Robert, 26, 360
Skolfield, Samuel, 26, 123, 359
Skolfield, Samuel, 26, 360
Skolfield, Thomas, 26, 73, 75, 359
Skolfield, Thomas, 26, 359
Skolfield, Thomas, 193
Skolfield, William, 26, 360
Slaughter House Point, 97
sleighing, 164, 178, 179

Smith, 99
Smith, Prof., 188
Snow, Capt., 206
Snow, Charles, 26, 359
Snow, Elisha, 42, 43
Snow, Harmon, 26, 360
Snow, Jesse, 26, 358
Snow, Jesse, 26, 358
Snow, Thomas, 26, 359
South, the, 185
South America, 234-238, 240-242, 271, 322, 324-328
Spain, 88, 122-124, 156, 157, 158-166
Spaniards, 110, 123, 163, 171
*Spartacus to the Gladiators,* 52
spatter work, 319, 320
Spinney's Brook, 33
Sprague, Mr., 97
Stanley Dock, 232
Stanwood, Robert, 359
Stanwood, William, 358
Start light, 261
steamers, 141, 142, 201, 253, 261, 262, 277, 291, 335, 338, 339
Stevens, Robert, 359
Stone, Daniel, 358
Stonington, 177
stove, 236
Stover, Alcot, 360
Stover, Lemuel, 360
Stowe, Harriet Beecher, 60, 61, 70, 78-81, 82, 83, 188, 189, 190, 351
Straits of Gibraltar, 122, 123
Street, Capt., 360
Strickland, Capt., 336
Stuart, Elizabeth, 38, 39
Stuart, Lady Eleanor, 38
sugar, 16, 31, 92, 110
Sumter, Fort, 196
Sunda Straits, 297-299
Sunday School, 276, 318
Suwa Sima, 300
Sylvester, Charles, 360

# Index

Sylvester, Henchman, 358
Sylvester, Isaac, 360
Sylvester, James, 360
Sylvester, Robert, 360
Syracuse, 158

*Tadesco*, bark, 35, 356
Tadousac, 83
Tappan, Amos, 358
tea, 303
*Teaser*, schooner, 199
telegraph, 303, 317
*Telegraph, The Brunswick*, 330, 341
*Tempest*, ship, 58, 69, 356
*Tennessee*, bark, 55, 355
Thames tunnel, 206
*Theobald*, 327
third mate, 273, 274
Thomas, Capt., 254
Thomas, Charles, 358
Thomas, William, 358
Thompson, Edward, 360
Thompson, John, 360
Thompson, Wildes, 360
Thorne, Mr., 93
*Three Brothers*, ship, 317
Thurlow, Capt., 109, 111
Thurlow, Mrs., 110, 111
Tierra del Fuego, 234, 323
Tokay light, 306
tooth extraction, 142, 202
Topsham, 72, 84, 280
Topsham Fair, 84, 138, 139, 148, 223, 322
Tortugas light, 98
town meeting, Brunswick, 71
Track Island, 213
Trade winds, 233, 247, 293, 314, 317, 323
Trick, Capt., 327
Trieste, 35, 109, 130, 136, 140, 141, 149-155, 157, 175, 268
Trinidad, 246
Trinity College, Dublin, 204

Troon, 93
Trott, Mr., 327
*Tudor*, ship, 242
Tunis, 126
Twelve-Rod Road, Brunswick, 134, 179, 279
*Tycho Brahe*, steamer, 339, 340
Tyler, Capt., 106
Tyne bridge, 260

*Ugland*, 327
*Uncle Tom's Cabin*, 60, 188, 352
*Undine*, 213
*Union*, ship, 36, 37, 355
United States Hotel, 182
*United States*, ship, 59, 75, 97, 170, 356
Uruguay, 276

Valparaiso, 237, 238, 268
Vancouver Island, 305
*Vanderbilt, Commodore*, steamer, 222
Venice, 11, 12, 119, 129-148, 156, 268
Venice, Gulf of, 127-129
Verde, Cape, 233
Villegagnon, Fort, 333
Virginia, 197, 204, 218, 248, 266, 272
*Vittoria, Hotel*, 132, 135, 136

Wales, 62, 231, 317
War of 1812, 8, 32-34, 90, 355
Warren, Mr., 119
Wars of the Roses, 28
Washington, George, 31, 32
Waterville, 187
Waterville College, 188, 195
*Watts, John*, ship, 229
*Wellfleet Harbour*, ship, 76
*West, George*, ship, 97
West Indies, 9, 16
Westcott, Capt., 76
Westminster Abbey, 206

# Index

whale feed, 311
whales, 296
wheat, 304, 306, 318
*Whisky for My Johnnie,* 295
whist, 204
Whitby light, 253
*White's Hotel,* Rio, 336
Whitmore, Amherst, 360
Wickham, Mrs., 331
Wight, Isle of, 261
Wilcox, Ephraim, 360
William, 193
Winchell, James, 228, 229, 257, 360
wishbone, 324
*Witch of the Waves,* 242
*Woods, Mary,* bark, 246
Woodside, Adam, 27, 360

Woodside, Arthur, 27, 360
Woodside, Benjamin, 27, 358
Woodside family, 180
Woodside, William, 26, 54, 91-93, 102, 353, 358
*Woodside, William,* bark, 45, 58, 88-100, 102-132, 146, 147-174, 177, 185, 187, 204, 356
Woodward, Isaac, 358
Woodward, John, 358
Woodward, Jordan, 359
world's fairs, 206, 207, 319

Yale, 345
*Yarm,* bark, 122
Yarmouth, 8, 337
Yokohama, 268, 290, 293, 301-304

*375*

# Afterword: Robert Coffin's Day

Paul David Nygard

On the afternoon of July 9, 1948, a crowd gathered at the campus of Bowdoin College in Brunswick, Maine to honor historian, novelist, essayist, Pulitzer Prize winning poet and resident English professor Robert Peter Tristram Coffin. In the past the people of Brunswick had generally maintained a hands-off attitude in regards to the activities of the Bowdoin community. Coffin himself once compared the often strained relationship between Bowdoin and Brunswick to the warlike atmosphere generated by the students and townspeople of medieval Oxford. But Rob Coffin was a home-town boy, born within the hailing distance of Maine Street, and it is understandable, then, that the town wished to be represented at the celebration of a writer whose poems and stories about a boyhood spent on a Casco Bay saltwater farm had helped establish a national fascination with life along coastal Maine.

A beautiful summer day only enhanced an occasion for which Bowdoin, hoping to also generate some publicity for the college, went all out. The campus's Walker Art Museum had organized an exhibit of Coffin watercolors and pen drawings, unveiled to the public that day at 2:00 p.m. The Rare Book Room of the Hubbard Library featured a display of the original manuscripts (on loan from the author) for most of the thirty-odd Coffin books published during the previous twenty years. Handsomely printed souvenir programs, each adorned with RPTC's picture, circulated throughout the campus, inviting visitors, some of whom had come a long way, to visit Memorial Hall at 3:00 p.m. for a lecture by the day's honoree. Finally, the Moulton Union, decorated with pine boughs and wildflowers, was the scene of a 4:00 p.m. reception for "Professor Coffin and Family" – hosted by Bowdoin President and Mrs. Kenneth Sills with the Bowdoin Wives Association providing refreshments of ice cream, cookies, and cake.

Professor Coffin himself was not on hand when some 700 people flowed into the lobby of the Walker Art Museum at 2:00 p.m. It was an eclectic group. Members of the Bowdoin faculty and their wives – who comprised the welcoming committee – shook hands with fishermen and farm folk from the shore areas, store clerks and housewives with children in tow from town, and from all over southeastern Maine, the summer residents and ladies book clubbers among whom R.P.T. Coffin was a subject of veneration. As 3:00 p.m. approached, most of the crowd drifted out of the museum and walked along the stone pathways toward the north end of the campus and Memorial Hall. Trooping past the bronze tributes to Bowdoin's Civil War dead just inside the building's main entrance, celebrants climbed the stairs to the second floor auditorium and settled into whatever seats were available. The best spots down front were reserved by the college for special out-of-town guests, the Coffin family, and those members of the faculty who wished to hear the lecture. At just past the top of the hour President Sills walked to the podium and, after welcoming everyone to the college, introduced the focus of all the excitement, Robert P. Tristram Coffin. The enthusiasm of those present, a family member remembered, was warm and sustained.

As the lecture unfolded, the style and magnetism that had made Coffin so popular on the national poetry-reading circuit was very much on display. Looking dapper in white cotton pants and shirt, navy-blue blazer, and his favorite blue tie, he thoroughly entertained the audience as he presented several of his long ballads under the title, "American Patterns." Many there were already familiar with the nuances of a Coffin recitation and chuckled in recognition as each appeared:

the rolling and lighting, with one hand, of a Bull Durham cigarette; the flourishing of his extravagant handlebar mustache; the frequent digressions into personal anecdotes, tall tales, or snatches of song; the clear love of performance that sparked in the lecturer's blue-gray eyes.

Still, some on hand could not help notice that, on this warm July afternoon, their friend and idol looked a little worse for wear. Though Coffin was only in his 56$^{th}$ year, his once brown curly hair was completely gray, his clothes hung on what had been a robust 5'8" frame, and anyone looking at his face could not help but take in the sunken eyes and weary expression. In his poetry and prose Coffin write regularly of the joys to be found in everyday life but, in fact, the previous few years had been heartbreakingly difficult for him. In 1945, within a few months, his beloved wife Ruth suffered a debilitating stroke and he himself nearly died from a heart attack. As he watched his wife fade away over the next two years, Coffin was himself plagued by continuous heart trouble and a painful gout condition. Added to these woes was the burden of looking after his frequently ill daughter, Peggy, and the responsibility of being the titular head of the rather large band of siblings, cousins, and other relations and their families that made up the Coffin family in southern Maine.

This role as the chief of Clan Coffin was rather complicated for RPTC (as his admirers called him) by the fact that he held a similar standing with another venerable Maine family – the Pennells. This connection began in the early 1920s when he was a professor of English at Wells College in upstate New York. Determined to maintain roots in his native state, Coffin purchased an old shipmaster's mansion in the Middle Bay area of Brunswick. This nine room, two-story salt box house with "an ell, applied to it behind, carriage houses and woodshed hitched to that, and, last, a barn as big as a cathedral," had been built in 1780 by William Pennell of the Pennell Shipbuilding family and later, in 1862, remodeled and enlarged. Set amidst a hamlet of white clapboard houses shaded by ancient elm trees, this slightly rundown structure had for Coffin the virtue of location, being both in his hometown and only a few steps from the sea. In addition, his new home stood directly across the road from the James Pennell House, a locale well-known in the region for its striking cupola (the setting of a Coffin poem) and the home of Rob's younger sister Alice and her husband Andrew Pennell. From the day of purchase Coffin considered his "Pennellville" residence his summer home, even after he returned to Brunswick to teach at Bowdoin in 1934. As he explained to a friend: "We could not live if we could not get back each summer. We have fixed it up as the best place to live and write."

    Clearly, too, given his lifelong interest in Maine history, ownership of this particular nineteenth century dwelling brought Coffin a most welcome link to a glorious past when ships and sailors from the Pine Tree State circled the globe and brought the world's riches back to ports and shipyards not unlike the one once maintained by the Pennells. As was the case with most of Maine's successful shipbuilding industry of the 1800s, the Pennell shipyard did not survive the shift from wood to steel hulls at the end of the century. By the early 1900s the family itself had lapsed by into a kind of genteel poverty, with the Pennell men struggling to make ends meets at a variety of employments while the women worked to keep bright a fast-fading grandeur. The grafting of R.P.T. Coffin, by marriage, onto the family tree was a Godsend for the Pennells for, through his celebrity, they hoped to revive past glories or at least have those glories known to the twentieth century.

Expectations were more than met in 1939 when Coffin wrote *Captain Abby and Captain John: An Around-the-World Biography*, a book based largely on the documents and papers left behind by a Pennell ship's captain and his wife who traveled the world between 1857 and 1877. Loaned to Coffin by K. Fred Pennell, John and Abby's son, these account books, letters, journals, and diaries provided the basis for an intimate and unusual look at a small but fascinating aspect of maritime America during the Age of Sail. As Coffin himself write, "Here are the bare bones of fine and brave and godly living," of a husband and wife "who followed the sea all their life together" but remained to the end faithful to civilization they knew back home in Maine.

In addition to being a history of the Pennell family, however, *Captain Abby and Captain John* also afforded RPTC the opportunity to contribute to the bicentennial celebration of Brunswick's 1738 incorporation as a township. In words suggestive of the spirit that imbued the discipline of history later in the century, Coffin wrote in his preface that he hoped to "excite others in Brunswick to do something similar for other people, other houses, other events that make up the whole and true history of the town of Brunswick. No real town history will be available until each section and each house have been explored with an eye not merely for facts but for human nature and the small but everlasting details of everyday living." Also, in evidence was the author's desire to champion the contributions of families like the Pennells (as well as his own) who claimed their origins in the shore areas of the town. Middle-class Brunswickians of the nineteenth century considered the shore people of their community shiftless "clamdiggers" and, therefore, their social inferiors – a sentiment that did not disappear with the economic ascendancy of the shipbuilding areas. Complicating those already hard feelings between the Shore and the Town was the fact that families like the Pennells had become shipbuilders and sea captains immersed in an international trading system. As such, they developed a more cosmopolitan outlook toward life, an attitude that often conflicted with the provincial views of the townspeople of Brunswick. Coffin captured what he was as the rub in a passage from *Captain Abby*:

> Some Brunswick citizens regarded the Pennells as stuck-up people, and they often shouted at them in town meetings a word not unheard today – "Bourbons!" For the Pennells naturally gravitated to the side of property themselves. But they were at heart plain and democratic Yankees, no Bourbons. If they wore good clothes, they earned them. And with their hands and by their own sweat. The women by sewing and ironing for a host of children, the men by driving nails and planing planks. They worked with their workmen on their ships. If they had fine ways and manners, it was because they thought fine manners and a sense of decorum were part of right living and thrifty living.

The resulting volume, when published by Macmillan Press, received generally positive reviews and sold well considering the United States was still feeling the effects of the Great Depression. Without question, *Captain Abby and Captain John* was and remains an enjoyable and moving account of a notable episode from the American past though the author, ever the showman, left much of his exuberant personality scattered throughout the telling of the tale. The Pennells, of course, were delighted and, over time, adopted their famous in-law as a kind of spiritual head of the family.

Taken all in all, however, the great contributor of Coffin's worn appearance in July 1948 was the self-imposed crusade he had maintained since his wife's death in April, 1947. Caught up in an extensive spring lecture tour of the American South, he arrived back in Brunswick only a short time before his own tribute. Part of the driving force behind his wanderlust was, without question, a desire to be away from the painful memories of his wife's long decline and death. The house at 44 Harpswell Street in Brunswick, he told an acquaintance, no longer felt like home. Yet Coffin was also stewing over a growing conviction that the influential literary critics of his day did not fully appreciate his talents – nor those of other Maine writers who, he believed, held similar insights on life and art. People such as himself, he was sure, along with Henry Beston, Elizabeth Coatsworth, Mary Ellen Chase, Kenneth Roberts, and Gladys Hasty Carroll were all making solid contributions to the world of American letters. Such achievements, Coffin *frequently* contended, deserved far greater recognition than that being offered on the pages of the prestigious journals or within the hallowed walls of academia. By 1948, traveling the poetry-reading circuit to cultivate his reputation and that of his Maine comrades had come to dominate his life. Robert Coffin Day resulted when many within the Bowdoin community decided to show their frequently absent Pierce Professor of English that, at least on home ground, his talents as a scholar and achievements as a writer were recognized and appreciated.

And on that warm July Friday, Rob Coffin seemed ready to believe it. Although he had, on and off, helped the organizers of the event, he was hardly prepared for the crowd of Coffin faithful on campus or the enthusiasm of the audience in Memorial Hall.

At the end of lecture, as soon as Coffin and his entourage of friends and family departed, several well-groomed escorts from the Student Union Committee led those remaining out of Memorial Hall and across the campus to President Sills's reception at the Moulton Union. The gathering was only supposed to last an hour or so but the festive mood of those on hand and the honoree's obvious relish for the limelight pushed it on toward twilight. Standing in the receiving line with his daughter Peggy, his sister Alice, and President and Mrs. Sills, RPTC shook the hand of every person who came to Bowdoin for his day. After the formalities of the receiving line ended, he circulated throughout the Union, talking, laughing, pausing to fill a request from a devotee for an autograph. Not once, but several times, he led clusters of admirers into the recently renovated student snack bar to view the Maine murals he had drawn and then donated to the school to embellish the decor.

Rob's obvious enjoyment of his Bowdoin tribute, however, changed nothing in regards to the peculiar restlessness that nagged him that summer of 1948. Simply put, Robert P. Tristram Coffin – poet, performer, and unrepentant egotist – hated to be ignored. How each newly published poem or story was received, and how his entire body of work would be treated by prosperity, mattered to him tremendously and all the tributes in the world, and there had been many over the years, did not meliorate his anxiety. True, he still possessed the national name-recognition that had been his since he won the Pulitzer Prize in 1936 for his book of poetry *Strange Holiness*. Each passing month still brought requests for a personal appearance from colleges and organizations along with numerous letters from both acquaintances and strangers who were moved in some way by his poetry and readings. And, as if compensation for an often lonely personal life, he enjoyed a tight circle of worshipful friends and former students. Coffin even found himself dubbed the "Virgil of Maine" in one of his publisher's publicity campaigns.

But, truth to tell, he found that appreciation of this sort could be problematic – and not just because of the sardonic smirks of Bowdoin students who sometimes referred to their professor of seventeenth century English literature as the "King of the Ladies Tea Circuit." Coffin had long considered himself to be part of an important literary tradition, the goals of which were loftier than the mere popularization of the charms of life lived along the rural New England coast. In fact, he saw himself and his fellow Maine writers as walking in the literary footsteps of Homer, Chaucer, and Shakespeare, sharing with those notable storytellers a determination to be "a reaffirmer of life and a believer in certain compact and lasting fundamental patterns that it is the salvation of mankind to believe in." Evidence that this belief was dearly held appeared throughout his writings, including his 1932 review of Mary Ellen Chase's book, *A Goodly Heritage*:

> In these days when Yahooism is too often mistaken for good health in literature, and well people are often represented as a little lower that the beasts, a book like *A Goodly Heritage* is a timely reminder that we are really, as we believed as recently as two decades ago, only a ittle lower than the angels. Here is life, simple as a Maine house and as subtle and complete as a Greek temple. One puts down this book with a reassurance that order is a law of being, that humor can be more than a guffaw, and that American living, even of a very modest sort, has been the chief American art.

For him, Chase's memory of her seacoast childhood exemplified the significance of the work that emerged from the Maine literary community in the 1930s and 1940s. More than well-crafted nostalgia, these writings highlighted what was being lost as modern life eroded the traditional patterns of American civilization. Such work, Rob felt, was important. But did America understand and appreciate what he and those of a similar mind were trying to do?

To be sure, what Ms. Chase herself described as the Maine renaissance did capture the attention of the American reading public. From the 1920s into the 1940s, Coffin and his fellow travelers produced a large body of work that expressly drew upon some aspect of Maine culture to illuminate what they considered a significant aspect of the overall human condition. As it turned out, these writings had the effect of beguiling a substantial depression-era audience who found comfort in poems and stories describing a place somehow set apart from the complex and uncertain nature of modern America. The popularity of Gladys Hasty Carroll's novel *As the Earth Turns* and Coffin's fictionalized autobiography *Lost Paradise* helped stimulate a national curiosity about life Down East that has never quite faded. At the same time, the authors of such books enjoyed a certain level of personal reward and notoriety. Coffin himself, by 1948, was the recipient of nearly every literary prize an American writer could hope to win and, from the late 1920s on, a month did not pass without at least one of his works appearing in some publication somewhere. He sold thousands of books and was in constant demand as a speaker.

But there, precisely, was the problem. The popularity of writers such as Coffin and Carroll was viewed by many literary critics, especially those influenced by modernism, as proof of the inconsequential nature of their talents. Commentators such as F.O. Matthiessen, for example, argued that prose and poetry lacking in a high degree of difficulty and complexity, that was popular with a mass audience in other words, was not great, or even good literature – certainly not mentioned in the same breath with a work such as T.S. Eliot's *The Waste Land*. What was equally damning in the eyes of the New Critics was the tendency of Coffin and his colleagues to use their work to delineate the positive aspects of American civilization. The modernist prose and poetry that appeared between the two world wars were often, among other things, elaborate explications of western society's ills. In an era when the contemplative mind was supposed to dwell on the dismalness of life, optimism was considered naïve and decidedly unintellectual. Poet ee cummings perhaps best stated the modernist case against Coffin, and those of a similar mind, when, asked to evaluate Rob's worth as a poet, he write: "People today… are not praising his [Coffin's] poetry, but rather his unique father-image. Within two or three decades his poetry will not appear in anthologies." Little wonder, then, that Coffin felt more than a little uneasy about his future literary reputation, especially with the modernist writers and critics emerging in the late 1940s as the guardians of the American canon.

As he left Bowdoin College that July evening to drive the nine miles to his Pennellville summer home, Rob Coffin no doubt felt much satisfaction over the success of his tribute. Still, the old restlessness remained and it was not long before it re-asserted itself. That fall, in his 17th Century Metaphysical Poetry and Prose course, a student referred to T.S. Eliot as "a contemporary metaphysician reminiscent of John Donne," an Elizabethan poet for whose work Coffin held a love as passionate as his dislike for the modernists. The result was a fifty minute diatribe about Eliot who, an agitated Coffin proclaimed, "had suffered no more than I" but insisted upon "whining and puling in a hopelessly obscuristic way."

And for that, Coffin added, "he gets the Nobel Prize." This incident illuminates, albeit harshly, Rob's fierce hostility to the direction western literature seemed to be taking under modernism, especially in the area of poetry. Since the mid-1930s he had argued that this, his favorite form of artistic expression, "ought not to be the private exercise of the intellect that some of the best known poets of our time have made. These poets have given poetry a bad name with their intellectual superiority, their retreat into patterns of disintegration and their sense of weariness and despair." To stem this tide, Coffin continuously called upon modern writers to obey the ancient laws of the Homeric and Elizabethan bards and seek out "the many fine designs of living" that abound in everyday life and "set them to the music of words and such words as men speak and understand." To this end, "I have set out to persuade and convince people of the fact that life is as zestful and lovely as I have found it."

As he no doubt anticipated, this stance did little to endear Coffin to the critics of his day, suggesting that such commentary was more than just a vain desire to re-claim the literary spotlight from his modernist rivals. Essentially, R.P.T. Coffin was an intelligent, reflective man who considered life, taken all in all, a good deal. In regards to his art, this optimistic assessment encouraged a sizeable output of stories, poems, and essays whose focus was those admirable qualities he thought marked his nation's civilization. Writers such as Walt Whitman, William Dean Howells, and Willa Cather all shared a similar interest, but their precedents brought Coffin limited comfort given the unbridled pessimism he believed modernism had instilled in American letters. Equally unsettling was the work of those preoccupied with T.S. Eliot's claim that "poets, in our civilization... must be difficult," an assertion that seemed in Rob's mind to offer full justification for their turning deliberate obscurantism from literary vice to virtue. The resulting poetry, functioning entirely independent of common experience and language, was found inaccessible by many, even those who decided not to skip graduate school. This rebuff of the common reader was very nearly criminal to Coffin whose own writings, featuring such traditional verse as "There is a strange holiness around / Our common days on common ground," possessed not a hint of the negativism and obscurity he felt insulated modern literature from the general culture that surrounded it.

Though some recent literary criticism does bemoan the current estrangement between writers and readers of poetry it is perhaps safe to say that Coffin's talents, themes, and theories had little lasting influence on the world of American letters. Furthermore, in a turn of events that no doubt had him spinning in his grave, the years following his 1955 death saw the almost complete eclipse of his literary reputation. If recalled today by the guardians of the western canon he is categorized as one of several regional artists who managed to achieve a minor level of national attention in the 1930s and 1940s. Nevertheless, neither Coffin's life nor his achievements deserve such a ready dismissal. The popularity on display during Robert Coffin Day encompassed nearly twenty-five years, offering at the very least insight into what once mattered to a specific, and significant, audience. Clearly, reading or listening to Coffin's poetry and prose got people thinking about the still undiminished potentials of American civilization – no small feat in a time of depression and world war. The merit of work that inspired such optimism seems easily recognizable but was critically overlooked then and forgotten since; a fate by all appearances shared by the author as well. And yet, something abides from every life and in the books, letters, and memories of family and friends Coffin left behind is found something extraordinary: a story worth knowing – one that provides, in the words of Rob's friend Henry Beston, "a rugged and vital picture... of existence."

William Pennell House,
Summer Home of R.P.T. Coffin